THE APOCALYPTIC PROPHECY

DAVID YONGGI CHO

THE
APOCALYPTIC
PROPHECY

CREATION
HOUSE
Orlando, FL

THE APOCALYPTIC PROPHECY by David Yonggi Cho
Published by Creation House
Strang Communication Company
600 Rinehart Road
Lake Mary, FL 32746
Web site: http://www.creationhouse.com

Unless otherwise noted, all Scripture quotations are from the
New American Standard Bible. Copyright © 1960, 1962, 1963, 1968,
1971, 1972, 1973, 1975, 1977 by the Lockman Foundation.
Used by permission.

Scripture quotations marked KJV are from the King James Version
of the Bible.

Scripture quotations marked NIV are from the Holy Bible,
New International Version. Copyright © 1973, 1978, 1984,
International Bible Society. Used by permission.

Library of Congress Cataloging-in-Publication Data

Cho, David Yonggi.
    The apocalyptic prophecy / David Yonggi Cho.
        p.   cm.
    ISBN: 0-88419-492-2
    1. Bible.   O.T.   Daniel—Commentaries.   I. Title.
BS1555.3.C44   1998
224'.507—dc21   98-4403
                                                                  CIP

89012345 BVG 8765432
Printed in the United States of America

Contents

SECTION ONE
THE BOOK OF DANIEL

SECTION TWO
THE BOOK OF REVELATION

SECTION ONE

THE BOOK OF DANIEL

Preface

THE BOOK OF DANIEL is the Old Testament's parallel to the New Testament's Book of Revelation. Daniel himself didn't fully understand the contents of his prophecy about the last days, but he faithfully wrote what he had received from God.

As early as 600 B.C. Daniel wrote a book of remarkably accurate predictions about things that would happen in the last days; he provided an outline of human history as well. In fact, the prophecies in the Book of Daniel about the centuries just after Daniel's time came true in history so accurately that modern critics who disbelieve that genuine prophecy can take place have asserted that all the fulfilled predictions had to have been composed *after* the events they describe, no earlier than the Maccabean period (second century B.C.). But through the guidance of the Holy Spirit we are assured that such assumptions about the impossibility of prophecy are wrong.

We who live in this apocalyptic age should well know how to interpret the signs of the times. It has been my strong desire to write this exposition of the Book of Daniel ever since I wrote one about the Book of Revelation, which you will find in Section II. I thank God for the fulfillment of this dream now, and I feel as if a heavy debt has been at least partially paid.

This exposition of the Book of Daniel has been written for lay readers in a popular style like a sermon, instead of in a scholarly style for specialists, just as my study of the Book of Revelation in Section II was written.

My sincere wish is that this study will become a guide that will enlighten the wisdom of the people who live in this apocalyptic age so that they may serve the Lord more fervently.

Section I of this book was first published in the Korean language in August 1976 under the title *Daniel.* It was also published by Creation House in 1990 under the same title. Section II was published by Creation House in 1991 under the title of *Revelation.*

—David [Paul] Yonggi Cho

1

The Character of Daniel

DANIEL, THE CAPTIVE
(1:1–2)

WHEN THE NORTHERN kingdom of Judah fell to Babylon's King Nebu-chadnezzar in 606 B.C., young Daniel was among the Jews who were taken captive and carried away to Babylon. But he was promoted to a high government position in Babylon, just as he would be when he was later carried as a captive to the Persian empire after it conquered Babylon. As an administrator in the courts of these kingdoms, Daniel gained wide respect both from his fellow Jewish exiles and from pagans. At the same time, he remained as a faithful servant of God throughout his lifetime.

Daniel was a prominent political figure of the era during which he served six kings successively in the Babylonian court: Nabopolassar (626–605 B.C.), Nebuchadnezzar II (605–562 B.C.), Amel-Marduk (562–560 B.C.), Nergal-Sharezer (560–556 B.C.), Labishi-Marduk, (556 B.C.), and Nabonidas (556–539 B.C.). Then after the downfall of Babylon, he served Darius the Mede and Cyrus in the Persian court.

Babylon, where Daniel spent most of his life, was the foremost city of the world in his day. Its glory as the capital of a powerful world empire continued for more than seven decades. According to archaeological findings today, it was an enormous city. Babylon was shaped like a square. The perimeter of its four sides totaled fifty-six miles, with the length of each side stretching fourteen miles. The city wall, made of brick, was as high as three hundred feet in some places and went down thirty-three feet beneath the surface of the earth so any enemies couldn't tunnel under it. It was eighty feet thick.

This city was famous for its fabulous buildings. It boasted the great temple of Marduk, the Babylonian god, and the luxurious palaces of Nebuchadnezzar. In addition, the famed Hanging Gardens, one of the so-called seven wonders of the ancient world, hung from and covered many arches and terraced slopes.

Nevertheless, just as Isaiah prophesied, Babylon was overthrown like Sodom and Gomorrah, and today nothing remains but its ruins. (See Isaiah 13:19–22.) Great Babylon disappeared with the magnificence of its kings, like passing clouds. Yet the revelation of God, which Daniel perceived and wrote, remained alive and is still held in our hands. That revelation is the Book of Daniel which we will study. To begin, let's look first at how the Israelites were conquered by the Babylonians and carried away as captives.

THE STATE OF ISRAEL

ISRAEL IS GOD'S chosen people. She is the posterity of Abraham, Isaac, and Jacob, who received the promise from God. God called Israel and loved her like the apple of His eye.

Yet God's chosen people were taken captive and carried away to Babylon, the sinful land which did not know the true God but served pagan gods. The treasure of the house of the Lord was taken as spoils, and the land that flowed with milk and honey was turned into a desolate place. Why was Israel forsaken and smitten by God in this way?

First, Israel was forsaken because the people forsook the Law and the promise of God. God gave the promise of His blessing as well as the Law to the Israelites through Moses, but they ignored the Law of God and lived as they pleased.

The Bible often compares God to a husband and the Israelites to the wife. The wife was wanton and left her husband like an adulterous woman. She declared that she was independent from her husband and disregarded the Law and the promise.

What if your own spouse, whom you had trusted and thought to be a vital part of your life, had become treacherous in that way? You would probably burn with jealousy and seek to help your spouse correct his or her ways. This is simply the nature of things. In such a situation, what spouse in the world would remain a mere spectator?

How much more, then, would the righteous God, our Father, do? So God, who had been waiting for Israel to repent and to return to Himself, finally used Babylon, a Gentile nation, to discipline Israel.

Second, Israel not only had broken the Law of God; she had violated the Sabbath and the sabbatical year. God had commanded Israel to work for six days of the week and rest on the seventh day, for it was holy to Him. (See Exodus 20:8–11.) God had also commanded the Israelites to set a Hebrew servant free in the seventh year when the six years' service was finished, no matter what the circumstances were under which he had been bought. (See Exodus 21:2.) Concerning the land, God had commanded that for six years they should sow the land and gather in its fruit, but that in the seventh year they should let it rest. (See Leviticus 25:1–7.)

Israel, however, did not keep these commands of God. So God clearly foretold that He would make Israel desolate as punishment for her wickedness. (See Leviticus 26:14–46; Jeremiah 34:12–22.)

Third, the nation worshiped idols. The first of God's commandments said, "You shall have no other gods before Me" (Exod. 20:3). But the Israelites committed spiritual adultery by serving the Baals and Ashtoreth, the Canaanite gods and goddesses, while they lived in the land of Canaan. How could God leave them unpunished?

Fourth, idolatrous nations inevitably degenerate into moral corruption. The moment they leave the righteous God, the power of God that makes them live according to conscience and the standards of morality leaves them. So this also happened to Israel.

When Israel thus left God and became adulterous and degenerate, God decided to destroy the nation. God had warned His people repeatedly through His prophets, such as Isaiah and Jeremiah. Nevertheless, Israel did not turn back from her wickedness. So God finally delivered Israel into the hand of Nebuchadnezzar of Babylon.

Babylon had to have God's permission to do this. Unless God permits it, human armies cannot smite as they wish. The beginning and the end of world history are both in the hand of God.

During the Korean War, for example, God delivered the Republic of Korea into the hand of the communists. Like Israel, Korea, in the providence of God, had been called to preach the gospel to the nations of the world. Yet like Israel, our nation forgot the command and covenant of God and walked the path of corruption and immorality. So God delivered us into the hand of the communists. Through these circumstances God made us undergo repentance and an awakening, which brought forth the growth of the Korean church.

Nevertheless, if our nation forsakes the commandment and covenant of God and departs from His holiness again, no one can say with certainty that God will not strike this land again. On the contrary, if we realize the burden God has given to us and serve Him well, obeying all of His commandments, we will receive wonderful blessings from God, blessings of heaven, and blessings of earth.

THE YOUTH WHO WERE ELEVATED TO HIGH POSITIONS (1:3–8)

BECAUSE GOD DELIVERED Jerusalem into the hand of Nebuchadnezzar, the king easily captured the city and took some of the articles from the temple to the temple of his own god. Besides this, he carried away most of the inhabitants of Jerusalem to Babylon as captives. Then from his captives, Nebuchadnezzar picked some young men who were handsome and intelligent to serve in his court.

From this we can conclude that Nebuchadnezzar was a wise king. When he conquered a country, he not only captured its material treasures like gold and silver; he also captured its human treasures. He made it a policy to take intelligent people from those he conquered to train them for the development of his own kingdom.

Among the young men chosen out of the royal family and nobility of Israel were Daniel, Hananiah, Mishael, and Azariah. For three years they were taught the language and literature of the Chaldeans in the school of the palace. Ashpenaz, chief of the court officials, gave new names to these young men after the names of Babylonian gods. Because they were captives and were specially favored by their conqueror, they could not refuse the pagan names given to them. Nevertheless, Daniel would show his Babylonian captors who the true God was through his consecrated life.

DANIEL'S UNFALTERING FAITH

IN THIS PASSAGE we notice how firm the faith of Daniel was. From ancient times the Jews were famous for loyalty to their religion. This may be one

4

of the main reasons why they have kept their integrity in spite of two thousand years of wandering all over the world.

Look at the unfaltering faith of Daniel. He was a young man specially chosen from among the youths to be admitted to the royal school of Babylon. Others may have taken pride in that. But Daniel clung to the faith of his forefathers, and he made up his mind not to defile himself like the heathen Babylonians.

The food was royal food, appointed by Nebuchadnezzar himself who ruled the world of his day. So it is not difficult to imagine the sumptuousness of his table. Yet Daniel determined not to eat this kind of food because of God's laws.

Heathens of Daniel's day had no restrictions on what foods they could eat. In Leviticus 11, however, the Mosaic law prohibited the Jews from eating certain kinds of food. For instance, the Jews could not eat insects; animals such as pigs, camels, and rabbits; marine animals without fins or scales; or birds which belonged to the eagle or owl families. So Daniel was afraid that he might unknowingly violate the commandment of God if he ate the royal food of the Babylonian court.

Another reason Daniel refused the royal food was that it had first been offered to idols before it was eaten. It was the custom of that day for all the meat and wine served to the king to be first offered to the Babylonian god Merodach. Accordingly, if Daniel ate the food, it meant that he acknowledged idols. So he refused. This problem of food offered to idols—which occurred in the New Testament church as well—may not be common in modern America. (See 1 Corinthians 8:7.)

But in some countries today, such as Korea, it can still be an issue. Daniel provides us with such an example. The Bible says that we must not eat food we think has been sacrificed to an idol or offered in a service of exorcism, as is traditional in the Korean culture. We may eat food as long as we do not know its source, but if we eat such food after we learn its source, 1 Corinthians 8 says we will fall into the temptation of Satan and find ourselves in agony because we feel guilty about it.

THE YOUNG MEN ARE REWARDED (1:9–16)

BECAUSE DANIEL RESOLVED not to defile himself with the royal food and wine sacrificed to Nebuchadneccar's pagan idols, he asked the chief official in the integrity of his faith, "Give us nothing but vegetables to eat and water to drink."

His supervisor was afraid. He might have considered the request profitable because he could keep the royal food and drink assigned to Daniel and his three friends as his own. But the request seemed to be dangerous because if the king saw the youths looking haggard, the king would have his head. Accordingly, the official did not accept Daniel's request.

Nevertheless, Daniel persisted and suggested a test of diet that would allow the official to determine whether the young men's health would suffer. Though they ate nothing but vegetables and drank nothing but water, at the end of ten days they looked healthier and better nourished than any of the young men who ate the royal food. So the chief official granted with pleasure Daniel's request to eat vegetables only. We can learn from this episode that if we resolve to maintain the integrity of our faith, God will *always* take care of the problems that may arise from our resolution.

THE SERVANTS GOD TRAINED (1:17–21)

As FOR these four youths, God gave them knowledge and intelligence in every branch of literature and wisdom; Daniel even understood all kinds of visions and dreams. Then at the end of the days which the king had specified for presenting them, the commander of the officials presented them before Nebuchadnezzar. The king talked with them, and out of them all not one was found like Daniel, Hananiah, Mishael, and Azariah; so they entered the king's personal service. As for every matter of wisdom and understanding about which the king consulted them, he found them ten times better than all the magicians and conjurers who were in all his realm. And Daniel continued until the first year of Cyrus the king.

Because Daniel and his three friends did not defile themselves and kept the command of God, despite the hardships of captivity in Babylon, God loved them and took care of them.

The Bible says in Deuteronomy 28:1–14 that a number of blessings will come upon a nation if that nation keeps the commands and law of God, neither turning aside to the right nor left, nor following other gods and serving them. That nation will be set high above all nations on the earth. The fruit of the womb and kneading trough among its people will be blessed. Though its enemies come from one direction, they will flee in seven. God will send rain on the land in season and will make the land produce bountiful crops. The people will lend to many nations, but will borrow from none. God will make the nation the head, not the tail.

The God who gave us such a promise is the faithful Creator of the whole universe. When He opens the door, no one can shut it; when He shuts the door, no one can open it.

God saw integrity in the faith of Daniel who trusted in Him. So He gave Daniel knowledge and understanding in all kinds of literature and learning, making him wiser than anyone else in the land. God does the same thing today. So when your children want to violate the Lord's day with the excuse that they must study, teach them this lesson. Make them first serve the Lord and then study in the remaining hours. The Lord will honor their integrity and bless their study.

Meanwhile, as parents, pray for your children every morning and night, laying your hands on them to bless them. All wisdom and understanding are blessings granted by God. If God lets His Spirit dwell upon a person so he or she may receive wisdom and understanding, that person can achieve great learning that no one in the world can challenge.

The same is true with business people—serving the Lord must come first. Too often we see Christian business people who are so absorbed in their business that they neglect their duty as Christians. They neither attend worship services nor give God their tithes, which is His due.

They forget God. Peace and joy disappear from their hearts. And since all the blessings of wealth come from God, is it possible for them to keep their wealth safely? Of course not. What good is it to accumulate money with so much trouble?

When we put out trust in the treasure of the earth, that treasure will disappear in just a brief time. But if we put our trust in God as our first and last, relying only upon Him and allowing Him to govern our lives, God will abundantly pour out His blessings upon us. We will receive the spiritual blessings of peace of mind and a joyful heart as well as the material blessing of earthly gain. I pray in the name of the Lord Jesus Christ that you may possess the kind of faith with integrity that Daniel had.

After the young men's three-year-training period in the court school was completed, Nebuchadnezzar put them to a test. When he did, the king was amazed to find that Daniel and his three friends were ten times better in wisdom and understanding than all the magicians and enchanters in Babylon. In addition, Daniel could understand visions and dreams of all kinds. So Nebuchadnezzar had them serve in the council of his court.

We must never forget that God set these young men in the highest positions in Babylon when they served Him first and kept His commands, even though they were prisoners from the small foreign country of Judah. So wonderful is God's providence!

2

Nebuchadnezzar's
Forgotten Dream

THE KING'S DEMAND
(2:1-13)

THE SECOND CHAPTER of Daniel deals with Nebuchadnezzar's spiritual dream that depicted coming events in world history. God gave Nebuchadnezzar this dream twenty-six hundred years ago to show the outline of world history from his time to the time of Jesus' coming to earth.

Even though the king was a daring man with a heroic temper, he couldn't sleep because the dream was so fearful and awesome. So the king desperately wanted to know the interpretation of the dream.

According to the Scriptures, Nebuchadnezzar must have been a wise king, for when he summoned the magicians and enchanters of his palace to tell him the interpretation of the dream, he didn't tell them what he had dreamed. He knew that when most people hear someone's dream they are usually able to provide a plausible interpretation of it. So, how much less difficult would it be for Nebuchadnezzar's Babylonian magicians and enchanters, he thought, who were specially trained to interpret!

When the king demanded that his enchanters and magicians tell the

9

interpretation of the dream without hearing what he had dreamed, they protested. But the king refused to change his mind and insisted that they should reveal the dream and its interpretation together. Only then would he know for certain that they could interpret the dream correctly.

Being pressed, the magicians slyly shuffled the responsibility to the gods. This made the king so furious that he ordered the execution of all the wise men of Babylon and the destruction of their houses. So the commander of the king's guard went out with the soldiers to execute his orders, and the situation became grave.

THE BOLD FAITH OF DANIEL (2:14–16)

THE FATE OF Daniel and his three friends, Shadrach, Meshach, and Abednego, hung by a thread. But notice here the boldness of those who trust in God. The people were frightened out of their senses by the king's command to execute all the magicians and enchanters of Babylon. But Daniel, who trusted in the eternal God, was unperturbed. Instead, he simply asked the king for some time to seek the Lord for the interpretation.

Daniel's response should remind us that we can trust God in difficult situations without panicking. In ordinary times there may seem to be little difference between the life of a Christian and a non-Christian. Once adversity comes, however, a great difference is manifested. Those who do not trust in Jesus Christ are easily frustrated and tend to complain. They grow uneasy and try to escape the circumstances, as Nebuchadnezzar's pagan magicians did. On the other hand, Christians can overcome crisis and hardship like Daniel, relying upon God with bold faith.

THE REVELATION OF GOD (2:17–19)

FACED WITH THE harsh and hasty decree of the king, Daniel called his three friends to him, and they held a prayer meeting.

Notice here that the prayer of two people is better than the prayer of one person, and the prayer of more than two is even better. The urgency of the king's decree might have sent him to a mountain to pray alone. But Daniel was a man who knew the power of corporate prayer. So he called his friends to pray together. This principle, which I call the "Law of Companions in Prayer," is still true today, especially for our families. The prayer of a couple is more desirable than the prayer of only one person.

And the prayer of the whole family is even better—especially when we are praying for revelation from God. If those who have fervent faith pray together according to this law, God will answer that prayer more quickly.

After the four friends prayed to God, God revealed Nebuchadnezzar's dream to Daniel during the night in a vision. I believe Daniel dreamed the same dream Nebuchadnezzar had dreamed. Accordingly, he could know everything in Nebuchadnezzar's dream.

When Daniel awoke the next morning, he praised God:

> Daniel answered and said, "Let the name of God be blessed forever and ever, for wisdom and power belong to Him. And it is He who changes the times and the epochs; He removes kings and establishes kings; He gives wisdom to wise men, and knowledge to men of understanding. It is He who reveals the profound and hidden things; He knows what is in the darkness, and the light dwells with Him. To Thee, O God of my fathers, I give thanks and praise, for Thou hast given me wisdom and power; even now Thou hast made known to me what we requested of Thee, for Thou hast made known to us the king's matter."
>
> —DANIEL 2:20–23

We can see in Daniel's response to God's revelation this example to follow: He had a heart of true gratitude.

DANIEL TELLS THE KING ABOUT GOD (2:24–30)

FINALLY DANIEL WAS brought into the presence of the king to tell him both the mysterious dream and its interpretation. Yet notice that Daniel did not come to simply tell the king the dream and its interpretation. He stood before the king with a determination to make the most of this opportunity to be a witness of the true God. The same should be true for us. Whenever we have a conversation with someone who is not a Christian, we should make it our goal to preach Jesus Christ through that conversation so the person may accept Him as Lord and Savior.

THE CONTENTS OF NEBUCHADNEZZAR'S DREAM (2:31–43)

SURELY THE KING was astounded by Daniel's accuracy as he began to interpret the king's dream. Daniel no doubt had the king's amazed attention as he went on to give the interpretation of each element of the dream.

Daniel's interpretation that the golden head in the dream was Nebuchadnezzar himself must have been a great shock to the king. Until then Nebuchadnezar thought he had become king by his own merit and by the blessing of his god Merodach. So he was understandably astonished when he heard that Daniel's God had make him a king. Yet he could not refute what Daniel had said, because Daniel had revealed every secret of Nebuchadnezzar's heart, which he had kept to himself.

The inferior kingdom that would arise after Babylon, which is represented by the breast of silver, will be dealt with more specifically in chapter seven. But we should note briefly here that it refers to the coalition kingdom of Media and Persia, which conquered Babylon at the time of Belshazzar. The breast of silver had two arms, representing the two members of the coalition. These two kingdoms alternately ruled what had been the whole region of Babylonia.

The belly of brass followed the breast of silver. This referred to the Greek age of Alexander the Great, who conquered the Medo-Persian kingdom. Babylon and Medo-Persia, which had ruled before the Greek empire, were Asian kingdoms. Alexander the Great, however, arose and conquered Macedonia in Europe, Iran and Syria in western Asia, and Egypt in Africa. He built the Greek empire by uniting the East and the West.

So the brass which formed the belly extended to the thighs and was divided into two parts because Alexander the Great built a kingdom that extended to the east and the west, which broke the coalition of the Medo-Persian kingdom. One leg refers to the West and the other to the East.

Next came the statue's legs of iron. After the fall of Alexander the Great, the kingdom he had built was divided into four parts by four generals who had been his staff officers. They lasted for only a short period and were conquered by Rome, which arose at that time. And because Rome established a kingdom, the territory that extended to the east and the west was represented by the legs of iron.

Daniel points out in particular that the kingdom of iron would be strong and would subdue the world. The Roman Empire was in fact the strongest and most terrible empire in history. Its army broke other nations to pieces, just like the legs of iron.

In addition, the feet and toes were made of both iron and clay. This signified that the kingdom would be divided. Part of it would be strong, and part of it would be weak at the same time.

THE AGE OF THE TOES

I BELIEVE THAT the age represented by the toes of mixed iron and clay refers to our present age. If that is the case, you may well ask, then what about the two thousand years that elapsed between the period of the iron legs—the time of the Roman empire, which saw the first coming of Jesus—and the present age?

This is the period I call the gospel age. And I believe that God did not disclose this gospel age of Jesus Christ when He gave revelation to the Jewish prophets, because these two thousand years are the age in which God calls His bride, the church, according to His special providence. This is why in Daniel's prophecy the description of the Roman empire is immediately followed by a description of the establishment of Christ's kingdom on earth—that is, Christ's coming to earth.

The ten toes of both feet therefore show that ten nations will be somehow united in the former territory of the eastern and western parts of the Roman empire. But this unity will be difficult to maintain because some of the member countries will be ruled by imperalist or authoritarian regimes, while at the same time other countries will be ruled by democratic governments. Such a unity—involving nations governed by different political philosophies—can only be incomplete.

You may ask whether such a period will actually come in history. If Daniel's book is an accurate and sure prophecy, then this age is without a doubt the very age of the toes. And if these toes—the ten nations—are on the way toward unity, we are sure to be approaching the end of the world.

What is happening around us? The movement to unify Europe in the former territory of the Roman empire has been briskly underway since 1958. The headquarters of the European Economic Community (EEC) was established that year in Brussels, Belgium. Its task has been to unify Europe economically, and plans are currently being laid for political unity as well.

We cannot predict presently with certainty when this political unity will be accomplished. Recent reports state there are currently fifteen participating countries, but things are changing rapidly. Only one thing is currently certain. Unless Europe is unified, it cannot survive. Its leaders know that it cannot compete with the superpowers of the world in its present fragmented condition. Consequently, by the divine providence which works in history and in nature, Europe is slowly marching toward a unity that will first be accomplished economically and politically.

At a certain day and hour in our lifetime, I believe we will hear through the news media that the unity of ten nations of Europe has finally been achieved. All over Europe they will have elected their representatives to the European Parliament, and the European Parliament will have elected the president of Europe. Then the drama of the End Times will speed up dramatically.

According to my understanding of other passages from the Bible, especially in Revelation, it is that period during which the Antichrist will arise and enter into a seven-year treaty of friendship with Israel. Then the Great Tribulation will start, and around that time the church will be taken up into heaven. The church will be swept up by the wind of the Holy Spirit, and eternal destruction and tribulation will come upon the people remaining on this earth.

THE STONE CUT WITHOUT HANDS
(2:44–45)

WHEN EUROPE HAS been unified, a stone that is not cut by human hands will strike the image according to its symbolic representation—that is, will bring down the pride of human empire—thereby bringing an end to history. In this time of the toes, we are told, God will set up a kingdom that will never be destroyed, nor will it be left to another people besides God's people. It will crush all human kingdoms and bring them to an end, but it will itself endure forever.

This kingdom is the eternal kingdom of Christ, and the stone that was cut out in heaven refers to Jesus Himself. The Bible says, "The stone which the builders rejected, this became the chief corner stone; this came about from the Lord, and it is marvelous in our eyes" (Matt. 21:42).

Jesus is the very stone that God uses to accomplish His purposes. Like the prophecy we will look at later in Revelation 19, this prophecy tells of things that will happen in the future when Jesus descends to this world riding on a white horse to bring an end to the war of Armageddon. He will come down with His saints who participate in the marriage supper. With them He will destroy all the armies of the earth and will throw the beast—the Antichrist—into the fire of sulphur, casting into hell all the people who have the mark of the beast. Then after all these things, He will set up His millennial kingdom.

These things will come true quickly. I believe they may happen before our generation passes. If they do, Paul tells us:

Nebuchadnezzar's Forgotten Dream

For the Lord Himself will descend from heaven with a shout, with the voice of the archangel, and with the trumpet of God; and the dead in Christ shall rise first. Then we who are alive and remain shall be caught up together with them in the clouds to meet the Lord in the air.

—1 THESSALONIANS 4:16–17

The prophetic fulfillment of Nebuchadnezzar's dream is coming to pass before our very eyes in current events. Daniel saw it twenty-six hundred years ago. We, however, know about it through historical events that have actually happened. So in that regard we now live in the happiest of all ages.

THE LESSON CONCERNING HUMAN HISTORY

THE PICTURE OF human history Daniel saw showed the deterioration of human civilization. Nebuchadnezzar's kingdom was gold, but the following kingdoms were increasingly inferior: silver, brass, iron, and finally clay.

Today many people say that with the improvement of education, human civilization will progress. Actually, however, it grows worse as time goes on, and its character has been progressively deteriorating into "clay." This is the reality Daniel saw through the revelation of God twenty-six centuries ago.

The imagery in Daniel also suggests that the world will become stronger militarily. In specific gravity, gold is 19; silver is 11; brass is 8.5; and iron is 7.8. In degree of hardness, however, silver is superior to gold; brass is superior to silver; and iron is much superior to brass. I believe this implies that the more human civilization develops, the more dreadful weapons and military power it will possess.

Furthermore, with regard to political forms, the imagery suggests that each kingdom's political power will be weaker. Nebuchadnezzar's kingdom of gold, for example, represented a government with supreme power. The king completely organized the entire domain of Babylon and held the fate of all its subjects in one hand.

But Medo-Persia, though it ruled a larger territory than Babylon, was weaker in political power. The weakening became more conspicuous in the Greek kingdom and in the succeeding Roman Empire.

The Roman dominions were eventually split in half, to the east and the west, under the reign of Valentinian I in A.D. 364. Then Rome finally fell to the invading barbarians. In the period of the toes, the iron and the clay are mixed together, implying that this period, our current period, will be characterized by a much weaker political power rather than totalitarianism.

NEBUCHADNEZZAR SURRENDERS TO GOD
(2:46–49)

WHEN DANIEL REVEALED the vision he had seen in his dream and interpreted it, Nebuchadnezzar was so impressed that he fell upon his face and worshiped Daniel. The king of this great kingdom actually came down from his throne to worship an exile! Since Nebuchadnezzar thought Daniel was a messenger of God, he commanded that offerings and incense be presented to the young man.

Of course, this behavior was not actually directed toward Daniel himself. Nebuchadnezzar sacrificed offerings, burned incense, and bowed himself down to the God of Daniel who gave him wisdom and understanding. He offered worship to God in the same way he normally worshiped his own god Merodach.

We must not misunderstand here and think that Daniel received worship as if he were God. Daniel knew that the object of the king's worship was actually the Lord Himself.

Afterward, Nebuchadnezzar set Daniel in a high position and made him ruler over the entire province of Babylon, placing him in charge of all its wise men. Moreover, at Daniel's request, the king appointed Shadrach, Meshach, and Abednego, who had prayed with Daniel, to be administrators over the province of Babylon.

Notice closely how much Daniel's circumstances had changed. He began as an exile attending a three-year course at the court school. Then he almost lost his life during the disturbance caused by Nebuchadnezzar's dream. But when he gathered together his friends and prayed to God, he received the divine revelation by which all the hardships turned into blessings.

This is the difference between those who believe in God and those who do not. When unbelievers are not able to solve the difficulty that comes to them, they are torn to death by the adversity. But believers of God can counter this difficulty with the concerted prayer of fellow Christians. Consequently, the difficulty is finally overcome, and they receive the miracle of God's turning everything into good in the end. In this way believers receive the blessings promised in Deuteronomy: They become not the tail, but the head; they do not decline, but rise; they do not borrow, but lend.

For that reason, we who believe in God give thanks in all the circumstances of our lives. For when good things come to us, we are grateful. And even though bad things come to us, we can be sure they will turn into good things.

3

The Fiery Furnace

NEBUCHADNEZZAR'S IMAGE OF GOLD
(3:1–7)

IN THE EIGHTEENTH year of the reign of King Nebuchadnezzar, twenty years after Daniel had become an exile, the king set up a ninety-foot golden image to be worshiped. I believe that image must have been the very same image Nebuchadnezzar saw in his dream. He was probably so puffed up by Daniel's interpretation signifying the golden head of the image as being himself that the king set up the image to show off his glory and power.

As grounds for this conjecture, we can cite the fact that a name was not given to the image. If it had been an idol to represent Merodach, it would have been named after Merodach. So I think it was just the nameless golden image Nebuchadnezzar had seen in his dream.

Nebuchadnezzar summoned all the leaders of the empire to the image's dedication to show off his glory and consolidate the political unity of his empire.

Today we might think it absurd that the king would command his people to worship an image. But Nebuchadnezzar was the sovereign ruler

19

of the Babylonian empire and held absolute power. Who dared to disobey his command? Neither the king nor his subjects would dare refuse, considering that the punishment for disobedience was to be thrown into a blazing furnace. No wonder all the officials lined up to worship!

But not everyone bowed before the image.

DANIEL'S FRIENDS REFUSE TO WORSHIP THE IDOL (3:8–12)

THREE PEOPLE IN the multitude that day stood upright while everyone else was prostrate. They were Daniel's three friends: Shadrach, Meshach, and Abednego. Daniel was saved from the disaster because he happened to be absent. But his friends could not break God's commandments: "You shall have no other gods before me. You shall not bow down to an idol." (See Exodus 20:3–4.) They could keep all the other commands of the king of Babylon, but they could by no means keep any command that was against the laws of God. This was their faith.

Their faith is a great model for Christianity today. When the government issues a command, we must obey that command as long as it is not against the commandments of God. There is no authority except that which God has established. It belongs to God to set up a nation and to appoint the one who rules the nation. Therefore, we must submit ourselves to all the governing authorities. (See Romans 13:1.)

Nevertheless, when the governing authority forces us to disobey God and compels us to worship an idol, putting other gods in God's place, we must obey God rather than submit ourselves to the worldly power. We must even risk our lives to keep the integrity of our faith.

When Shadrach, Meshach, and Abednego obeyed God rather than Nebuchadnezzar, trouble soon came. These Jewish men had been a thorn in the side of the Babylonian nobles because they were foreign exiles who were highly favored by the king. Consequently, the Babylonians had been watching for every opportunity to find fault with them.

Immediately they brought their accusations to the king. And the accusation was not a simple one. They brought three charges against Daniel's friends.

The first accusation was that they did not pay homage to the king. The second accusation was that they did not serve the god of the king. The third accusation was that they did not worship the image the king had set up.

In other words, their accusations were that the Jewish men had no respect for the king, did not serve him, and publicly opposed him. Thus their behavior was an infringement upon the sovereignty and authority of the king; in short, it was treason. So for the sake of his dignity and honor, Nebuchadnezzar had to punish the three men.

THE CONFESSION OF FAITH OF DANIEL'S FRIENDS (3:13–18)

WHEN NEBUCHADNEZZAR thought that his sovereignty was being challenged before his own subjects and the diplomats from foreign kingdoms, his rage knew no bounds. Yet Shadrach, Meshach, and Abednego had served as governors of the province for more than fifteen years. During that period they had obtained a good reputation for administration based on wisdom and mercy. If they had been low-level officials, Nebuchadnezzar might have shouted that they should at once be thrown into the furnace. But because they were high-ranking officials who commanded respect both in and outside of his kingdom, Nebuchadnezzar suppressed his surging rage and gave them a second chance.

The king's words to them meant basically this: "In the past the God of the Jewish people revealed to me the interpretation of my dream through Daniel. Can He deliver you from the burning furnace?" This was the last chance he could give them and still save face.

The officials and foreign guests in his court were all holding their breath, watching the development of the incident with keen interest. I can imagine how the king's face grew red with anger. Meanwhile, the Babylonians who had accused the three Jews were singing a triumphal song in their hearts.

> Shadrach, Meshach and Abednego answered and said to the king, "O Nebuchadnezzar, we do not need to give you an answer concerning this. If it be so, our God whom we serve is able to deliver us from the furnace of blazing fire; and He will deliver us out of your hand, O king. But even if He does not, let it be known to you, O king, that we are not going to serve your gods or worship the golden image that you have set up."
>
> —DANIEL 3:16–18

What a solemn and bold confession of faith this is! Numerous martyrs and saints who suffered persecution in the history of Christianity received great courage from the integrity of faith and bold confession of these three. Their example of faith should inspire and encourage us as well.

THE KING BECOMES FURIOUS (3:19–23)

WHEN NEBUCHADNEZZAR heard the three Israelites confess their faith, he became so furious that his complexion even changed. Those who stood in the presence of the king all trembled because they knew harm might come to them as well.

Nevertheless, I believe that Shadrach, Meshach, and Abednego, whose fate hung by a thread, were calm and full of smiles. They were firm in their faith that God could easily deliver them from the burning furnace. Their solemn attitude showed that even if it were not God's will to deliver them, they could never be brought to worship the image.

These three men truly loved God. Their great love of God made them ready to die for Him rather than lose the integrity of their faith. What we should learn from them is this: Even if the same crisis should come to us, forcing us to acknowledge Jesus at the cost of our lives, we should never waiver in the confession of our faith.

In the journey of life we sometimes fall into sin because of our weakness. But if we come back to God and repent of our sins, He forgives us. When we compromise in this area, breaking the commandment "You shall have no other gods before me," God is grieved and angry, because this is a matter which concerns His majesty.

For this reason, when we are put to the test by those who would demand that we worship another god, we must never compromise. Rather, we must resist even at the risk of our own lives. This is the fundamental reason Christians have never been able to embrace that now-faltering ideology called communism. Communists deny the existence of God and worship their ideology as god. So we cannot make any concessions to communism. Instead, we must continue to fight against it, no matter the cost.

ANGER LEADS TO FOOLISHNESS (3:24–25)

IN HIS RAGE Nebuchadnezzar shouted at his subjects, "Heat up the furnace seven times hotter than usual!" Anger is always accompanied by such foolishness. In calmness of heart we can say wise words, while in anger we utter foolish ones.

Here Nebuchadnezzar's rage made him a fool because his command was counterproductive. If he had wanted to maximize the pain of the three men, he could have lowered the heat of the furnace so that it would not kill them instantly. But he did the opposite.

Full of anger, Nebuchadnezzar continued to speak foolish words and do foolish things. Notice that the king commanded the three men to be thrown into the *midst* of the blazing furnace. If the three had been thrown into the *mouth* of the furnace, that would have served the purpose just as well. It was just a decision made in anger.

In order to carry out this command of the king, several soldiers had to raise the three men one by one and throw them. The result was the unfair death of several soldiers who were consumed by the fire while trying to carry out the command. So the king's anger led not only to foolishness but finally to tragedy.

Though this is but a small example, here is an important lesson we must realize: We must not under any circumstances make decisions in anger because a decision made in anger leads to failure.

THE FOURTH MAN (3:24–27)

ONCE THE THREE men were thrown into the furnace by the command of Nebuchadnezzar—the king of Babylon who held such power that he dictated to the world—everyone, including the king himself, assumed that the three men had died. But only the ropes binding the three men were burned up by the fire, because the man who is with God does not die.

The rope is a symbol of royal power dominating the whole world. Only that symbol of power was burned up like bits of straw, while Shadrach, Meshach, and Abednego danced in the midst of the fire. Then Nebuchadnezzar saw a fourth man like "a son of the gods" walking around with them in the fire, and he was astonished (v. 25).

Human beings cannot obstruct what God does. God was watching this scene in heaven as He heard the unyielding confession of faith spoken by Shadrach, Meshach, and Abednego.

You see, Nebuchadnezzar used the expression "a son of the gods" not knowing who the man was. But the fourth man in the fire was Jesus Christ. When the men had been dragged to the furnace, the Son must have said to the Father, "Father, I will go down to the earth. We cannot let those who have such uncompromising faith die. We must show them that the God of the universe lives."

Then, when Shadrach, Meshach, and Abednego fell into the fire at the command of the furious Nebuchadnezzar, the Son of God also jumped into the fire.

What is impossible to the God who made heaven and earth? Just as He would later command the physical elements and cause the furious storms to become calm, He took charge of the fire and commanded it to do no harm to God's children, however hotly it burned. (See Mark 4:39.)

This story should remind us that when we suffer persecution, we meet Jesus. If we stand before the Lord with uncompromising faith, this fourth man, Jesus Christ, will always be with us because He said, "Lo, I am with you always, even to the end of the age" (Matt. 28:20). So even today God wants to deliver us miraculously out of the fire.

A ROYAL SUMMONS (3:26–27)

NEBUCHADNEZZAR WAS struck dumb with amazement to see how that the rope, which was a symbol of his power, honor, and dignity, had been burned up, while the three men he had ordered executed were running around in the flames free. He discovered that his power and authority did not originate with himself, but with God.

Not one sparrow will fall to the ground apart from the will of God. When Pilate asked Jesus, "Don't you realize I have power either to free you or to crucify you?" Jesus answered, "You would have no power over Me except what is given to you from above." (See John 19:10–11.) Neither Pilate nor Nebuchadnezzar nor any other ruler has any power over God's people except what God has allowed them to have.

When Nebuchadnezzar and his officials realized what had happened, the king's rage turned to fear. With a trembling voice he summed them to come out, calling them "servants of the Most High God" (v. 26).

When Shadrach, Meshach, and Abednego heard this, they came out immediately, and the fourth man disappeared. They obeyed the king's command to come out even though he had ordered them thrown into the furnace, because the power to rule the kingdom of Babylon was nevertheless given by God. Although they could by no means obey the royal command to worship an idol in opposition to God's commandment, they still obeyed the other commands given by the king; it was their duty as the king's subjects, according to the will of God.

We should also follow the example of these Hebrew's attitudes. While we live in this world, we preach the gospel with all our might and try to change our environment according to our vision of success. But we also

24

have a duty to submit ourselves to the government we have elected.

Of course, if an official commands us to betray God, we must resist unto death. Otherwise, we must submit to and pray for the political leaders of our country. They are human beings just as we are, so we must help them with our prayers so they may receive God's wisdom and understanding to lead the nation.

When Shadrach, Meshach, and Abednego came out of the furnace, the king and his officials crowded around them to touch their clothes and their bodies. Seeing that the fire had not harmed them, they were further amazed to discover that even the smell of fire was not on them. The king wondered, "How on earth could such a thing be possible?"

NEBUCHADNEZZAR PRAISES GOD (3:28–30)

NEBUCHADNEZZAR AT LAST praised the one true God, saying:

> Blessed be the God of Shadrach, Meshach, and Abednego, who has sent His angel and delivered His servants who put their trust in Him, violating the king's command, and yielded up their bodies so as not to serve or worship any god except their own God. Therefore, I make a decree that any people, nation or tongue that speaks anything offensive against the God of Shadrach, Meshach and Abednego shall be torn limb from limb and their houses reduced to a rubbish heap, inasmuch as there is no other god who is able to deliver in this way.
>
> —DANIEL 3:29–30

He even went so far as to threaten anyone who spoke against God in his kingdom. Notice here that in the king's thinking God had become the God of Shadrach, Meshach, and Abednego—the personal God of these men. In a similar way the Bible says that God was the God of Abraham, Isaac, and Jacob, for He was the God experienced personally by each of these patriarchs throughout their lives.

God wants to become your personal God as well. You should live your life in such a way that other people will speak of God as *your* God. Let them put your own name behind His. When the living God comes into your own life to work so that you experience Him personally, signs and wonders will appear.

Notice as well that even though Nebuchadnezzar decreed that no one should speak anything against God, he still did not say that everyone should believe in God. This is an indication that he still had pride in his heart. Later, however, we will see him completely yielding to God and confessing that everyone should believe in Him.

What was the result of this episode with the furnace? The king promoted Shadrach, Meshach, and Abednego. Consequently, the whole kingdom of Babylon came to serve a handful of Jewish exiles as their masters. Daniel and his three friends took all the key posts of the court.

This story illustrates vividly that when God is with us we become the head, wherever we may be. We don't need to worry, because in all things God works for the good of those who love Him. (See Romans 8:28.)

4

Nebuchadnezzar's Insanity and Recovery

NEBUCHADNEZZAR'S SECOND DREAM (4:1–3)

TIME AND AGAIN God gave His revelation to King Nebuchadnezzar through dreams. In Daniel chapter 2, through the dream of the golden image, God showed him what would happen in the future of the world, and Daniel interpreted the dream for him clearly.

Daniel 4 is set in the context of Nebuchadnezzar's decree of God's judgment that resulted in the king's becoming insane for seven years. When Nebuchadnezzar had finally recovered, he was so overwhelmed with gratitude that he issued the decree giving praise to God.

THE KING RELIES ON DANIEL FOR THE INTERPRETATION (4:4–9)

THE BOOK OF Daniel makes it clear that even a wicked man like Nebuchadnezzar can be broken enough in heart to believe in God, considering that he appointed a man like Daniel as chief of governors—a man with a pure faith of integrity who met with God every morning and evening. Our influence as believers is greater than we realize. This is why Paul says, "For the unbelieving husband is sanctified through his wife, and the unbelieving wife is sanctified through her believing husband" (1 Cor. 7:14). The marriage relationship represents the greatest influence of this kind. Accordingly, when one spouse has faith, the other is necessarily affected.

The influence of a Christian is like the mustard seed. It looks small, but when the seed is sown it grows to become a big tree. Our influence is also like yeast. Only a little bit of yeast in a large wooden kneading bowl is enough to leaven the whole dough.

Under the influence of Daniel's faith, the stubborn and wicked man Nebuchadnezzar became a new man after he had recovered from his insanity. His unbelief was completely broken, and he became a worshiper of God. The greeting at the beginning of his decree and the peals of praise to God that follow even resemble those in the New Testament epistles of that great man of faith, the apostle Paul: "May your peace abound! . . . How great are His signs and how mighty are His wonders!" (vv. 1, 3).

One primary concern of a heathen ruler was to establish his kingdom and to preserve the throne for his posterity from generation to generation. But instead Nebuchadnezzar confessed that *God's* kingdom "is an everlasting kingdom, and His dominion is from generation to generation" (v. 3).

This is an extraordinary transformation. Nebuchadnezzar had been responsible for the fall of Israel. He had sent an army to overthrow the nation and to destroy the temple of God. Yet through Daniel, an exile whom he had brought to his court, he came to believe in God and to praise Him.

This is the power of faith. When Jesus heard Peter confess faith in Him, He said, "Upon this rock I will build My church; and the gates of Hades shall not overpower it" (Matt. 16:18). Who is this rock? He is the person who confesses as Peter did, "Thou art the Christ, the Son of the living God" (Matt. 16:16). Anyone who believes and confesses today, "Thou art the Christ, the Son of the living God," is the same kind of rock, and upon this rock Jesus builds His church.

Furthermore, Jesus referred to Himself as the stone when He said, "He who falls on this stone will be broken to pieces; but on whomever it falls, it will scatter him like dust" (Matt. 21:44). Jesus dwells in you and me. So when unbelievers "bump" against believers, they are spiritually broken to pieces and are brought to repentance.

Of course, we are speaking here of the kind of Christian who lives faithfully, having Jesus at the center of his or her life. Sadly enough, there is another kind of Christian who leads a worse life than a non-Christian, though he or she may profess faith in Jesus Christ. Such a person is a shame to Him.

The Bible says, "Faith, if it has no works, is dead, being by itself" (James 2:17) and "You shall love your neighbor as yourself" (Matt. 22:39). To love God and your neighbor are the basic principles of Christianity.

Why does the Bible emphasize faith with works? Through faith at work, we can let our neighbors see God. King Nebuchadnezzar of heathen Babylon saw the God of Shadrach, Meshach, Abednego, and Daniel. Because of their faith at work, he could become like these children of God.

The same is true today. People around us are watching us. Whether we are an elder or a senior, deaconess or a deacon, whether we are a home cell group leader or a church member without any leadership responsibilities, they are observing our behavior. They want to see God in us.

In the midst of this world with all its problems there is no one to turn to, so they want to believe in our God. Show them God, as Daniel and his friends did. Through faith and behavior worthy of the name of God's children, show them God their creator. "Let your light shine before men in such a way that they may see your good works, and glorify your Father who is in heaven" (Matt. 5:16).

For the glory of Christ, this should be the attitude of a Christian: If someone forces us to go one mile, we should go two; if someone wants to take our tunic, we should let him have our cloak as well; if someone strikes us on the right cheek, we should turn to him the other also. (See Matthew 5:39–41.) In the eyes of the people in the world, these behaviors may seem to make us losers. But since God is for us, who can be against us? (See Romans 8:31.) We will have God as our strength, and He will bless us.

Therefore, we must diligently learn the pattern Daniel set forth. His faith had such integrity that it even impressed the pagan king Nebuchadnezzar and showed him God. In this way, through the quality of his life, Daniel was an excellent preacher of God. I pray in the name of Jesus that you too may become a precious saint like Daniel who reflects God in your daily life.

THE CONTENTS OF THE DREAM (4:10–18)

AT THE BEGINNING of the king's dream, the events of the dream must have been pleasant and unworthy of his calling in the interpreters to examine. But suddenly, at verse 13, the dream became a nightmare.

The angel's shouting from heaven disturbed the peacefulness of the dream, and Nebuchadnezzar was terrified. When he awoke he knew it was a divine revelation. So he called for all the magicians, enchanters, and astrologers of Babylon for an interpretation. But none of them could do it, because demons cannot interpret a divine revelation.

We should keep this in mind as we pray. When we pray in our common language, our prayer is understood by both God and the devil. But when we pray in tongues, our prayer is understood by no one but God unless He gives an interpretation: "For one who speaks in a tongue does not speak to men, but to God; for no one understands, but in his spirit he speaks mysteries" (1 Cor. 14:2).

For that reason, if we are filled with the Holy Spirit and can pray in tongues, we should endeavor to pray that way often. It is the prayer our spirits offer directly to God, and it brings us great benefit.

DANIEL'S INTERPRETATION (4:19–27)

WHEN NONE OF the magicians and the enchanters were able to interpret the dream for him, Nebuchadnezzar called for Daniel. But when Daniel learned the meaning of the dream, he was so terrified that he was mute for a time. So the king had to encourage Daniel not to worry and to tell the interpretation of the dream. Comforted by this, Daniel began to interpret the dream, wishing that the thing would not happen to the king.

The beginning of the interpretation was complimentary rather than troubling. But then Daniel went on to reveal the rest of the interpretation.

To summarize: Daniel first revealed that the tree represented Nebuchadnezzar. Next he said that the one who came down from heaven was a divine messenger and that his words revealed what would happen to the king— namely, that the king would be insane for seven years and would live in the field eating grass like cattle after being driven from the royal palace. Then, said Daniel, the king's pride would be broken, and he would acknowledge the sovereignty of God. Afterward, the king would be brought back to his throne.

Next Daniel gave his advice to the king. He said that Nebuchadnezzar should change his ways and act righteously.

We should keep in mind that it was hard to find righteousness in the kings of that day. They had such absolute power that they could seize the possessions of their subjects on a whim. They even held the power of life and death over them, so their tyranny knew no limits.

Nebuchadnezzar had used his power to mobilize a large number of poor people in forced labor to build the city of Babylon, and they had been terribly mistreated. Under such circumstances, Daniel advised the king to cease from oppressing these poor people.

NEBUCHADNEZZAR'S PRIDE (4:28–30)

HERE NEBUCHADNEZZAR describes what actually happened to him. Twelve months after he had dreamed the dream, the king went out on the flat, spacious roof of the palace and looked down upon the city of Babylon.

The sight of the city which spread before him near and far must have been impressive and beautiful. Modern archeologists who have excavated this site say that it was one of the architectural wonders of the world's ancient civilizations. It was a magnificent city built by the hard labor of people enslaved from the countries Babylon conquered.

Looking out over the sight, the king proudly threw back his shoulders and boasted about it. What he said was similar to Satan's proud words when he rebelled against God. Being puffed up, the devil claimed:

> I will ascend to heaven; I will raise my throne above the stars of God, and I will sit on the mount of assembly in the recesses of the north. I will ascend above the heights of the clouds; I will make myself like the Most High.
>
> —ISAIAH 14:13–14

Because of his proud rebellion, Satan fell from heaven and into hell. The Bible says, "Pride goes before destruction, and a haughty spirit before stumbling" (Prov. 16:18).

God brings the arrogant low and exalts the humble-hearted—not only among His chosen people, but among the heathen as well. So we should not be surprised that God humbled this man and that the king's pride led to his downfall.

THE KING'S HEART IS CHANGED (4:33)

AS SOON AS Nebuchadnezzar uttered his arrogant words on the roof of the palace, he heard a voice from heaven. As soon as the words had been spoken to Nebuchadnezzar, his human heart departed; the heart of a beast was given to him instead.

The total transformation of a human heart can be tragic, as in the case of this king. Yet the change can take another direction as well, bringing great benefit. For example, when John the Baptist preached, "Repent, for the kingdom of heaven is at hand" (Matt. 3:2), the biblical Greek word for *repent* means "to change the thoughts of one's heart"—a change that leads to salvation.

So the condition of our heart is important because our heart determines our behavior. If people dwell on murder in their hearts, they will eventually commit murder. If lewd thinking creeps into their hearts, they will sooner or later translate it into sexually immoral action.

On the other hand, if people's hearts are sanctified, their behavior will be sanctified, too. If they have faith in their hearts, they will behave accordingly. If their hearts become positive and prosperous, actions that bring them success and victory will necessarily follow.

The heart must be changed before the life can be changed. And a change of environment does not necessarily bring a change of heart. Instead, a change of heart will bring a change of environment.

The Bible says, "Watch over your heart with all diligence, for from it flow the springs of life" (Prov. 4:23). The heart must be kept in such a way that pride cannot possess it. And a bad heart must be renewed by the blood of Jesus Christ to become a good one.

When we repent and change our hearts in Jesus Christ through hearing the Word of God, our lives become totally different. That is why the apostle Paul said, "Therefore if any man is in Christ, he is a new creature; the old things passed away; behold, new things have come" (2 Cor. 5:17). If we are born again to become positive, active, and creative people, and if we fill our hearts with things that are rich and victorious according to the Word of God, our lives and even our environment will bear the same fruit.

For that reason, keep the Holy Spirit always in your heart and let Him be the master of it. Fill your heart with the Word of God so that your faith may grow. And your environment will be changed beautifully in proportion to the growth of your faith.

NEBUCHADNEZZAR RECOGNIZES GOD'S SOVEREIGNTY (4:34–37)

WHEN WE READ that Nebuchadnezzar raised his eyes toward heaven, we can understand this to mean that he surrendered himself to God and came to admit the sovereignty of God. He fully realized now that God could exalt him or bring him low, and that God was able to spare his life or destroy it.

Then the heart of the beast left him, and his sanity was restored. He bowed down to God and prayed, giving thanks and praise. And he committed his life to the sovereign God.

Then after he recovered, a group of his subjects headed by Daniel brought him back to the throne and once more served him as the king. In fact, Daniel was responsible for ensuring that Nebuchadnezzar was able to return to his throne after an absence of seven years.

Daniel's prophecy had been heard by all the people in the court. They knew from his words that the king's insanity was temporary, that he would return to rule, and that the whole episode happened by divine providence. If Daniel had not prophesied this, King Nebuchadnezzar would have died. His enemies would have followed the insane man to the field and killed him to usurp the throne. But because Daniel prophesied what God would do, no one dared attempt an assassination. They were afraid of Daniel's prophecy and of the God whom he worshiped.

At last Nebuchadnezzar repented of his arrogance. Acknowledging God's sovereignty, he finally became a man who trusted in God.

Notice here again our important point: Even such a wicked and ruthless man as King Nebuchadnezzar fell by Daniel's prayer and became one of God's people. From a merely human perspective, the prayers offered by Daniel may have seemed as futile an effort as trying to sweep the sea with a broom. Nevertheless, this terrible king of a heathen kingdom who had previously worshiped Merodach, believing that he was above all gods, surrendered himself at last to the true God. This transformation speaks for the patience of Daniel's prayers.

So we should always remember Daniel's example. Even though we sometimes seem to receive no immediate answer to our prayers, we shouldn't lose heart. Daniel did not receive the answer to his prayers even within a year or two. He had to pray constantly for King Nebuchadnezzar for twenty years.

Our prayers are bound to be answered. So pray in bold faith. As the Scripture says, "Believe in the Lord Jesus, and you shall be saved, you and your household" (Acts 16:31). Do not cease praying for the redemption of the members of your family. Even the ruthless heathen Nebuchadnezzar surrendered. How much more will your relatives? I pray in Jesus' name that you may pray for them in faith and finally receive the answer you desire.

5

Belshazzar's Banquet

THE DESECRATION OF THE TEMPLE VESSELS
(5:1–4)

I N THIS TEXT Nebuchadnezzar is called Belshazzar's father, but he was
actually Belshazzar's grandfather. In the Aramaic language the word
we translate *father* frequently meant "ancestor," and *son* often meant
"descendant."

So King Belshazzar was actually a viceroy of his father, Nabonidas,
who was at the oasis city of Terna, recuperating from mental illness.

At that time Darius, the king of Media, came with his Medo-Persian
army of irresistible force to besiege Babylon. But Babylon was an adamant
city, enormous and strongly built. Since the city also had provisions for several years in preparation for such a siege, it refused to yield. And, because
the Euphrates River ran beneath the city, Babylon seemed invincible.

Even so, King Belshazzar was restless. He feared that the soldiers and
even the generals of his army might be demoralized while the city was
under siege for such a long time. The king racked his brain to solve this
problem and finally decided to give a banquet for his subjects to pacify
them. So he prepared a great feast for one thousand of his nobles.

When Belshazzar had gotten drunk, a foolish idea came into his mind. He commanded his servants to bring forth the vessels of gold and silver that had formerly been used in the sacrifices to God at the temple in Jerusalem—vessels that his ancestor King Nebuchadnezzar had taken as spoils. Then Belshazzar and the others present drank wine from them in the name of their pagan gods.

This was a blasphemous desecration. Nebuchadnezzar himself had not even dared to touch them, much less do such a thing. But Belshazzar was so drunk that he became foolish and forgot the fear of God. How then could God ignore what they had done?

In the Bible we see that when people violated any of the last six of the Ten Commandments—those regulating human relationships—God forgave them and gave them opportunity for repentance. But when people violated any of the first four commandments, which dealt with their relationship to God, God's judgment often came more quickly. No wonder then that the judgment of Belshazzar and his guests was swift.

Japan's defeat in Word War II is a good example of this truth. During the war, the emperor of Japan proclaimed that World War II was the war between the Japanese god of Amateras and the God of the Christians. Because Japan had thus profaned the holiness of God, God made that nation the victim of a horrible atomic bombing, and it finally had to surrender.

Likewise, the Nazi leader Adolf Hitler proudly claimed that later history would record him as a god, if there was any such being like a god. And God struck him down.

For decades now the communists have been arrogant. They have blasphemed God and denied His existence. They have devastated churches, prohibited education about God, and forbidden the worship of God. So we are not surprised to be seeing now in our generation the downfall of communism and its disappearance from this stage in history—for they have attacked the very nature of God.

Of course we know that God forgives all the faults Christians commit against their brothers and sisters. But if they pull down the church, which is the body of Christ, God will swiftly judge them. When Ananias and Sapphira, for example, tried to deceive God and the church by keeping some money to themselves, God struck them dead on the spot (Acts 5:1–11). For this reason, we should always examine our relationship with God to find anything amiss before Him.

Of course, as for the fourth commandment that regards the Sabbath day, Jesus said, "The Son of Man is Lord of the Sabbath" (Matt. 12:8). So to us who believe in our Lord Jesus Christ, every day is the Sabbath day. And the day when Jesus Christ was resurrected is the Lord's day, so we must keep it holy. Consequently, the Bible says that we should not let anyone judge us with regard to the Sabbath day (Col. 2:16).

If, however, we violate any of the other three commandments dealing with our relationship to God—"You shall have no other gods before Me," "You shall not make for yourself an idol," "You shall not take the name of your God in vain"—immediate judgment will come upon us. Not only Christians but also non-Christians will be judged if they violate any of those commandments. So even though you may fall and make mistakes in other aspects of your faith life, never violate any of those first three commandments.

THE DIVINE JUDGMENT (5:5–12)

As SOON AS King Belshazzar profaned the vessels of the temple, God's divine judgment was given. In the middle of the merrymaking, suddenly there was heard a sharp shriek: "Look at that wall!"

Belshazzar evidently sensed that the handwriting he saw there was an ill omen and may have guessed that it had to do with his act of desecration. Since he was a viceroy to his father, his offer to make anyone who could interpret the handwriting's message the third highest ruler in the kingdom meant he was offering the position of chief administrator, immediately below himself—so concerned was he to understand what was written.

His fear understandably increased all the more when none of his wise men could interpret the writing. As we said before, they were unable to help him because demons cannot interpret a revelation from God.

Amid the chaos of the banquet, the shouts of the king, and the murmuring of the guests, the queen entered and spoke wise advice: Call Daniel. Evidently Daniel was living in retirement at that time, having withdrawn from active politics because of his old age.

DANIEL'S INTERPRETATION (5:13–31)

RECEIVING THE ROYAL order, Daniel came in hurriedly. Notice that though the king gave Daniel the same promises of wealth and promotion he had given the others, Daniel turned them down. He already knew from the contents of the writing that such promises were meaningless, because the end of Babylon was imminent.

Instead, Daniel, though only a Jewish exile, gave a bold history lecture to the heathen king of Babylon, the world power of that day. Now that Daniel was quite old, he had no lingering affection for anything but to serve God. Nor was he afraid of death. So he sharply rebuked King Belshazzar.

"Don't you know," Daniel said, "what happened to your father—how God humbled him? You are his blood relative and saw it with your own eyes. Haven't you learned your lesson yet? No! Far from learning a lesson, you even blasphemed God by drinking wine from the sacred vessels. Therefore, God will judge you. Now there is no time even for repentance. That writing on the wall forebodes an impending judgment!"

When Daniel finished lecturing Belshazzar, Babylon was already doomed and without hope. God had opened the way of forgiveness to King Nebuchadnezzar, but he did not give King Belshazzar a chance to repent. Nebuchadnezzar's pride caused him to undergo divine "training" for seven years during his insanity, and he did not blaspheme God as Belshazzar did. But because Belshazzar blasphemed God, the Holy Spirit left him, and the way of forgiveness for him was closed.

The Bible says that all the sins of people will be forgiven except one: Whoever blasphemes against the Holy Spirit will not be forgiven either in this world or in the world to come (Mark 3:29). The sin of blaspheming the Holy Spirit is the sin a person commits by calling the work of the Holy Spirit the work of a demon. Those who do this often do it out of envy and jealousy, even though that person knows it is the work of the Spirit. If a person calls the Holy Spirit a demon, the Holy Spirit leaves that person.

I once knew a man who blasphemed the Holy Spirit and was forsaken by Him. He and I were saved together in the city of Pusan in Korea, and we both preached on the streets. He was such a Spirit-filled man that everybody called him "Holy Ghost Boy." Many people envied him and wished to be filled with the Holy Spirit as he was.

But later when I came to Seoul to become a pastor, he went out into the world. Worse yet, he blasphemed against the Holy Spirit by saying that the things he had experienced up to that time were not the works of the Holy Spirit, but the works of a demon. So the Holy Spirit left him.

Then when he went into the army, he did all the wicked things of the devil. Later, he was tormented with an extreme agony of heart as if he had been in hell. It seemed that he could hardly bear the pain. So he called on me when I was pastoring my church in the city of Seodaemun.

This man opened his heart to me and said that he had been writhing

38

with agony of heart. I can still remember his words: "Pastor Cho, for God's sake, help me! As an old friend, have pity on me and make me get out of this pain. Though I have tried hard, I can neither repent of my sin nor believe in Jesus again. My heart seems to be burning, and my soul seems to be in hell several thousand miles away from me. For God's sake help me!"

So I took hold of him and did everything I could do to help him repent, only to fail, because the Spirit had already left him.

"No one can say, 'Jesus is Lord,' except by the Holy Spirit" (1 Cor. 12:3). If we believe in Jesus and confess that Jesus is our Lord while the Holy Spirit dwells in our hearts, we can repent of our sins, and they will be forgiven. But when the Spirit leaves us there will be no more chances. Such was the state in which King Belshazzar found himself. His hour of destruction came, and he could not find a way out.

Today all who do not have Jesus will find themselves in the same situation if they have not received Him when their hour of destruction comes. Now is the age of grace when whoever repents of sin and confesses that Jesus is Lord will be saved. "Behold, now is 'the acceptable time,' behold, now is 'the day of salvation'" (2 Cor. 6:2).

But all who reject such an opportunity for salvation will later stand before the judgment seat of Jesus and will hear the stern voice of the Lord condemning them. By that time God's hand will have already written their judgment on the wall. There will be no hope. Only the eternal pain of hell will be waiting. So I pray in Jesus' name that you will never forsake Jesus once you believe in Him.

After his "history lecture," Daniel read the writing on the wall and interpreted its meaning. Upon hearing Daniel's interpretation, King Belshazzar went out of his mind and ordered that Daniel should be rewarded. That very night, however, the city of Babylon fell. On the very same night that Belshazzar blasphemed God, Medo-Persian armies changed the course of the Euphrates River, which had passed through the middle of the city. Then, as soon as the river dried up, the enemy invaded it like surging waves.

Belshazzar was slain, and Babylon fell. When Belshazzar's father, King Nabonidas, heard the news, he rushed with an army to rescue his son. But he too was defeated in battle and became a prisoner. Thus, as Jeremiah and Isaiah had both prophesied, Babylon was destroyed within twenty years.

6

Daniel in the Lions' Den

THE FALSE CHARGE AGAINST DANIEL
(6:1–9)

WHEN DANIEL WAS quite old, approaching ninety, he was once again promoted to the position of administrator—this time in the kingdom of Darius the Mede. After the conquest of Babylon, King Darius had divided his kingdom into one hundred twenty provinces and appointed one hundred twenty satraps to rule the provinces, setting three administrators over them to supervise the collection of royal revenue. Among the three administrators, Daniel was most likely the oldest.

Daniel had no worldly desires. He was honest, and as he served the king with such integrity of heart, Darius grew greatly attached to him. Furthermore, though Daniel was old, he was inferior to none in sagacity and excelled in every matter. So the king planned to set him over the whole kingdom. But not everyone was pleased with his plans.

Two of the king's other administrators were evidently jealous of Daniel. They probably complained that the young people did not have the opportunity to be promoted because of him. Moreover, Daniel was an exile who had been taken captive from Judah, so his prominence and power seemed an insult to native citizens. Consequently, those two administrators conspired together with the satraps against Daniel, and they probably reasoned with them with words like these: "If Daniel becomes the chief administrator, we'll have to serve him. We won't be promoted, and you won't be either," they probably said. "So we must knock him down from the position—but how? Since he doesn't desire worldly gains or political ambition, there's only one way we can bring any charge against this man. We've noticed that he prays to his God three times a day without fail, opening the windows toward Jerusalem. So let's find a way to make this the basis for charges against him."

Then those who had thus conspired hatched a plot.

> Then these commissioners and satraps came by agreement to the king and spoke to him as follows: "King Darius, live forever! All the commissioners of the kingdom, the prefects and the satraps, the high officials and the governors have consulted together that the king should establish a statute and enforce an injunction that anyone who makes a petition to any god or man besides you, O king, for thirty days, shall be cast into the lions' den. Now, O king, establish the injunction and sign the document so that it may not be changed, according to the law of the Medes and Persians, which may not be revoked." Therefore King Darius signed the document, that is, the injunction.
>
> —DANIEL 6:6–9

This pleased King Darius, for he thought that he would make the most of this opportunity to unify the empire, establish official discipline, and elevate his own authority. So he consented to make it a decree and signed it with his royal ring so that it could not be changed.

The two administrators who had seen this must have danced with joy. They thought they had finally caught Daniel in a trap and that they would soon win the confidence of the king.

Of course, Daniel must have known well about this matter. A candidate for the chief administrator of the kingdom could not have been ignorant of what was happening. He knew exactly what the edict forbade and what punishment it threatened. So how did he respond?

DANIEL'S FAITH DISREGARDED PERIL (6:10–15)

DESPITE THE THREAT of death, Daniel went home, opened the window toward Jerusalem, and prayed on his knees three times a day as usual. We should not be surprised, for even his enemies had been certain that he would still pray, however severe and strict the royal decree might be.

If Daniel had departed just a little from his convictions, he could have avoided danger. He did not have to open the windows in full public view while he prayed, for God is not bound to any such external conditions. If he had prayed clandestinely after the others went to bed instead of insisting on his custom, or praying three times at a set hour, he could not have been charged with disobeying the law. But Daniel would not compromise even a little. Consequently, he was accused. "Daniel, who is one of the exiles from Judah, pays no attention to you, O king, or to the injunction which you signed, but keeps making his petition three times a day" (v. 13).

The administrators knew that the king could not change the law without subverting his own authority and his nation's traditions. So they had him trapped into passing the death sentence on Daniel.

The king realized belatedly that an evil scheme lay behind the decree, and he was deeply distressed. Now we must keep in mind that in those days it was considered a matter of little consequence for a king, who typically put little value on human life, to throw a lawbreaker into the lions' den. Yet King Darius was distressed. Evidently Daniel's loyalty to Darius and the firmness of his faith in God were so great that the king was deeply impressed and moved.

So Darius determined to rescue Daniel and made every effort until sundown to save him. He probably analyzed the decree closely in the hope of finding some clause by which he might possibly rescue the old man. When Darius delayed, however, Daniel's accusers came again to the king and pressed him with a reminder that the law of the Medes and Persians could not be changed. They implied that if the king did not carry out the decree he had issued, he would have difficulty in ruling over the kingdom. In this way the king found himself bound by the decree he had issued, even though he was absolute in power. And because of Daniel's faith in God, he was put to the test.

DANIEL'S TEST OF FAITH (6:16–18)

THE LOVE OF Darius toward Daniel is evident in these verses. This heathen king who was ignorant of God was so deeply moved by the integrity of Daniel's character and the firmness of his faith in God that he made a confession of faith before Daniel. In essence, he said, "Daniel, though I have tried hard all day long to deliver you, it's beyond my power to deliver you. But I'm sure that your God will deliver you from the lions' den."

Our own proclamation of Jesus through our life of faith should bear fruit like this. Daniel, who had made King Nebuchadnezzar of Babylon surrender himself to God, now changed King Darius of the Medes and Persians as well.

Listen to the king's confession of positive faith. "But I'm sure that your God will deliver you. . . . " We should also have this faith that Daniel possessed so that others will believe in our God and confess faith along with us.

When the king had given his orders against his will, the two administrators and the one hundred twenty satraps were perhaps afraid that the king might change his heart and rescue Daniel. So after Daniel was thrown in the lions' den they had a stone placed at the mouth of the den and sealed with the royal signet ring, adding the seals of the nobles as well. Finally they could rest easy, thinking that the matter was over. Surely, they said, the lions would tear old Daniel to pieces.

How distressed King Darius was after he had ordered Daniel's death! He spent the night restlessly, while a still and solemn atmosphere hung low around the whole palace.

GOD'S PROTECTION (6:19–23)

AT THE FIRST light of dawn, the king arose and hurried to the lions' den. Though he hoped on the one hand that the God of Daniel had surely delivered him, his question showed that he could not quite believe it. But Daniel's response dispelled his doubt.

Notice how even in the lions' den Daniel maintained the courtesy that he had always shown in the presence of the king. Evidently, he had spent the previous night with a calmness of heart—which is more than we can say for the king.

Daniel's words—"My God sent His angel and shut the lions' mouths"—would be echoed centuries later by another man of great faith, the apostle Paul. When Paul was sailing for Italy, the ship he was on was overtaken by a storm and drifted for two weeks. But while the others on board feared, Paul declared, "And yet now I urge you to keep up your courage, for there shall be no loss of life among you, but only of the ship. For this very night an angel of the God to whom I belong and whom I serve stood before me . . . " (Acts 27:22–23).

It was not only in the time of Daniel and the apostle Paul that God sent delivering angels. God still sends His angel to deliver those who trust in Him and serve him with sincere hearts. As God shut the mouths of the lions, quenched the power of fire in the furnace, and stilled the raging storms in the sea, He will still protect us from all kinds of trials.

Today, as in Daniel's day, the angels of the Lord are the messengers sent by God to protect and serve the heirs of God who are saved. If our eyes were opened and we were able to see into the spiritual world, we could see the angels standing around us; for wherever the people of God gather together, the angels of the Lord always surround them.

JUDGMENT AGAINST DANIEL'S ENEMIES (6:24)

HOW FEROCIOUSLY THOSE lions must have leaped upon Daniel's enemies when the king had them thrown in the den instead! They must have been ravenously hungry, because the angel had kept them from eating all night.

And here is another important lesson. Notice here: Those who do not believe in Jesus may lay a snare for Christians, but they will always get themselves ensnared instead. Who would have thought that the schemers themselves would be thrown into the lions' den that had been prepared for Daniel? Think of what happened in the Book of Esther. Who would have thought that Haman would be hanged on the gallows that he himself had prepared for Mordecai?

Remembering this, those who believe in the Lord will have nothing to fear. If we keep the integrity of our faith, even though we walk through the valley of the shadow of death, the rod and staff of the Lord will comfort us, and He will prepare a table for us in the presence of our enemies (Ps. 23). Since God is with us, who can be against us?

THE FAITH OF KING DARIUS (6:25–28)

DANIEL'S DELIVERANCE FROM the lions' den was so impressive that King Darius immediately wrote a decree to all the people throughout the empire. This decree was a wonderful confession of faith, just as the earlier decree of King Nebuchadnezzar of Babylon had been. God is not only the God of Judah and Israel, but He is also the God who controls the history of all human beings.

King Darius did not see God, but he did see the God of Daniel. Nebuchadnezzar did not see God either, but he did see the God of Shadrach, Meshach, and Abednego.

The same is true today. Many people don't know God, but they do know about your God. They picture God in their minds through your words and behavior. So just as King Darius called God the "God of Daniel," you should live in such a way that others will call God "your God." Let them see your God in such a way that they confess, "We must fear this person's God."

Even though Babylon conquered Judah and carried many of its people as captives to their land, Babylon's kings and kingdoms knelt down before the God of their captives and surrendered to Him. In the same way, our spiritual faith still has greater power than the atomic or hydrogen bombs of the world because we serve the God of Daniel.

Korea is perhaps located disadvantageously from a geopolitical standpoint. But as long as Korea serves the God of Daniel, the Lord God Almighty who is with us, we have nothing to fear. The God of Shadrach, Meshach, and Abednego, the God of Daniel, and the God of the apostle Paul is our God and is with us all. No lion will open its mouth to devour us.

> If God is for us, who is against us? He who did not spare His own Son, but delivered Him up for us all, how will He not also with Him freely give us all things? Who will bring a charge against God's elect? God is the one who justifies; who is the one who condemns? Christ Jesus is He who died, yes, rather who was raised, who is at the right hand of God, who also intercedes for us. Who shall separate us from the love of Christ? Shall tribulation, or distress, or persecution, or famine, or nakedness, or peril, or sword?
>
> —ROMANS 8:31–35

7

Daniel's Vision
of the Four Beasts

THE FOUR WINDS OF HEAVEN
(7:1–2)

D ANIEL CHAPTER 7 deals with the revelation Daniel received in a dream during the first year of Belshazzar, king of Babylon, which was fourteen years before Babylon fell. First, Daniel saw in this dream the four winds of heaven churning up the great sea. The winds of heaven signified the providence of God and God's sovereignty over human history. That the winds came from heaven meant human history goes on within the boundaries of the divine will. In other words, whatever rebellion the devil may raise, it cannot make any change in the course of human history that God has not allowed. "The great sea" in the Bible always refers to the Mediterranean. So the phrase "the four winds of heaven were stirring up the great sea" set the scene for a forecast of historic events that by the providence of God would unfold in the countries surrounding the Mediterranean Sea.

THE LION WITH THE WINGS OF AN EAGLE (7:3–4)

THE FIRST BEAST that came up from the sea, a lion with eagle's wings, referred to Babylon. It corresponded to the golden head of the statue King Nebuchadnezzar had seen in his dream.

Why was Babylon represented as a lion with eagle's wings? Sculptures of such a creature stood before the gate of the Babylonian palace. An eagle is king among the birds of the air, while a lion is king among the animals on the earth. So this creature reflected the absolute power of the Babylonian monarch and the perfect organization of the Babylonian bureaucracy. It also meant that Babylon would conquer all the known world of the day with the swiftness and power of eagle's wings to become a mighty power.

But while Daniel watched the lion, its wings were torn off, and it was lifted from the ground so that it stood on two feet like a human being. This referred to the mysterious incident that happened to King Nebuchadnezzar when his arrogance caused him to be judged by God with insanity for seven years.

The eagle's wings that were torn off meant that Nebuchadnezzar's power had departed from him. Yet when he recovered, he did not become like an animal, but like a human being.

In this vision, God depicted each kingdom and the king of the world through the image of a beast. But when Nebuchadnezzar deeply repented of his folly, acknowledging the divine sovereignty, God made him stand up like a human being. Then Nebuchadnezzar, who repented before God, became a beautiful person in God's sight. So the first beast Daniel saw referred to his own age, the age of Babylon.

THE BEAR WITH THREE RIBS BETWEEN ITS TEETH (7:5)

DANIEL SAW THIS vision during the reign of Belshazzar, the last king of Babylon. The second beast in the vision, a bear, revealed the age that was next to come. It represented the kingdom of the Medes and Persians, which would rise through the conquest of Babylon and last about two centuries, to 331 B.C. Like a bear, the Medes and Persians were stupid and tactless, but they were strong. When they waged a war, they needed little strategy; they just pushed with the power of sheer numbers in their enormous army, which ranged from a hundred thousand up to a million. The number they mobilized in their campaign against the Greeks amounted to a million, with one-half of the army serving as a regular battle force and the other half as supporting troops.

The Medo-Persian empire was not only stupid and tactless, but it was also cruel. It conquered many countries, trampling them under their feet.

The bear in the vision was raised up on its side. This showed that, although the Medes and Persians were a coalition of two kingdoms, their empire leaned to one side, the side of Persia. For Persia, which was built later than Media, came to supremacy and eventually defeated the Medes. The silver breast and arms beneath the golden head in Nebuchadnezzar's dream also corresponded to this coalition of the Medes and Persians.

In the vision the bear also had three ribs between its teeth. These three ribs signified the strong nations conquered by the Medo-Persian empire: Babylon, Lydia, and Egypt. The voice that said, "Devour much meat," represented the divine grant given to the Medo-Persian empire to have dominion over many neighboring countries. According to that divine grant, the Medes and Persians conquered many small nations in the Near East, expanding their territory far greater than the territory Babylon had once possessed. This lasted for more than two centuries, but the empire finally fell, and the third beast appeared.

THE LEOPARD WITH FOUR WINGS AND FOUR HEADS (7:6)

IMAGINE THE THIRD beast. A leopard is a fast animal, and this leopard had four wings on its back. What could be faster than a flying leopard?

This creature referred to Alexander the Great, the Greek general who conquered Medo-Persia and gained control of much of the world. He was the greatest conqueror the world had ever seen, occupying a vast territory in a short amount of time. Alexander rose from Macedonia in Europe and conquered large portions of Asia and Africa, sweeping like a storm all the way to the borders of India.

Legend has it that Alexander wept while sitting at the bank of the Indus River because there was no more land to conquer. But soon after that he died of a fever in Babylon at the age of thirty-three.

The four heads of this leopard referred to Alexander's four generals, who represented the collective leadership system of his empire. In Alexander's conquest of the world, these four generals played a central role. Then after Alexander's death, they divided the entire Greek kingdom among themselves. Thrace and Bithynia went to the first general, Lysimachus; Macedonia and Greece to the second, Cassander; Syria and Babylon to the third, Seleucus; and Egypt, Palestine, and Arabia to the fourth, Ptolemy. In this way Alexander's empire was divided into four kingdoms that constantly warred against each other.

THE BEAST WITH TEN HORNS (7:7–8)

THE FOURTH BEAST Daniel saw was terrifying and powerful. It had large iron teeth and ten horns. This beast referred to the Roman empire, which succeeded Greece and brought the whole world under its power.

The city of Rome, which began as a small village on the River Tiber in Italy, began to extend its territory through wars with its neighbors in the fourth century B.C. By the turn of the second century B.C., it had conquered Spain and Carthage. Then it continued to further its conquests, adding Macedonia, Greece, and Asia Minor to its dominions. Eventually Syria and Jerusalem fell to Rome, as well as the European lands which today make up the countries of Great Britain, France, Belgium, Switzerland, and Germany.

By the early years of the second century after Christ, the Roman empire was at the height of its prosperity. Its vast territory included almost all of Europe, and its power reached to the border of India. Thus Rome succeeded in building the largest empire in human history. Yet even Rome fell to invading armies in A.D. 410. No human kingdom lasts forever.

In Daniel's vision, this terrifying fourth beast crushed and devoured its victims and then trampled underfoot what was left. This showed that Rome, driven by the lust for conquest, would relentlessly pursue a policy of expansionism, crushing its subjugated countries. In fact, the massacre of subjugated people took place frequently in the Roman empire, with thousands of people often being killed at one time. Those who survived the massacres, hundreds of thousands of them, were carried off as prisoners and sold as slaves. Thus in the wake of the Roman armies, civilization was often reduced to ashes.

As we noted before, the two-thousand-year period that followed the age of Rome does not appear in Jewish prophecy. Jesus came to this world during the age of Rome, and the two thousand years that come between that time and the Second Coming of Jesus are the age of the gospel, the period in which all humankind can be delivered by the cross of Jesus Christ. So because this period has nothing to do with Judaism, God did not show it to the prophets of the Old Testament.

When the two thousand years of the church age have come to a close at the end of the world, then, according to Daniel's vision, ten horns will suddenly come up from the head of the terrifying beast that is Rome. Next a little horn will come up among the ten horns, uprooting three of them. In the vision this horn had human eyes and a mouth that spoke boastfully.

This part of the vision paralleled Nebuchadnezzar's dream by also showing that at the end of the world ten kingdoms will be unified in the former territory of Rome. Twenty-six hundred years ago, Daniel prophesied accurately the historic fact that ten kingdoms would arise from the former territory of Rome.

The little horn, which came up among the ten horns, referred to the Antichrist. This Antichrist will arise and oppose God, toppling three kingdoms and unifying the remaining seven. As we shall see in coming commentary, all of these things are elaborated upon in Revelation 13.

As we noted before in chapter two, the last part of this world's history will begin with the unification of the ten kingdoms of Europe, Rome's former territory—and that unification is underway right now. Daniel saw this in his vision twenty-six hundred years ago, but he did not know then what it meant. We, however, are living in the very age of that prophecy, so we can observe with our own eyes how ten kingdoms arising in Europe are coming together in the European Economic Community.

When ten countries in this former territory of Rome are thus unified politically, economically, and militarily, a supreme leader will arise and conquer three countries out of ten. After that he will subdue the remaining seven countries, bringing all of Europe under his feet. He will dictate to the world, speaking boastfully to God. Then, as we will see in our coming study of Revelation, he will launch a campaign against the Jews.

As we have also noted before in chapter two, around the time when the unification of ten countries is completed in Europe, we Christians will be taken up into heaven all at once. That is why we should pray all the more to receive the fullness of the Holy Spirit as the time draws near.

THE JUDGMENT AGAINST THE ANTICHRIST (7:9–12)

As SOON AS the era of ten horns passed in Daniel's vision, the judgment against the little horn, the Antichrist, approached. At this time Daniel saw the judgment seat of God, the Ancient of Days, set in place. Those who attended Him were angels, and those who stood before Him were the bride of Jesus Christ—that is, the saints who had been resurrected and had gone to heaven.

51

THE APOCALYPTIC PROPHECY

The Bible further says in Daniel's vision that the court was seated, and the books were opened. This judgment signifies the one that will take place shortly after the Tribulation Jesus prophesied (Matt. 24:21). From the moment the Antichrist completes the unification of Europe, the Tribulation will begin, and the Antichrist will reign for seven years.

According to my interpretation of this passage and the Book of Revelation, after the Tribulation, Christ and His faithful saints will descend from heaven; then right after the battle of Armageddon, Christ will take captive the Antichrist and his false prophets. After judging them, He will cast them into the lake burning with fire and brimstone.

This judgment against the Antichrist which Daniel saw twenty-six hundred years ago is also mentioned in Revelation 19. During that period, any individual or nation with the mark of the beast will also be judged. But there is a particular order in the events of the judgment according to John's vision in Revelation chapters 19 and 20.

First, as we will look at in great detail in section two of this book, the Antichrist and his false prophets will be taken and cast into the lake burning with fire and brimstone.

Second, the other beasts of the ten kingdoms will be stripped of their authority but allowed to live for a period of time until the kingdom of one thousand years begins (Dan. 7:12). Then they will be judged and cast into hell, where they will remain for a thousand years.

Third, after that thousand years, the judgment of the great white throne of God begins. At this time all the dead will rise to be judged finally, and they will be cast into the lake burning with fire and brimstone.

THE EVERLASTING KINGDOM OF CHRIST (7:13–14)

WHILE JESUS WAS in this world, He frequently called Himself the Son of man. Here Daniel says, "With the clouds of heaven, one like a Son of Man was coming." The "one like a Son of Man" whom Daniel saw in the night visions was Jesus Christ Himself.

The clouds of heaven represent not only glory but also the crowds. Accordingly, in this scene Jesus comes down from heaven not only in glory but accompanied by His bride, the multitude of His saints. This event takes place after the judgment in which Jesus Christ takes over the thousand-year kingdom from His Father.

Some day we will be with God and will be His heirs. The Bible says it this way: "The Spirit Himself bears witness with our spirit that we are

52

children of God, and if children, heirs also, heirs of God and fellow-heirs with Christ, if indeed we suffer with Him in order that we may also be glorified with Him" (Rom. 8:16–17).

The dominion that we inherit as fellow-heirs with Christ will be eternal, and His kingdom will be an everlasting kingdom. I pray in the Lord Jesus' name that none of you lose the blessing of inheriting this dominion and kingdom.

THE INTERPRETATION OF THE FOURTH KINGDOM (7:15–28)

THE VISION OF the fourth kingdom troubled Daniel's heart because he didn't know what it meant. He had been able to interpret the meaning of the other beasts, but this one was quite different. So he approached the angel who had brought him the vision and asked its meaning.

Though Daniel had trouble understanding the angel's response, the beast is not beyond our understanding because we have already studied about it. It is obvious from the angel's explanation of the vision that the fourth kingdom refers to Rome. The ten horns signify the ten kingdoms that will rise in the former territory of Rome at the end of the world. The little horn signifies the Antichrist. According to that explanation, the Antichrist will first unify the three kingdoms, then he will expand his dominion over the other seven kingdoms.

After he has arisen, the Antichrist will wage war against the saints of God. Here "the saints" refers to two groups: the Jews and the Christians who were not prepared when Jesus descended from heaven. Those Spirit-filled Christians who had prepared themselves and waited for the coming of Jesus will have already been taken up into heaven around the time of the Antichrist's appearance.

According to Daniel in verses 25–28, the Antichrist will also try to change the set times and the laws. He will dislike the present name of our era, A.D. or *anno Domini,* which means "in the year of the Lord." Thus he will loathe to hear words like "A.D. 1999," because it means "in the year of the Lord 1999," a year in the era whose beginning is Jesus Christ. He will also change laws in order to place himself at the center of law, and he will institute a new era. From this time on, the Jewish people will be delivered into the hand of the Antichrist for "a time, times, and half a time" (7:25), and they will go through the Tribulation. We will deal with this in great detail in our commentary on Revelation 11 and 13. During the first three and one-half years of the Tribulation there will be natural disasters. During the second three and one-half years the Antichrist will set up his own idol in the temple of God in violation of the seven-year treaty that he had previously agreed upon with the Jews. Then he will launch a dreadful campaign against the Jews.

But verse 22 says that the Ancient of Days—that is, God—came and pronounced judgment in favor of the saints. Verse 26 says the Antichrist will be taken and destroyed. All the world will become the kingdom of Christ, according to verse 22, when it will be given to the saints. This will happen at the last judgment.

For us the Book of Daniel is no longer a sealed book (12:4), but an open book. What Daniel could not understand, we can now see clearly. Nevertheless, the devil is furious that we know in advance through the study of these books and prayer the things that will happen in the future. That is why many pastors hesitate to examine the Book of Daniel. They are afraid of being attacked by the devil in spirit or in body. Even so, every believing saint can now clearly know the contents of the Book of Daniel that history has opened, which once was sealed.

Today you and I live in this wonderful age believing in Jesus. Is there anything for which we could be more grateful?

8

A Ram and a Goat

THE SECRET OF A RAM WITH TWO HORNS (8:1–4)

THE RAM WITH two horns in this vision of Daniel signifies the Medo-Persian empire. Strange as it may sound, the kings of the Medo-Persian empire wore helmets that looked like rams' horns instead of a crown when they went into battle. Accordingly, this prophecy accurately depicts the Medo-Persian kings going to war.

Referring to the Medo-Persian empire, Daniel's vision showed the horn that grew up later as becoming longer than the first. This revealed that even though Media came to power earlier than Persia, it was conquered by Persia, which by annexing it built a united empire.

The Medo-Persian empire was located in the East between Egypt and Asia. It expanded its territory by conquering Greece westward, Babylon northward, and Egypt southward. This was prophesied in verse 4.

THE GOAT FROM THE WEST (8:5–8)

WHEN THE RAM with two horns increased greatly, charging toward the west, north, and south, suddenly a goat came running. This goat refers to the Greek empire, and the horn between the eyes signifies Alexander the Great, whom we have mentioned before.

Before this king's conquest of the Medo-Persian empire, the Greeks had themselves been invaded by the Persians, who had waged a campaign with a great army that was one million strong. Since then, Greece had waited bitterly for revenge. Finally, the opportunity arrived. When he was only thirty, Alexander, the son of King Philip of Macedonia, led a sizable army on an expedition against the Medo-Persian empire. Yet compared to the vast army of the Medo-Persians, the Greeks were numerically inferior.

Daniel said that the goat was so strong and fast it ran even without touching the ground. That is how Alexander's army swiftly advanced and defeated the large army of Persia at the Granicus River of Asia Minor in May 334 B.C.

A year and one-half later, in November 333 B.C., Persia again raised an army and fought with Greece at Issus by the northern tip of the Mediterranean Sea. But their troops were smashed by Alexander. Then in October 331 B.C., two years later, Greece and Persia had a final showdown at Guagamela near Nineveh, where Alexander trampled Persia once and for all.

Thus the ram, which stood for Persia, was completely conquered by the goat, which stood for Greece. The vision further showed that the large horn of this goat was broken off, and in its place four prominent horns grew up toward the four winds of heaven. This showed that Alexander would die young and that his empire would be divided into four parts by his four generals, as we saw in chapter seven.

A LITTLE HORN (8:9–12)

NOW WE HAVE a story about a little horn that is quite mysterious and difficult to understand. The little horn in this vision is different from the one that appeared in chapter 7. This second prophecy of a little horn was already fulfilled historically, but at the same time it stands for the Antichrist who is yet to come.

After the world was divided by the four generals of Alexander the Great, two of the four resulting kingdoms eventually emerged as major forces: Syria, taken by Seleucus, and Egypt, taken by Ptolemy. These two kingdoms were constantly engaged in hostile actions.

Israel was sandwiched geographically between the two kingdoms. So when Egypt came up to fight Syria, Israel was trampled underfoot. And when Syria went down to fight Egypt, Israel was also stamped down. Thus the sufferings of Israel were beyond description.

Under these circumstances, according to Daniel, a little horn came up out of one of the horns. The description that follows in Daniel's account fits a king of Syria perfectly named Antiochus Epiphanes, who was eighth in the Seleucus dynasty (175–164 B.C.).

Antiochus rose to prominence among the four horns. He defeated Egypt, and on his way home, he subdued Jerusalem. After Jerusalem surrendered, he set himself up against God and cruelly trampled Israel underfoot. "The host" in Daniel's vision refers to the Jews whom this conqueror cast down in defeat.

Antiochus murdered several of the political and religious leaders of Israel, including the high priest Onias III, the religious star of the Jews in that day. Moreover, he set himself up to be as great as the Prince of the host—that is, God. He forbade the daily sacrifice in the temple. And he desecrated the sanctuary with an altar offered to the Greek deity he worshiped. On it he sacrificed swine's blood, an abomination to the Jews. No worse sacrilege could be imagined.

Yet he went further. He abolished the Mosaic law, which was held to be most sacred by the Jews. He also forbade circumcision and imposed a pagan lifestyle upon them. Anyone who refused to obey Antiochus or rebelled against him was subject to death.

These events parallel what will come to pass in the last days: the rise of the Antichrist in the Tribulation and his conquest and cruel treatment of Israel. The tragedy that already happened once in the history of Israel will be repeated in the future by the Antichrist.

In that day, the Antichrist will break down the altar in the sanctuary, setting up in its place his own idol. Then he will force the Jews to worship the idol and will take away the daily sacrifice that is offered morning and evening. And he will abolish the law of Moses, imposing a pagan lifestyle on the Jews.

THE BLASPHEMY OF THE LITTLE HORN (8:13–14)

THE WORDS OF the angels came true in history. The persecution against the Jews began in 171 B.C. and continued until Antiochus finally died on an expedition to Media in 164 B.C. As soon as he died, Israel was released from Syrian bondage. The temple was purged, and the daily sacrifice was restored. The number of days from Antiochus's conquest of Israel to his death was exactly twenty-three hundred, the number prophesied here.

Because this is a double prophecy that was once fulfilled in history, and will yet be fulfilled again at the end of the world, this passage shows clearly that some day the Antichrist, like Antiochus Epiphanes, will arise to destroy Israel and to desecrate the sanctuary. As we have already seen, that period will be "a time, times, and half a time" (7:25).

GABRIEL'S INTERPRETATION
OF THE VISION (8:15–27)

WHEN DANIEL SAW this vision he was distressed because he could not understand it. But then he heard a man's voice from the opposite side of the river commanding Gabriel to explain it. As an archangel heralding divine messages, Gabriel was one of the highest among the angels along with Michael, who was captain of the heavenly host. So this must have been the voice of Jesus, for no one but He had the authority to give orders to Gabriel.

In verses 17 through 22, Gabriel explained the significance of the vision according to the historical outline we have already presented. Then he went on to say that at the latter part of the period of the four kingdoms arising out of Alexander's kingdom there would arise a fierce enemy of the Jews. This was Antiochus Epiphanes, but because he was a type of the Antichrist, what is said here about him can also be applied to the Antichrist who is to come.

A DESCRIPTION OF THE ANTICHRIST (8:23–25)

WE ARE TOLD first of all that the countenance of the Antichrist will be stern. So the president of the United Europe prophesied here will be a hard man, hard enough to control all of Europe and to sway the world.

The angel goes on to say that he will be a master of intrigue. This shows that he will manipulate the ten countries of Europe as he wishes because of his great political ability.

The Bible also says here that the Antichrist will become very strong, but not by his own power. This aspect is explained by Revelation 13, which we will study in the second section of this book, that the dragon who is the prince of the air—that is, Satan—will flee away from Michael the archangel. When he comes down to earth, he will enter into the

Antichrist. Then the Antichrist will immediately turn into the beast and, receiving extraordinary ability and supernatural power from Satan, will grip all of Europe in his hands.

As we have previously noted, the Antichrist, who will have achieved the unification of Europe, will then enter into a seven-year treaty with Israel. He will help Israel rebuild the temple, which was destroyed by the Romans, at the top of Mount Moriah. He will take advantage of Israel, using the nation for his own purposes for three and one-half years until he has enough political power to stand by himself.

Then the Antichrist will suddenly turn into the beast, claiming that he is a god. Having his own idol built in the sanctuary, he will force the people to worship it. But monotheistic Israel will never obey that command. Consequently, this will lead to the campaign against the Jews during the latter half of the Tribulation.

Referring to this time, Jesus said:

> Therefore when you see the abomination of desolation which was spoken of through Daniel the prophet, standing in the holy place (let the reader understand), then let those who are in Judea flee to the mountains; let him who is on the housetop not go down to get the things out that are in his house; and let him who is in the field not turn back to get his cloak. But woe to those who are with child and to those who nurse babes in those days! But pray that your flight may not be in the winter, or on a Sabbath; for then there will be a great tribulation, such as has not occurred since the beginning of the world until now, nor ever shall. And unless those days had been cut short, no life would have been saved; but for the sake of the elect those days shall be cut short.
>
> —MATTHEW 24:15–22

Thus the Antichrist will persecute the Jews, opposing God while claiming that he is Christ for the second half of the Tribulation. Yet the time will come to an end when he is broken, but not by human power.

THE BATTLE OF ARMAGEDDON

WHEN WILL THIS Antichrist fall? During the war of Armageddon (Rev. 16:16). A vast army will come from the east, mainly from China, and the army of the Antichrist will move from Europe to fight with them. Thus there will be a bloody war in Israel.

Nuclear bombs will be used, and blood will flow like a river. At that very moment, Christ will come with His saints. Then the army of the Antichrist and the eastern army that has come from China and other Asian countries will stop fighting and will compromise to fight against Christ in concert. This will be described in great detail when we study Revelation. But the Antichrist will be taken and his entire army will be destroyed by the sharp swords which come out of the mouth of Jesus Christ. Finally, the Antichrist, who has been taken by the hand of Christ, will be thrown alive into the lake of fire burning with brimstone, along with his false prophets.

THE END OF THE AGE

WHEN GABRIEL TOLD Daniel to "keep the vision secret, for it pertains to many days in the future" (v. 26), he meant that, since the things of this vision did not concern Daniel's own age, he had to keep this vision to himself. Meanwhile, the vision was so shocking that after Daniel saw it he lay ill for several days.

Today the vision is no longer secret. We are now at the threshold of the End Times. Before long, the grace-filled gospel age of Jesus Christ will come to an end by a move of the Holy Spirit.

This period of two thousand years was kept secret to the prophets. Yet the end of it was foretold in Joel, when he said that God would pour out His Spirit upon His servants, both men and women (Joel 2:28–29). That happened at the beginning of this century when the latter rain of the Holy Spirit came down to earth in the Pentecostal outpouring. Soon that work of the Holy Spirit will cease, and the harvest time will begin, though we don't know at what hour.

Around the time when this gospel age and the period of the Spirit's outpouring have come near to an end, Israel has risen again, regaining her nationhood. This happened in 1948. The fig tree is a symbol of Israel, so Jesus said: "Now learn the parable from the fig tree: when its branch has already become tender, and puts forth its leaves, you know that summer is near; even so you too, when you see all these things, recognize that He is near, right at the door" (Matt. 24:32–33).

The fig tree, Israel, wandered among the nations for a long time but has finally become a nation once more and put forth leaves. Before long the ten countries of Europe will be united and one ruler will come out of them. There are currently some sixteen nations interested in this coalition. But when the time is right, there will only be ten. He will conclude the seven-year treaty with Israel. With the conclusion of the treaty, both the church age and the time of the Gentiles will end. Then will start the time when God gives the final exhortation to the Jewish nation.

Listen to the news that comes today from Europe, and you will realize how accurately and swiftly these scriptures are being fulfilled. Not much time is left to preach the gospel. We don't know exactly how many years are left, but we can be sure that we are now standing at the threshold of the End Times.

9

Daniel's Prophecy of Seventy Weeks

JEREMIAH'S PROPHECY (9:1–2)

W E SHOULD NOTE that even though Daniel had such deep revelation from God, he did not neglect the study of the Scriptures. In contrast, when some people pray and receive a little bit of revelation from God in answer to their prayers, they talk big about this and that, based solely on the revelation, and lay aside the Bible.

The books or scrolls Daniel saw here refer to Jeremiah. As he read the prophet prayerfully in order to find out what would happen to Israel in the future, he came across a passage with a wonderful promise in it:

> "Moreover, I will take from them the voice of joy and the voice of gladness, the voice of the bridegroom and the voice of the bride, the sound of the millstones and the light of the lamp. And this whole land shall be a desolation and a horror, and these nations shall serve the king of Babylon seventy years. Then it will be when seventy years are completed I will punish the king of Babylon and that nation," declares the LORD, "for their iniquity, and the land of the

Chaldeans; and I will make it an everlasting desolation."

—JEREMIAH 25:10–12

This prophecy said that Israel would be taken captive to serve the Babylonian kings for seventy years. It also predicted that after this period, when God's appointed time was fulfilled, God would punish Babylon and grant freedom to Israel. So Daniel was deeply moved by this passage.

As we noted before, the primary reason the Israelites were carried away as captives and had to suffer for seventy years was that they had repeatedly broken the Sabbath. So God repaid them for their deed. The Sabbath law had three strict stipulations.

First, the people were to work for six days, but on the seventh day they had to cease from work. Second, after having kept a fellow Israelite as a slave for six years, they had to set him or her free in the seventh year. And third, when they plowed a field, they might plow it for six years, but in the seventh year they had to let it lie fallow. God promised a harvest that would provide Israel extra provisions to support them during this fallow year if they would obey this command.

But the Israelites habitually broke all the Sabbath laws. So God allowed the nation to be taken captive and exiled so the land, which had been denied its Sabbath up to that time, could rest for seventy years.

We must recognize that the commandment to work for six days and rest on the seventh was not given to afflict us, but to bring us benefit. This is the law of the God who created the universe and who knows what is best for us. So today we should also live according to this divine law. Otherwise, compulsory rest will come to us as it came to Israel when the nation was sent into captivity for seventy years.

Daniel felt his heart burning when he read the verse from the prophet which promised that his people would return home from captivity after seventy years, once the land had rested and the Jews had repented of their ways. The day when he could go home was drawing near. All that remained was for the people to repent, so Daniel began to intercede for his people.

THE SECRET OF ACCEPTABLE PRAYER (9:3–4)

DANIEL'S PRAYER WAS extraordinary. Whenever I read it, I can feel his heart torn to pieces and bleeding for his nation. It was a prayer accepted by God.

We should learn from Daniel's example the secret of prayer that is acceptable to God. Whatever divine promise we may have, unless we pray, it cannot come true. Prayer is an essential condition for the fulfillment of the divine promise.

Through the prophet Jeremiah, God had no doubt promised Israel that after seventy years He would destroy the king of Babylon and send the Israelites home. This promise, however, rested on the premise that God's people had to first understand the divine promise and then to pray. The promise was not an unconditional one that would be automatically fulfilled.

Even though the Bible has as many as thirty-two thousand five hundred promises, they can be fulfilled only when we know about them and pray for their fulfillment as Daniel did. If we assume an indifferent attitude, saying, "May this be done as You will," not a single promise will be fulfilled in our lifetime. The creative work of God will not take place until the promise of God, which comes down from heaven, and the prayer of God's people, which goes up from earth, meet and join together.

DANIEL'S EXTRA EFFORTS

AFTER DANIEL KNEW the promise of God recorded in Jeremiah, he resolved to plead with God fervently. He did not want to do a halfhearted job.

We must pray the same way today. Without firm resolve in our prayer, we cannot receive an answer. If we pray halfheartedly, just saying, "Amen, we believe," our prayer will not rise up to heaven before God.

To ensure that God would answer his prayer without fail, Daniel made some extra efforts. The first one was fasting. The truly powerful prayer is one joined with fasting. When we pray earnestly, even to the extent of restraining our strong human instinct for eating, our prayer will not fail to rise to God. But if we pray while still satisfying our desire for food and sleep, our prayer cannot go beyond the level of an ordinary petition.

The second extra effort was sackcloth. By putting away comfortable clothing and putting on coarse cloth, Daniel showed that he was thoroughly repenting.

In fact, he went one step further to humble himself. He prayed with ashes on his head.

The kind of firm resolve Daniel had is an essential part of acceptable prayer to God. Especially when we pray about a critical problem that faces us, we cannot break the strength of the devil unless we are prepared to please God in prayer and in petition, in fasting, sackcloth, and ashes.

DANIEL'S CONFESSION OF SINS (9:5–6)

IN THREE ASPECTS, Daniel's prayer sets an example for us. The first aspect is the confession of sins.

No human being lives without sin. The Bible says, "There is none righteous, not even one . . . for all have sinned and fall short of the glory of God" (Rom. 3:10, 23).

It is not sinners who are sent to hell by God; rather, it is those sinners who do not repent. So the most dreadful thing is not sin, but the impenitent heart.

For that reason, when we come to God we must first pray penitently, confessing our sins. When God sees us turning to Him, confessing our sins, He does not forsake us. Instead He has compassion on the contrite heart that seeks His forgiveness.

Listen to Daniel's prayer of repentance. Perhaps no one was more faithful to God than Daniel, who maintained the integrity of his faith. But he chose to bear upon his shoulders in confession not only his own sins, but the sins of all the Jews.

We should learn to imitate Daniel's attitude. Like him, we should confess not only our own sins, but the sins of our country and our people as well.

Daniel said in his prayer, "We have sinned, committed iniquity, acted wickedly, and rebelled, even turning aside from Thy commandments and ordinances" (v. 5). What is our sin? It is violation of the law of God. If we know the law of God and yet break it, we commit a sin.

Daniel also confessed the sin of indifference that the people committed against the word of the Lord. He said the Jews had not only broken God's laws, but that they had also failed to listen to God's servants, the prophets. Daniel repents especially on behalf of past leaders of Israel, lamenting bitterly as if it were his own sin.

In order to offer acceptable prayer to God, we too must examine ourselves to determine whether we are breaking the law of God. Then, if we find that we are, we must confess it. In addition, we should confess not only our own sin but also the sins of our family members when we bring them to God in prayer.

Confession is essential to our spiritual life. When some people today try to receive the Holy Spirit, they fall victim instead to an evil spirit because they do not make thorough confession of sins before they pray to receive the Holy Spirit. Because sin still remains in the hearts of these people, the Holy Spirit cannot enter. To make matters worse, because their hearts are wide open, an evil spirit may enter, seeking after sin, to oppress their hearts.

For that reason, when we come to Jesus Christ to receive special grace after we are forgiven of our sins through faith in Him, we must first confess all the sins we can remember and wash them away with the precious blood of Jesus. If we put on purity when we pray to God, the devil cannot enter our hearts.

The devil is just like a fly. He hates clean places. Just as we remove a dirty garbage can to keep flies from gathering around it in our homes, we should treat sins as if they were garbage cans, removing them from our hearts. If we fail to do this, we have no reason to complain of being tempted by the devil.

THE PRAYER OF A BROKEN HEART (9:7–15)

A SECOND ASPECT of Daniel's prayer is that it is the prayer of a broken heart. He was so ashamed of the sins of his people that he could only cry out that Israel deserved the shame and disgrace to which it was subjected. He pointed out Israel's stubbornness, admitting that even though Jerusalem itself had become a ruin by the unprecedented judgment of God, Israel deserved the judgment: because the nation had neither repented nor sought God's grace even down to the last moment when it was carried away to a heathen country.

Do you know what true repentance is? It requires that we avoid making an excuse for our sin or complaining about the present ill we may be suffering because of our sin. Those who are genuinely penitent say: "Lord, I deserve this trouble I have. Righteousness belongs to You, but to me the punishment. Yet, in comparison with the sin I have committed, even this is rather a light punishment. Thank You." A prayer like this is a prayer coming from a broken heart.

PRAYER FOR FORGIVENESS AND RESTORATION (9:16–19)

THE THIRD ASPECT of Daniel's prayer is that he entreats God's forgiveness and restoration. He appealed to the righteous acts God had performed for the Jews up to that time. So even though the nation was suffering its deserved shame, he pleaded with God to remember the holy city Jerusalem and to have mercy on it. And he asked God to restore the ruined sanctuary for His own sake.

In all these ways, then, we should pray as Daniel did, keeping in mind the three aspects of his prayer we have discussed. And when we pray a prayer of confession, we should not get our prayer out of focus by being distracted. We must make our prayer succinct, reflecting these three elements illustrated by Daniel's prayer.

In addition, we should make a thorough confession of sins for our family and our country, because the Bible clearly tells us:

> Behold, the LORD's hand is not so short that it cannot save; neither is His ear so dull that it cannot hear. But your iniquities have made a separation between you and your God, and your sins have hidden His face from you, so that He does not hear.
>
> —ISAIAH 59:1–2

Finally, we should beg God to give us an opportunity to live exerting our utmost effort for the Lord's name and His glory. "Only for the Lord"—this should be the central theme of our final supplication.

I pray in Jesus' name that you too may learn to pray as Daniel did.

GABRIEL'S ANSWER TO DANIEL'S PRAYER (9:20–23)

DANIEL'S PRAYER WAS so well-prepared and firmly based on the three elements we have discussed that the divine answer came down powerfully from the throne of God. The archangel Gabriel was sent to bring that answer to Daniel.

The recorded prayer of Daniel is brief because it is only the gist of what he prayed. Actually, Daniel prayed all day long, from morning until the evening sacrifice. Then about the time of the evening sacrifice Gabriel appeared.

According to the Bible, Jacob had a dream in which he saw a stairway resting on the earth with its top reaching to heaven and angels of God ascending and descending on it (Gen. 28:12). These angels of God, who travel back and forth between heaven and earth, number more than ten thousand times ten thousand, and they are His ministering spirits sent out to render service to God's people (Heb. 1:14). So when we pray to God, God answers our prayer by sending these hosts of heaven.

Whenever we pray an appropriate prayer to God, God's command is immediately given. But it takes time for angels to bring it to us. God is omniscient, omnipotent, and omnipresent, but angels are not. So don't get discouraged even when you fail to receive a quick answer to your prayer.

DANIEL'S SEVENTY YEARS (9:24–27)

WHEN GABRIEL CAME to Daniel with God's answer to his prayer, he spoke about the seventy weeks in Jeremiah's prophecy. This short passage illuminates a great deal of biblical history and provides a key to the understanding of the entire Bible.

If we had to read the passage alone with no one to explain it to us, we would find it the most difficult puzzle in the world. But when we read these words in the light of what we have studied so far in the previous chapters of Daniel and with what we are told in the Book of Revelation, their meaning is fully revealed.

As we can see from Gabriel's opening words of interpretation (v. 24), this prophecy centers upon the Jewish nation. I believe this because the history of God's people as recorded in the Bible always serves as a clock for the history of the entire world. That is, just as we look at a clock to know the time, so we must look at the history of the Jews to understand the timing of world history, for God reveals the history of the world through the Jewish nation.

Because a week is composed of seven days, the term "seventy weeks" here means seventy times seven days, or four hundred ninety days. But what is the significance of this four hundred ninety days?

According to the Book of Numbers, when the spies returned from the land of Canaan after exploring it for forty days, they gave a bad report about the land so the Israelites who heard them grumbled against God. For this reason, God was enraged and sent Israel back into the wilderness, saying, "According to the number of days which you spied out the land, forty days, for every day you shall bear your guilt a year, even forty years, and you shall know My opposition" (Num. 14:34).

Using the same formula for calculating the length of Israel's judgment in Jeremiah's time, seventy weeks or four hundred ninety days would refer to four hundred ninety years. The following verses indicate that there would be sixty-nine weeks from the decree to rebuild and restore Jerusalem until the time of the Messiah. The last week, the seventieth week, refers to the Great Tribulation that is yet to occur. In all, seventy weeks or four hundred ninety years are determined for the period from the return of the Jews from captivity to the millennial kingdom which will be started when Jesus Christ returns to this world. In all these ways, four hundred ninety is a providential and historical number for the Jews.

WHAT WILL HAPPEN AFTER FOUR HUNDRED NINETY YEARS?

THE BIBLE SAYS that the transgression of the entire nation of the Jews would be finished after seventy weeks, or four hundred ninety years. This time was decreed to finish all the transgressions of Israel committed against God, to put an end to the sin which originated with Adam and Eve, and to atone for wickedness forever.

These things took place when sins were destroyed once and for all by the precious blood of Jesus Christ that He shed on the cross, and everlasting righteousness was brought in. At that time all the visions and prophecies were sealed. Now, after all these things have taken place, Jesus Christ is to be anointed and is to come again to take over the earth. Then at last the world will be completely changed into the kingdom of God.

Therefore, those who criticize the Bible today must be silent before this prophecy of Daniel. If the Bible were a book not recorded by divine revelation, but fabricated by human beings, then how could Daniel, writing twenty-six hundred years ago, pinpoint events that would happen in our own age and are still to happen in the future? Certainly Daniel did not prophesy past things, but rather future things.

THE COMMANDMENT TO RESTORE AND TO BUILD JERUSALEM (9:25)

THE MESSIAH OF this passage refers to Christ. These words tell about the first coming of Jesus.

Gabriel told Daniel that the anointed king would be born in Israel after seven weeks and sixty-two weeks, or sixty-nine weeks. During the first seven weeks Jerusalem would be restored and rebuilt, then the king would be born sixty-two weeks after that time. So our concern must be to determine when the commandment was given to restore and rebuild Jerusalem.

In Ezra 1:1 we read that the decree to restore and rebuild Jerusalem was issued in the first year of King Cyrus of Persia. The words of the decree are recorded there:

70

Now in the first year of Cyrus king of Persia, in order to fulfill the word of the LORD by the mouth of Jeremiah, the LORD stirred up the spirit of Cyrus king of Persia, so that he sent a proclamation throughout all his kingdom, and also put it in writing, saying, "Thus says Cyrus king of Persia, 'The LORD, the God of heaven, has given me all the kingdoms of the earth, and He has appointed me to build Him a house in Jerusalem, which is in Judah. Whoever there is among you of all His people, may his God be with him! Let him go up to Jerusalem which is in Judah, and rebuild the house of the LORD, the God of Israel; He is the God who is in Jerusalem. And every survivor, at whatever place he may live, let the men of that place support him with silver and gold, with goods and cattle, together with a freewill offering for the house of God which is in Jerusalem.'"

—EZRA 1:1–4

Thus Cyrus's decree to allow the Jews to return to their native land was the divine answer to Daniel's prayer. As prophesied by Jeremiah, exactly seventy years after the exile, God had Cyrus of Persia issue the decree to send the Jews to their native land, allowing them to restore and rebuild the sanctuary—but not the city of Jerusalem.

Yet the prophecy that came to Daniel tells us that the date of the Messiah's appearance must be calculated from the date of the issuance of the decree to restore and rebuild Jerusalem. This was given in the month of Nisan in the twentieth year of King Artaxerxes. Converted to dates on our modern calendar, this corresponds to March 14, 445 B.C. We can know this from Nehemiah chapters 1 and 2.

Daniel's prophecy says that there will be seven weeks and sixty-two weeks from the issuance of the decree to restore and to rebuild Jerusalem until the coming of the Anointed One, the ruler. The Hebrew word for week can also be translated "seven." Sixty-nine "weeks" could also be understood to mean sixty-nine sevens. Calculate this for yourself:

$$(7 \text{ years} \times 7) + (62 \text{ years} \times 7) = 483 \text{ years}$$

The prophecy says that Jerusalem would be rebuilt "with plaza and moat" in seven sevens. And later those words came to pass: It did actually take seven sevens, or forty-nine years, for Jerusalem to be restored.

In addition, the prophecy says that the Anointed One, the Messiah, would come when sixty-two weeks had passed. This was also fulfilled in history. Sixty-two weeks represents four hundred thirty-four years; and four hundred thirty-four years after Jerusalem was rebuilt, Jesus entered the city riding on a donkey, where a large crowd gathered to welcome Him as a king. This is the day we call Palm Sunday.

Daniel's prophecy even shows the accurate date of Jesus' entry into Jerusalem. On the Jewish calendar, one year was three hundred sixty days instead of three hundred sixty-five days (as in our present calendar). Leap year came around every four years as it does now. So if we add seven weeks and sixty-two weeks—that is, four hundred eighty-three years—to March 14, 445 B.C. (the month of Nisan, the twentieth year of King Artaxerxes), taking into account the necessary adjustments for the differences in calendars, we get April 6, A.D. 32. This is the approximate time, if not the very day, when Jesus entered Jerusalem as a king. Praise the Lord! If Daniel's prophecies had not been a true revelation from God, they could not have been so precisely accurate.

> Then after the sixty-two weeks the Messiah will be cut off and have nothing.
>
> —DANIEL 9:26

The prophecy further says that after the sixty-two weeks, the Anointed One would be cut off. Thus Daniel even predicted our Lord's crucifixion.

But why would the Messiah, that is, Christ the Son of God, be cut off as soon as He entered Jerusalem as the king? This king did not die because of His own sin. He voluntarily bore our wickedness, our vileness, our despair, and our curse. He died on the cross by His own free will to prepare an eternal place for us. How amazing is the Lord's grace!

THE PEOPLE OF THE PRINCE THAT SHALL COME (9:26)

ACCORDING TO DANIEL'S vision, after the Messiah was cut off, Jerusalem and the sanctuary would be destroyed. This actually happened in A.D. 70. After the Crucifixion of Jesus, the Jews rebelled against Rome to obtain freedom, but the revolt was quickly quelled by a Roman army dispatched under the leadership of Titus. The prophecy goes on to say that the end will come like a flood, war will continue until the end, and desolations have been decreed. While suppressing the revolt, the Roman army destroyed Jerusalem so completely that no stone was left on another. It is said that half a million Jewish youth were killed in this revolt against the Romans and that blood ran like a river in Jerusalem.

As we said before, because the church age—that is, the time from the first coming of Christ to His Second Coming—has nothing to do with the history of the Jews, God removed it from the prophecy of the Jews.

Of these seventy weeks prophesied by Daniel, the first sixty-nine weeks are already fulfilled: Jerusalem was restored and rebuilt during the seven weeks; sixty-two weeks after that the Anointed One, Jesus Christ, appeared and was cut off; and "the people of the prince," namely the Roman general Titus, destroyed Jerusalem. During the following two thousand years, humanity has lived in a world that has become desolate by a succession of wars like the coming of a flood.

THE LAST WEEK (9:27)

SUDDENLY THERE APPEARS in verse 27 a single week. This one week refers to seven years.

Who then is the one who will "make a firm covenant with the many"? Considered in context, "he" refers to "the prince" in verse 26—that is, the Roman leader. The power of the Roman empire no longer exists today. So how can the Roman leader come and confirm the covenant with the Jews for seven years? Actually, we have already examined this mystery.

Remember the age of the toes of the golden image which King Nebuchadnezzar saw and the age of the ten horns of the fourth beast which Daniel saw? They both signify the ten nations in a unified Europe that will rise again in the former territory of Rome. As we have seen, today is the last age, and the unification of ten nations is rapidly taking place in the former territory of Rome.

When a unified Europe is thus achieved, the Antichrist referred to in verse 27 will arise from it. He will confirm a covenant with many, which refers to the Jewish nation. But it was necessary that Israel first regain its status as a nation to bring forth the fulfillment of this seven-year treaty.

As recently as half a century ago, the Jews were still a wandering people in exile. At that time the last week of Daniel's seventy weeks must have seemed like a dream. But now all that has changed: Israel is once again a nation after being reborn in 1948, and it is waiting for confirmation of the treaty of seven years.

"In the middle of the week" (v. 27) refers to the same period that John calls "a time and times and half a time" in Revelation (12:14)—that is, the first three and one-half years. When these three and one-half years pass, the Antichrist will put an end to sacrifices and offerings in the temple at Jerusalem. Then in a wing of the temple, he will set up an abomination that will cause desolation.

As we have seen before, he will set up his own statue in the temple to deify himself. Then he will force the Jews to bow down to the idol or else be put to death. But the Jews who have kept the law of Moses will defy the command, and a brutal massacre will follow.

Referring to this time, Jesus said there would be a great distress, unequaled from the beginning of the world. But only through such a tragic and painful tribulation will the Jews be finally broken so they surrender themselves to Jesus Christ as their Savior.

Finally, God's wrath will be poured out, and when the second half of the Tribulation ends, Jesus Christ will come down to the earth to judge it and begin the millennial reign.

We now live at the end of the last age. Therefore, watch and pray, because you do not know exactly when the Bridegroom will come (Matt. 25:1–13). But since the night is far spent, the coming of the Bridegroom must be imminent. And you must be ready to partake of the wedding supper of the Lamb.

When the Lord Himself comes down from heaven with a loud command, with the voice of the archangel and the trumpet call of God, you will be changed and be caught up together in the clouds with the dead in Christ who have risen first to meet the Lord in the air (1 Thess. 4:16–17). Make sure there is oil in your lamp.

10

The War in
the Spiritual World

DANIEL'S FINAL VISION
(10:1–9)

F OR THREE WEEKS Daniel mourned and prayed while observing a partial
fast. The revelation he then received, recorded in chapter 11, was
about war in the spiritual world. On the other hand, the revelation in
chapter 12 concerned war in the human world.

By this time Daniel was eighty-six years old. If he still had any lingering hopes, they were probably for the restoration and rebuilding of
Jerusalem and the temple and the return of the Jews to their native land.
In fact, three years before this time Ezra and Nehemiah had led the Jews
back to their homeland to restore the nation. But Daniel continuously received news that the work of rebuilding the temple was being delayed by
the interference and false accusations of countries neighboring Judah. So
when Daniel heard this news, he became so distressed that he made up
his mind to pray for the salvation of his native land.

Consequently, Daniel and several others went to the Hiddekel River,
which is now called the Tigris River, to pray. He ate no choice food until
the three weeks were over. Since he was almost ninety years old, he was

too feeble for a total fast. Following his example, if anyone today finds that total fasting is too hard, that person should try a partial fast—that is, limited eating.

Daniel abstained not only from choice food, but also from meat and wine. He ate only plain food, just enough to keep himself alive. In addition, he refrained from anointing himself and dressing up.

Here we need to look at the scene behind the stage of the physical world—that is, the spiritual world. More often than not we lose heart in prayer, concluding that the answer will not come. But our Lord wants us to recognize what is happening in the spiritual world so we can have hope to wait just a little longer.

Our prayer is our struggle. When we fight on the earth, the angel who has the answer of God for us also fights in the air. The devil, who is the prince of the air, is encamped between humanity and the throne of God. His demons are desperately endeavoring to block our prayers from reaching heaven.

Nevertheless, if we keep praying on the earth, the angel will catch the cord of our prayer and come to us, breaking through the stronghold of the devil. This is what happened to Daniel. A full twenty-one days had passed before he received an answer to his prayer.

THE ANGEL WHO CAME
(10:5–9)

THE ANGEL WHO came to Daniel with an answer to his prayer must have had a very high position. His appearance, as Daniel described it, was dazzling, even overwhelming. But even though the description sounds somewhat like John's description of Jesus in Revelation, it was not Jesus who appeared to Daniel. If it had been Jesus, He could have come quickly, penetrating the encampment of the devil. But since it was an angel, he was detained by the devil for twenty-one days before he finally came.

Daniel saw the angel because his spiritual eyes were open. But those who prayed with him did not see the angel, although they were so terrified that they fled and hid themselves. Sometimes we find ourselves in the same situation as those men. Though nothing is to be seen in the room where we are, it seems as if we can actually feel the presence of the Lord. At other times while we are praying, we feel as though an angel is at our side.

THE WAR IN THE SPIRITUAL WORLD
(10:10–21)

THE ANGEL REFRESHED Daniel and set him on his feet so he could hear clearly the angel's detailed explanation about the war in the spiritual world. This war is described in only one other place in the Bible:

> For our struggle is not against flesh and blood, but against the rulers, against the powers, against the world forces of this darkness, against the spiritual forces of wickedness in the heavenly places.
>
> —EPHESIANS 6:12

Our faith can be successful only when we fully grasp this secret of the spiritual world.

We should take note that on the very first day Daniel set his mind to gain understanding and to humble himself before God. Daniel's words were heard and the angel came in response to them. When we repent of our sins, admit that the judgment God has passed upon us is just, and humbly beg God for His mercy, God's answer will come swiftly in response to our prayer.

Nevertheless, it took twenty-one days for the angel to come to Daniel. We read here that the prince of the Persian kingdom resisted the angel twenty-one days, so the angel was detained. The king of Persia was a human being who lived on the earth. How then was it possible for the angel of heaven to be detained for twenty-one days by a human being?

Here lies a deep secret of the spiritual world. We must realize that behind this earthly king of Persia was a demonic force also called the king of Persia. The demons were encamped in the air over that throne, and they took possession of the king of Persia and his people, exercising strong influence over them.

On the first day Daniel started his prayer (which continued for the following three weeks accompanied by a partial fast), the cord of his prayer went up to heaven, and God sent an angel in response to it. But the devil obstructed the passage of the angel with all his might because he was afraid that he might lose his domain by the advancement of the kingdom of God.

From this we know that behind the human kingdoms of the earth there is always a struggle between Satan's demons and the angels of God. For that reason we Christians must view rulers such as Kim Il-Sung, chieftain

77

of the North Korean puppet regime until his death in 1994, in the light of this spiritual reality. Kim was notorious for his cruelty and wickedness, even in the communist bloc. So we should not be surprised that behind him, and Kim-Il-Jong, his son who is his successor, is the prince of his kingdom, encamped in the air. The fact is that the devil was behind Kim Il-Sung, manipulating him.

Consequently, the way to bring down a communist regime like that of North Korea is to compel the angel of God to bring God's answer to us through our fasting and prayer—before we resort to military arms. The object of our spiritual struggle is the devil who manipulates Kim Il-Jong. If our prayer is brought up to God, and the angel of God comes down to take prisoner the prince of the communist nations in response to our prayer, communism will be brought low like a castle of sand. We saw this principle at work in the overthrow of the former Soviet Union, the world's largest communist nation, several years ago.

Such prayer warfare is being waged even now. The North Korean regime has kept a vigilant eye on the Republic of Korea to invade it, but it has not been able to succeed in the years since the Korean War—for it has always been ensnared by its own trap. The prayers that the faithful Christians pray day and night in the mountain and in the field, in the closet and in the church, have bound our true enemy, the devil, who is behind the leaders of North Korea. This is a sign that because of our prayers the devil who manipulates North Korean leaders will be defeated by the angel of heaven. Whatever strategy North Korea may use, it will be kept at bay in the future as long as our prayers continue, for the prince of North Korea has already been defeated by the angel of God.

Though the angel was resisted for twenty-one days by the prince of Persia, the unceasing prayers of Daniel on the earth allowed Michael—who was in charge of God's army—to come. Backed up by his help, the angel was able to defeat the prince of Persia and come down to Daniel after three weeks.

With this scene in mind we should remember that throughout all the ages those who pray for their country and their people are the true patriots, men and women of prayer who have fervently dedicated themselves to a vigil of fasting and prayer. We should pray day and night for the leaders of our country. And in order to deliver our twenty million compatriots suffering in North Korea, we Christians in South Korea should pray first that God's angels in heaven may defeat the demons who are behind North Korea, winning the victory in the war of the spiritual sphere.

78

In a similar way, when we are praying for the repentance of family members, we should also take the victory in the war of the spiritual world. Exhortation and persuasion with worldly wisdom cannot bear any fruit.

For example, a spirit of rebellion and defiance will cause children to be even more resistant to authority when parents discipline them. At such times, parents should pray that the demons who are behind their children be cast out. A person is completely changed when the demons are cast out and the Spirit of God comes in. The Bible says that when Philip preached the gospel to a city in Samaria, evil spirits came out of many with shrieks, and many paralytics and cripples were healed (Acts 8:5–8). Today evil spirits must first be cast out to heal those who are paralyzed and crippled spiritually and make them children of God.

In order to make a nation stand upright, the evil prince that is behind the nation must be driven away through prayer. The demon which seeks to steal and kill an individual or a family must also be bound through prayer. After healing a boy possessed with a demon, Jesus said, "But this kind does not go out except by prayer and fasting" (Matt. 17:21).

Above all things, we Christians must first start with prayer to break the stronghold of demons. Then the Spirit of God will come to indwell us, and the angels of the Lord will attend us. If we achieve victory in the spiritual war so the inner person of the one we are praying for is changed, that person will be a good Christian and will love God. A child will obey his or her parents; a spouse will have a love for family members and neighbors.

The apostle Paul taught us how to win a sure victory without fail in such a battle: "With all prayer and petition pray at all times in the Spirit, and with this in view, be on the alert with all perseverance and petition for all the saints" (Eph. 6:18). Whoever wins in this battle of prayer for the spiritual world also wins in the physical world. Whoever loses in the battle of prayer also becomes a loser in the physical world.

THE WAR CONTINUES TODAY

THE ANGEL OF God fought with the prince of Persia, but his fight did not end there. He fought with the prince of Greece as well, and his fight will continue with the kingdom of Satan and with his power to the end of the world. So we should pray unceasingly to help angels win in the spiritual war.

The individual who prays will no more fall than the family or the nation who prays. But the nation that fights only in the physical world is bound to fall.

It is no accident that Korea has ten million Christians. I believe God wants to use the Korean church to send out missionaries to every nation and people in the world to preach the gospel that they may be saved through repentance. So the Korean church must cease denominational contention. This is utterly destructive. And we must concentrate our efforts instead to pray that the nation may receive more abundant grace and be filled with the Spirit, so the fire of revival may grow. And we should pray that the Korean church may become united.

Christians in every land would do well to pray the same way. We are all generals engaged in spiritual war. And Michael, the captain of God's host, stands by our side.

11

The Kings of the
South and the North

PERSIA AND GREECE
(11:1–4)

C HAPTER 11 BEGINS with an interesting statement by the angel. This messenger said that he had stood with Darius the Mede to confirm and strengthen him in his first year as king. Now let's think for a minute about the meaning of this passage.

When the Medo-Persians conquered Babylon and set up their kingdom, the demons took possession of this kingdom and manipulated it to try to destroy all the captive Jews within its borders. As their first manipulative act, the demons stirred up all the administrators and satraps of the kingdom to bring charges against Daniel to King Darius. They probably intended to begin an extensive extermination of the Jews as soon as Daniel was killed in the lions' den. But thanks to Daniel's prayer, the angels of God defeated the demons who were in possession of the kingdom so that an angel could get into the lions' den and shut their mouths.

Consequently, King Darius was so impressed by this incident that he immediately began to adopt a pro-Jewish policy. First, he ordered that the administrators who had accused Daniel be thrown into the lions' den along with all their households. Then he issued a decree to all the people in the kingdom commanding them to worship Daniel's God.

Thus the Jews could live well, even in the land where they had been carried as captives, because an angel took his stand to support King Darius and strengthen him.

THE KINGS WHO WILL APPEAR IN PERSIA

NOW LET'S PAY attention to the words of the prophecy itself. The revelation first told about the kings who would appear in Persia. It was in fact fulfilled in later history.

The first king who appeared was Cambyses (529–522 B.C.); the second king was Pseudo-Smerdis (522–521 B.C.); the third was Darius I Hystaspes (521–486 B.C.); and the fourth king was Xerxes I, who reigned from 486–465 B.C. During his reign Persia reached its highest glory. Xerxes was also called Ahasuerus and was the same king who appeared in the Book of Esther.

At the time of the fourth king, the Medo-Persian kingdom—which had become extremely rich—set up a strategy to invade Greece. As I pointed out earlier, after a four-year preparation, the empire mobilized an army of one million. Then it set out on its campaign against Greece in 480 B.C., but it was defeated in humiliation by Greece. As a result, Persia began to decline after Xerxes I and finally fell to the Greeks.

A MIGHTY KING WHO IS TO COME (11:3–4)

THE KING DESCRIBED here, who defeated Xerxes, is Alexander the Great, whom we also discussed in an earlier chapter. Once again, this prophecy was accurately fulfilled in history down to the last detail: At the height of his power Alexander's kingdom was "broken up" and divided among his four generals. His kingdom did not fall to his descendants; they were assassinated. Thus Daniel's prophecy told about events of history that were still two hundred to four hundred years in the future.

THE WAR BETWEEN THE KINGS OF THE SOUTH AND THE NORTH (11:5–6)

AS WE HAVE noted, two of the kingdoms resulting from the division of Alexander's empire attained prominence over the others: Egypt and Syria.

The king of the South in this passage is Ptolemy Soter I, who ruled Egypt from 323 to 285 B.C. The king of the North was Seleucus Nicator I of Syria, who ruled from 312 to 281 B.C.

Seleucus Nicator was at one time driven out of Syria by Antigonus, who ruled Babylon. So he sought refuge with Ptolemy Soter of Egypt. Aided by Egypt, he defeated Antigonus and became the king of Syria, ruling its vast territory stretching from Asia Minor to India. Thus at first he received help from Egypt, but his kingdom later became stronger than Egypt, thereby opening the door to a war that lasted for the following one hundred fifty years.

The details of verse 6 came true in later history. In order to cement diplomatic ties with the king of the North (that is, of Syria), Ptolemy II Philadelphus, king of the South (that is, of Egypt, 285–246 B.C.), wanted to marry his daughter Berenice to Antiochus II Theos of Syria (261–246 B.C.). Antiochus II had married before and already had a wife. But Ptolemy pressured Antiochus until he finally divorced his wife Laodice against his own will to take Berenice, princess of Egypt, as his new wife. However, Antiochus could not forget his former wife, Laodice. So later, when his new father-in-law died of illness, Antiochus brought Laodice back to the palace.

All this time Laodice had been waiting bitterly, watching for the opportunity to take revenge. So as soon as she was brought back to the palace, she murdered Antiochus, Berenice, and their son, Antiochus III. Then she conspired to make her own son ascend to the throne of Syria so she could rule the kingdom through him.

Read verse 6 once again to see how precisely every detail was fulfilled. What an accurate prophecy this was—as it had to be, because it was given by God.

SYRIA AND EGYPT CONTINUE TO FIGHT (11:7–15)

THIS VERSE IS a prophecy of the things that would happen three hundred years after Daniel's time. After Ptolemy II died, the brother of Berenice—the princess who had married Antiochus—ascended to the throne of the Egyptian kingdom. He became Ptolemy III Eurgetes (246–221 B.C.). Since he had waited for the opportunity to avenge the death of his sister, he finally raised a great army and made an expedition against Seleucus II Callinicus (246–226 B.C.) of Syria—the son of Laodice, his sister's murderer. But Syria was badly defeated by Egypt.

After this great war, acts of hostility ceased for several years as Syria regained strength. Then Syria raised a large army and made an expedition to Egypt in 240 B.C. But Seleucus II Callinicus was beaten again—exactly as the words of verse 10 had predicted.

When Seleucus II Callinicus of Syria thus failed in his expedition against Egypt, he fell sick and died of an illness. But his sons succeeded in the task. His first son, Seleucus III (226–223 B.C.), made several expeditions against Egypt, only to fail and die young. But he was followed by his younger brother, Antiochus III (223–187 B.C.), who defeated Egypt and took the Egyptian-held regions as far as the border of Gaza.

Note again that Daniel's prophecy concerning these sons actually took place three hundred years after he received it. Phase after phase of this prophecy was fulfilled in history! Thus the Word of God is true, and not the smallest letter, not the least stroke of a pen, will fall to the ground.

Verses 11 and 12 speak of how Ptolemy Philopater (221–203 B.C.) of Egypt, who had lost his territories to Antiochus III, eventually waged war against him in 217 B.C. with an army of seventy thousand. In the Battle of Laphia, near the border of Palestine, Ptolemy crushed Antiochus.

Antiochus not only lost his large army in this battle, but he also had to hide himself in the desert, where he was almost taken captive. He narrowly escaped from death and fled—just as verse 11 had prophesied.

On the other hand, if the king of Egypt who had defeated Antiochus III at Laphia had gone on to Syria itself, sweeping everything in his way, he could have conquered the kingdom. But after he had slaughtered tens of thousands of enemy soldiers, he was filled with pride and ceased pursuing the enemy. Accordingly, after that time Egypt once again began to decline. This fact Daniel prophesied in verse 12.

Antiochus III, who narrowly escaped death in the desert, at last returned home. Bitter and seeking revenge, he prepared to make another expedition against Egypt. The long-sought opportunity finally came. Mysteriously, Ptolemy Philopater of Egypt and his wife died with no apparent cause in 203 B.C., and their only son, Ptolemy V Epiphanes, succeeded to the throne. But he was only a little child.

Seizing this opportunity, Syria invaded Egypt several times, like the flow of a tide. The prophecy recorded in verse 13 refers to this event.

At the time Israel was subject to Egypt, and the garrison of the Ptolemaic general Scopas was defending Jerusalem. Scopas showed much favor to the Jews, aiding them in refurbishing the temple and helping them in many other ways.

Nevertheless, when Syria invaded Egypt, many of the Jews stood with Syria against Egypt. Their plan was to take advantage of the conflict to drive Egypt from the country. But the plan ended in failure. Because of this endeavor, Israel was branded a robber and an ungrateful nation. This event was prophesied in verse 14.

The Egyptian army of Scopas fought with the Syrian army in Farnia at the upper stream of the Jordan. But they were greatly defeated and had to retreat to the city of Sidon, which was known as the strongest fortress in the world at that time. Even so, the Syrian army attacked Sidon by building siege works all around the city, and the fortress finally fell between 199 and 198 B.C. Scopas surrendered.

Thus Syria came to possess all the regions of Palestine and even Gaza at the border of Egypt, just as Daniel had prophesied. Elite Egyptian generals like Eropas, Manacles, and Demonius tried hard to rescue Scopas when he was under siege. But they failed.

ROME ENTERS THE PICTURE (11:16–20)

SYRIA, ONCE IT had crushed Egypt, brought to trial the Jews who had earlier rebelled against it, and Jerusalem once again came under the control of Antiochus III. Nevertheless, when Antiochus perceived the danger of Rome's advance east from Italy, he determined to make peace with Egypt, for he thought that further conflict with Egypt might threaten the security of his kingdom.

Accordingly, in order to carry out his plan, he gave his beautiful daughter Cleopatra in marriage to the seven-year-old King Ptolemy V Epiphanes of Egypt in 192 B.C. Her father hoped to gain control of the Egyptian throne through this marriage.

But Cleopatra sided with Ptolemy against her father in several matters, so Antioch's plan to make peace with Egypt failed. This situation was prophesied in detail in verse 17.

Eventually Antiochus gave up on Egypt and instead met with a Roman envoy who was traveling eastward at Lysimachus. The envoy proposed to Antiochus that he should surrender and pay tribute to Rome. But Antiochus answered proudly: "Asia has no interest in Rome, nor will she obey the command of Rome."

Having been thus insulted, Rome waited for the opportunity to take revenge on Antiochus. Meanwhile Antiochus, who had always succeeded up to that time in his expeditions to Egypt, made an expedition west into

Europe, emulating Alexander the Great. His intention was to bring Greece under his control. But his European campaign ended in failure.

The Syrian advance was first checked at Turmophy, north of Athens, in 191 B.C. Two years later Syria was again badly defeated by an army led by the Roman consul Scipio at Magnesia, alongside the Maeander River southeast of Ephesus.

Antiochus III returned home disheartened from the failure of this campaign. Some time later he was murdered by an assassin while attempting to plunder a temple in the province of Elymais.

These historical facts also square with Daniel's prophecy in verses 18 and 19.

After the death of Antiochus III, Seleucus IV Philopater succeeded to the throne. He surrendered to Rome and paid a tribute of several thousand talents every year. But when he had difficulty finding the fund for the tribute, he imposed heavy taxes on his own people and sent tax collectors to his tributary territories as well.

Seleucus sent a man named Heliodorus to be the tax collector for the Jewish nation. He was to seize the funds from the temple treasury in Jerusalem, but he died abruptly without any apparent cause. This is just what was predicted in verse 20.

ANTIOCHUS EPIPHANES (11:21–35)

VERSES 21 THROUGH 35 is the key to the prophecy in the Book of Daniel. The little horn which appears in 8:9–14, 23–25 of this book, namely Antiochus Epiphanes, arrives on the scene. He is a type of prophecy's coming Antichrist: He was a king who arose from Syria, and he devastated the temple of Israel.

In fact, he was a contemptible person who did not rightfully inherit the throne. When Seleucus IV Philopater died unexpectedly, he left two sons behind. The first son, Demetrius, was being held in Rome as a hostage. His second son, Seleucus, was still a young boy.

When their uncle Antiochus Epiphanes (175–164 B.C.) heard this news in Athens, he returned to Antioch under the pretext of becoming his nephew's regent. But after his return, he hired a man named Andronicus to kill his young nephew. Then he put Andronicus to death on a charge of treason, and he himself took the throne.

Consequently, his succession was not a rightful one but was accomplished by intrigue, as this prophecy had foretold.

Antiochus Epiphanes struck Egypt with a mighty army in 170 B.C. and crushed its forces in the region between Gaza and the Nile delta, which today is called Rasbaron. He also murdered Onias, the high priest of Israel, breaking the treaty of alliance he had made with him. This is the one referred to by Daniel in verse 22 as "the prince of the covenant."

Thus Antiochus Epiphanes routed Egypt and ended the conflict with that nation. Then competition for the throne broke out in Egypt between his two nephews, the sons of Cleopatra. While Ptolemy Philometor and his young brother Ptolemy Euergetes were thus engaged in a fierce contest for the throne, Antiochus Epiphanes seized the opportunity to extend his power. He helped Ptolemy Philometor to become king—with the stipulation that Egypt would become subject to him in return. In this way Antiochus consolidated his power.

After winning the hearts of his followers through the distribution of the spoil he had obtained from frequent pillages, Antiochus Epiphanes mobilized an army and made another expedition to Egypt to attack his nephew. Egypt resisted strongly, but Syria made successive attacks.

During that time many treaties were agreed upon between the Egyptian king and the Syrian king. But even though they were close relatives (uncle and nephew), none of the treaties were kept, and they waged war against each other continually. Finally, Antiochus Epiphanes pounced on Egypt and seized much wealth from the country. Then, on his way back home, he also seized the treasures in the temple of Jerusalem.

Verses 29 through 35 prophesy of the events of 168 B.C., when Antiochus Epiphanes invaded Egypt again, breaking their treaty. At that time, however, Egypt was under the regency of Rome.

Outside Alexandria, the Syrian king was confronted with the Roman envoy Gaius Popilius, who gave him a peremptory command. The envoy, who had already deployed his fleet in the Mediterranean, drew a circle where Antiochus Epiphanes stood and said, "Now choose before you come out of this circle, whether you will evacuate Egypt or attack her."

Epiphanes could not by any means resist the command of Rome. So he withdrew, full of anger. On his way home he stopped and took out his vengeance on Jerusalem. He destroyed the temple, violating the former covenant. He suspended the daily sacrifice and set up an altar to Zeus Olympius, the pagan god he worshiped. But worst of all, he ordered a sow to be sacrificed under the abominable winged image.

Then the Jews arose in revolt under the leadership of Judas Maccabeus and his brothers. During the revolt, eighty thousand Jews were killed, forty thousand Jews were sold as slaves, and another forty thousand Jews were carried off as captives. This was a great tragedy Israel suffered because of war between the kings of the South and the kings of the North. And it was all prophesied centuries before by Daniel.

Throughout this entire chapter of Daniel we can see how Daniel's prophecy was fulfilled in history down to the last detail. Yet some people do not believe that the Book of Daniel was recorded two hundred to four hundred years before the incidents of the prophecy actually took place. Because they do not believe that prophecy is possible, they assert, "The Book of Daniel is spurious, a fake prophecy that in reality was recorded after the things of the prophecy actually had happened. How otherwise could it be so accurate?" But it is their own assumption that genuine prophecy cannot take place that causes them to be so foolish.

THE KING OF THE LAST TIME (11:36–39)

ANTIOCHUS EPIPHANES, who produced this last series of tragedies, prefigures the Antichrist who will arise in the last days, for the last Antichrist will come and behave in the same way.

Up to verse 35 the prophecy was concerned with the war between the king of the South and the king of the North. But beginning with verse 36, the focus suddenly shifts to the Antichrist who will appear at the end of time. As we have said, the two thousand years of the church age were hidden to the Jewish prophets. So we will get a better look at the Antichrist's coming in our study of the Book of Revelation.

But here, in verse 36, we do find a clear description of the Antichrist who will appear during the Great Tribulation. He will do as he pleases. He will exalt himself above all, claiming that he is divine. He will oppose the Lord God with unheard-of things. For seven years he will prosper. And that period will continue until the time of wrath is complete.

Thus Antiochus Epiphanes, who was dealt with in the passage up to verse 35, is immediately followed by a depiction of the Antichrist, who imitates him.

The ensuing passage from verse 37 to verse 39 foretells how the Antichrist will arise. It says that he will show no regard for the God of his fathers or for the desire of women, nor will he regard any god, but will exalt himself above them all. Here the God of his fathers refers to the Lord God of Israel. It was the dream of every Jewish woman that she might find favor from God and conceive the Messiah in her own womb.

So Daniel is saying that the Antichrist will have regard neither for God nor for his Messiah, Jesus Christ.

Here the details of the Antichrist's background are more clearly revealed. The Antichrist, like Antiochus Epiphanes, will come from Syria and will be a Jew. He will appear on the European political scene as a prominent politician, and he will accomplish the unification of ten European countries with his sternness and intrigue.

Daniel says that he will honor the god of forces, which means that he will worship Satan. The Bible shows that he will honor Satan with gold and silver, with precious stones and costly gifts. It also shows that he will build a strong fortress and conquer the whole world with the help of a foreign god—that is, through the strength of Satan. He will honor those who follow him, and he will distribute the land in return for a bribe.

THE LAST WAR OF THE EARTH (11:40–45)

THE PROPHECY FOLLOWING verse 40, combined with insights from the Book of Revelation, shows that the Antichrist will gain power while he rules over Europe for the first three and one-half years, but he will also face rebellion in Africa when the Tribulation passes into its second phase. When the rebellion arises in the confederate nations of Africa, centering in Egypt, the Antichrist will make Jerusalem his headquarters for suppressing this uprising. He will make the temple of Jerusalem desolate and will set up his own image in it, destroying every Jew who does not bow down to it. Thus he will imitate Antiochus Epiphanes. In this time of tribulation, however, the Jews will retire into a safe place prepared by God. This shelter is the city of Petra in Jordan, which was formerly the land of the Moabites and Ammonites. At this time God will bless the Jews by working a miracle, allowing them to flee away only one mile at a time. This we can see in prophetic detail in Revelation 12.

For that reason, some British and American Christians are storing up at Petra a large quantity of canned food and Hebrew Bibles so that the Israelites may eat the food and read the Bible during the second three and one-half years of tribulation. Petra is a shelter God has prepared for His people, a natural fortress impregnable to every attack by the enemy. Moreover, according to the prophecy, whenever the Antichrist's army attempts to advance, the earth will open its mouth and devour it.

Consequently, the Antichrist will have to turn his attention in the direction of Africa, especially Egypt. When he is about to strike Egypt, Libya, and Ethiopia so that he can conquer and unify them, he will be alarmed by bad reports from the east and the north. The alarming news will be that the Euphrates River has dried up and a vast army of Asian people, led by China, is invading his country. As we will also see, this will come to pass as the result of Revelation's sixth bowl (Rev. 16:12).

While advancing to the southwest, this army from the east will shower nuclear bombs. It will encounter the Antichrist's army at the Valley of Jehoshaphat. This will be the Battle of Armageddon, which we have mentioned before. It will be a conflict on a scale unprecedented in human history.

At the very moment when the Antichrist destroys Israel and is engaged in the terrible war with the army from the east, placing his headquarters between the Mediterranean and the Dead Sea ("the seas") on Mount Zion ("the beautiful Holy Mountain"), his end will come. Suddenly heaven will be opened, and Jesus will come down riding on a white horse. Countless numbers of redeemed people in white linen will follow Him. By the sharp sword that comes out of His mouth, the Lord Jesus will kill at once every person who has the mark of the beast. Then after overcoming the Antichrist, the age of Jesus Christ and His saints will begin.

12

Israel and the End of History

THE GREAT TRIBULATION
(12:1)

W E HAVE DISCUSSED earlier how the seven-year Tribulation is divided into two parts, each three and one-half years long. When the second part of the Tribulation comes to the Jews, Michael the archangel will arise and lead them to the fortress of Petra in Jordan. The Antichrist will pursue them, setting in motion every weapon and piece of equipment he has.

If the Jews were to resort to running in that situation, it would not be long before they were all overtaken and put to death. But God will show them special favor through providing a way to escape. John says in Revelation:

> And when the dragon saw that he was thrown down to the earth, he persecuted the woman who gave birth to the male child. And the two wings of the great eagle were given to the woman, in order that she might fly into the wilderness to her place, where she was nourished for a time and times and half a time, from the presence of the serpent.
> —REVELATION 12:13–14

Here the woman stands for the Jews. This prophecy shows that they will be enabled to flee swiftly to Petra. During this flight they will not be alone, but Michael the archangel will protect them. Those who escape to Petra will be the ones who are chosen among the Jews, and they will be those who love Jesus Christ.

THE RESURRECTION (12:2–3)

WHEN CHRIST DESCENDS to this earth after the second three-and-one-half-year period is concluded, the great resurrection begins. Those who are beheaded during the seven years of the Tribulation, especially the Jews, will arise to receive everlasting life. But remember that before the Tribulation will have begun, those who rest in the earth will have risen first, with the voice of the archangel and the trumpet call of God. Then after that those who are still alive will be caught up together with them into the air to take part in the wedding of our Lord Jesus Christ.

So those who rise at this point, at the end of the Tribulation, will be the martyrs who will be killed by the Antichrist during the Great Tribulation.

Meanwhile, all the sinners who have opposed Christ will be killed by the sword that proceeds from His mouth, and they will be shut up in hell for a thousand years. Then the dead, great and small, will rise to stand trial before the great white throne. As soon as it is determined that their names are not recorded in the Book of Life, they will be thrown into the lake of fire burning with sulphur.

Then "those who have insight will shine brightly like the brightness of the expanse of heaven, and those who lead the many to righteousness, like the stars forever and ever" (12:3). "Those who have insight" refers to the people who wisely put off the lust of the flesh, the lust of the eyes, and the pride of this world. (See 1 John 2:16.) They are the people who wait for the coming of the Lord in constant watching and prayer.

Who then are they who will "lead the many to righteousness"? They are today's pastors, missionaries, home cell leaders, elders, senior deaconesses, deacons, and ordinary Christians engaged in the propagation of the gospel of Jesus Christ to many people. These are the Christians who spend their time and energy to encourage other believers to cultivate a stronger faith while teaching sinners who are ignorant of the truth the path of life to make them turn around. These people will shine forever, for they will shine with Christ.

When our Lord comes to this earth, He will reward us according to our labor. As the sun has one kind of splendor, the moon another, and the stars another, and each star differs from another in splendor, so the reward God will give each of us will differ in glory (1 Cor. 15:40–42). So I pray in the name of our Lord Jesus Christ that you will preach the gospel to many people in order to receive a prize that will shine forever.

THE END OF THE REVELATION (12:4)

DANIEL DID NOT receive this revelation for his own sake or even for his own generation, but for us who live in the time of the end. He was told to close up and seal this revelation for us.

The Book of Daniel was thus closed to the people who lived before us, so it was impossible for them to understand this book. By now, however, much of the revelation has passed into history, and Daniel is an open book to us. The time of the end is the very time when people go here and there swiftly, and knowledge increases. So the present time in which we come to possess the full knowledge of the Bible, by opening the seals from the Bible and by the increase of knowledge, is the very time when we are at the threshold of the End Time.

THE FINAL PERIOD AND
CONCLUDING INTERPRETATION (12:5–13)

IN HIS CONCLUDING vision Daniel heard a conversation about the End Time. One man asked another, "How long will it be until the end of these wonders?" (v. 6).

The answer was given in words we have read before: "It would be for a time, times, and half a time" (v. 7). This refers to the second period of three and one-half years in the Tribulation, during which the Antichrist and his soldiers "finish shattering the power of the holy people," that is, the Jews (v. 7).

But Daniel could not understand these words, so he asked what would be the outcome of these events. But the only answer he received was to go his way, because the words were hidden and sealed until the End Time.

But that is not the case for you. Happy are you who live at this closing time of the age of grace, because the words of Daniel are open to you.

In 1948 you may have witnessed Israel's rebirth as a nation after two thousand years of wandering.

Daily in your morning paper you read about the progress Europe is making toward unification.

You have succeeded in interpreting the secret of Daniel, and you are aware that when Europe is unified, from out of it will come a leader who is the Antichrist foreshadowed by Antiochus Epiphanes. And you know that the Great Tribulation, the final week of Daniel, will begin as soon as he concludes a seven-year goodwill treaty with Israel.

Happy are you as well because you know that the people of God who believe in Jesus Christ will have been taken up into heaven by this time. You also know that seven years after that, the sanctuary of Israel will be destroyed and the power of the holy people will be broken. Then the people of God who have been taken up into heaven will come down to the Battle of Armageddon with Jesus Christ, who will take captive the Antichrist and the false prophet. Though you will not be on this earth during the Tribulation, you know quite well what will happen during this period.

So blessed are you who are among the wise at this time of the end! You understand the Word of our Lord, and you are clean, for you have been washed by the precious blood of Jesus Christ. The foolish people will not be able to understand this secret that you know, even if they are given it in their hands and are taught about it.

UNDERSTANDING THE DIFFERENT NUMBER OF DAYS

THIS VERSE AGAIN confirms what will happen at the end of the world through the activity of the Antichrist. Now note here that verse 11 says, "And from the time that the regular sacrifice is abolished, and the abomination of desolation is set up, there will be 1,290 days." But the period of three and one-half years we have mentioned is equivalent to one thousand two hundred sixty days. So why are thirty days added here?

Here is the answer. Jesus will indeed come down one thousand two hundred sixty days after the abomination is set up, and that is exactly three and one-half years. But before Jesus comes down, many people will have been killed in the Battle of Armageddon. In addition, when Jesus descends, He will destroy all His enemies who have gathered there with the sword that proceeds out of His mouth. So the number of people who will have been killed will roughly amount to three hundred million. Along with their bodies on the battlefield will be the weapons and the equipment they have left, which will be heaped as high as a mountain.

Once our Lord comes and casts the Antichrist and the false prophets into the lake of fire, the battleground will have to be cleared of all the bodies and equipment. It will take thirty days for all these things to happen.

Then in verse 12, forty-five days are added for a total of one thousand three hundred thirty-five. The forty-five days is the period needed for God to separate the sheep from the goats (Matt. 25:31–46). Thus after His coming, for thirty days Jesus will put in order this world which has been destroyed. Then He will judge it in another forty-five days. After that, the millennial kingdom will begin on this earth. It will take one thousand three hundred thirty-five days for all these things to be accomplished.

ARE YOU READY?

EVEN SO, THE church will not need to wait until then. By this time we will have been taken up into heaven and will have descended with Jesus Christ when He comes down to put this world in order and to judge it. Afterward, we will reign with Him for a thousand years. When the period of this millennium is thus fulfilled, the new heaven and new earth, which are eternal, will wait for us.

Let me take the liberty of posing a few questions to you who have now finished reading this book:

- Have you prepared the oil of the Holy Spirit in your life for the coming of the Bridegroom?
- Are the members of your family all saved?
- Have you brought your neighbors to the path of salvation?

We are just now passing over the threshold into the End Time. The Lord is doing new things, and we must be ready.

SECTION TWO

THE BOOK OF REVELATION

13

The Revelation of Jesus Christ

A GENERAL PREFACE TO THE BOOK OF REVELATION

N OW THAT WE have studied the prophet Daniel's End-Time revelations given in the fifth century B.C., we can now complete our study in the book section with the first-century revelations given the New Testament prophet John.

The very first verse of the Book of Revelation reveals its title. It is "the Revelation of Jesus Christ." After His Resurrection from the dead, when He was glorified, Jesus dictated this word of revelation to His disciple John to be given to the church He had redeemed with His precious blood.

Many people have either interpreted Revelation the wrong way or turned their faces from it. However, such an attitude is dangerous because it hinders the Word of God from growing in their lives. Since the Book of Revelation was recorded through the direct dictation of Jesus Christ Himself, we should receive it with godly and thankful hearts and study to understand its full meaning.

Revelation's purpose was to show God's servants that the events reserved for the last two thousand years of world history would come to pass shortly. God said He wanted this revelation taught to Christians so they might enter the eternal heaven through watchfulness and prayer. Because the Book of Revelation came directly from God, we know its message is certain, for the word God speaks is always fulfilled. It's being fulfilled even now, and it will surely be fulfilled in the future. Moreover, God gave this revelation to Jesus, who in turn sent an angel to deliver it to the apostle John.

THE SCENE RECORDED BY THE APOSTLE JOHN

THE GOD OF TRINITY AND THE
CERTAINTY OF CHRIST'S REDEMPTION (1:4–6)

THE FIRST THINGS Jesus emphasized when He dictated the Book of Revelation were the triune Godhead and the certainty of His redemption. "Him who is and who was and who is to come" mentioned by John refers to the eternal God, our Father. "The seven Spirits who are before His throne" refer to the Holy Spirit in the state of His fullness, for seven, the perfect number, was used to describe Him. In addition, John said this revelation came from Jesus Christ, who is "the faithful witness, the first-born of the dead, and the ruler of the kings of the earth." With that, John was making it clear that this revelation came from the God of the trinity.

"[Christ] has made us to be a kingdom, priests to His God and Father," John wrote, and he gave glory to Christ by saying, "To Him be the glory and the dominion forever and ever."

In the days of Paul, and especially after his death, many churches in gentile lands began to return to their former yoke of the law from which they had been set free. The Christian doctrine that people are saved by faith in Jesus and that salvation is purchased by His precious blood had become weakened. Many gentile converts had been persuaded to accept a legalistic faith by Jews who had come down from Judea. Those legalists taught that unless the gentile believers became circumcised and kept the days, months, and holy days after the manner of Moses, they could not be saved.

Under those circumstances, John, inspired by the Holy Spirit, emphasized that people are saved not by their deeds in accordance with the Law, but by the blood of Jesus, who loved them even unto death. By having John emphasize that we are made priests unto God and His kingdom, Jesus made it clear that our salvation is a divine gift of His grace.

The Revelation of Jesus Christ

THE SECOND COMING OF JESUS CHRIST (1:7)

THE RETURN OF Jesus mentioned here is not His coming in the air but His coming to earth after the Great Tribulation, when everyone will see Him, including those who pierced Him. At the Rapture of the church Jesus will not reveal Himself to the world, but will come only to gather the believers as they rise to meet Him in the clouds (1 Thess. 4:17).

Jesus will come like a thief in the night and take away His chosen children, like priceless treasures, to heaven. Unsaved husbands will awake in the morning to find their wives missing, or wives will find their husbands missing. Some pilots will suddenly disappear from their aircraft. In schools, some of the teachers and pupils will be missing.

Moreover, Matthew 24:40–41 tells us, "Then there shall be two men in the field; one will be taken, and one will be left. Two women will be grinding at the mill; one will be taken, and one will be left." Jesus' faithful believers will hear the calling of the Holy Spirit and will be taken. Though we don't know the day or the hour, it's certain our Lord's coming in the air is close at hand.

Christ's coming to earth with His saints will take place seven years after the Rapture. Verse 7 of the first chapter says, "He [Jesus Christ] is coming with the clouds." The clouds mentioned here are not ordinary clouds; these have a significant meaning. The glory of the Lord will appear like clouds, but it seems reasonable to interpret the verse as saying those clouds signify the flapping of the white robes on the saints who will return with Him.

The Bible uses the same figure of speech to describe a large number of people in Hebrews 12:1. Therefore when Jesus comes with all His saints (1 Thess. 3:13), with many thousands of His saints (Jude 14), it will appear as if Jesus is coming wrapped up in the clouds.

After we've been taken up into heaven and have participated in the great wedding feast of the Lamb (Rev. 19:6–9), we will return to earth. The site for the Lord's coming to earth the second time will be the Mount of Olives outside Jerusalem.

What does it mean that "every eye will see Him, even those who pierced Him; and all the tribes of the earth will mourn over Him"? It means the word of prophecy recorded in Zechariah 12:10 will be fulfilled: "And I will pour out on the house of David and on the inhabitants of Jerusalem, the Spirit of grace and of supplication, so that they will look on Me whom they have pierced; and they will mourn for Him, as one mourns for an only son, and they will weep bitterly over Him, like the bitter weeping over a first-born."

God will give the spirit of repentance to the Jews. They will look at the nail prints in Jesus Christ's hands and the marks of the spear in His side. They will recognize that this was the Messiah whom they had reviled and crucified under false accusations. They will weep bitterly out of contrition and remorse. The Gentiles who have lived so far according to the lust of the flesh, the lust of the eyes, and the pride of this world (1 John 2:16) will likewise shed tears out of fear of judgment and destruction.

THE ETERNITY OF JESUS

"THE LORD" RECORDED in verse 8 refers to our Lord Jesus. "Alpha" and "Omega" are the first and last letters of the Greek alphabet, just as A and Z are in the English alphabet.

Jesus is the One who was, the Creator who existed from the infinite past. He is not just another saint who was born two thousand years ago. Further, He is still alive, and He is concerned for our well-being. He is constantly interceding for us (Heb. 7:25). Out of His tender mercy He fills all our needs. John also emphasized that He holds the whole universe in His hands.

JOHN, WHO WAS IN THE SPIRIT (1:9–10)

IN VERSE 9 John identified himself. He wrote this Book of Revelation around A.D. 95. By this time the other apostles had all been arrested, tried, and martyred.

John was exiled to the isle of Patmos. This island swarmed with atrocious criminals who came from all parts of the Roman empire. There were no grass or trees. John probably also suffered bitter insults from his fellow prisoners in the daytime, and at night he was vexed among the felons who quarreled with abusive words. In the midst of such a confused and chaotic environment, however, John could still be in the Spirit through prayer. It was on one Lord's day as he was praying that he received Jesus' revelation.

How about you? Could you become similarly inspired? No matter how unfavorable your circumstances might be, they're probably not as bad as those of the apostle John on the isle of Patmos. We must pray without ceasing that we may be inspired by the Holy Spirit in spite of our surroundings. Without His help, no one can understand the deep meaning of divine revelation.

First Corinthians 2:11 tells us, "For who among men knows the thoughts of a man except the spirit of the man, which is in him? Even so the thoughts of God no one knows except the Spirit of God."

Except by the Holy Spirit, no one can unveil the secrets of God. Not a word! So God put John in the Spirit to show him His deep mysteries. Because this revelation was not written by human wisdom and experience but by the full inspiration of the Holy Spirit, it is the accurate Word of God, free from all errors as John originally penned it.

Those who recorded other books of the Bible also wrote under the inspiration of the Holy Spirit (2 Tim. 3:16). Therefore, every verse and every word of the Scripture became the Word of God and was free from all human error.

THE SOUND OF A TRUMPET (1:10–16)

JOHN WROTE THAT when he was in the Spirit, he heard a loud voice like a trumpet. The sound meant that God was about to give him a special message.

THE SEVEN CHURCHES IN ASIA MINOR

THE GREAT VOICE said, "Write in a book what you see, and send it to the seven churches: to Ephesus and to Smyrna and to Pergamum and to Thyatira and to Sardis and to Philadelphia and to Laodicea" (v. 11).

In those days there were more than a hundred churches in Asia Minor. Of all those churches, why did Jesus choose only seven?

First, I believe each of those many churches could identify with one of the seven, which had their own particular characteristics.

Second, through those seven types of churches, Jesus wanted to illustrate the two-thousand-year history of the church from the time of John to the present. The church age would be divided into seven periods, represented by one of the seven churches.

THE SEVEN GOLDEN CANDLESTICKS AND THE PICTURE OF JESUS

WHEN JOHN TURNED to see the voice that spoke to him, he saw seven candlesticks burning brightly. Those candlesticks were made of beaten, pure gold and signified the church, which lights up the world.

In the midst of the seven candlesticks John saw Jesus and beheld Him with a strong yearning. Previously he had thought of Jesus as being far away in a remote heaven. But he saw the Lord right in front of him. Today Jesus is still present at our side.

Let's examine the picture of Jesus in verse 13. First, He was "like a son of man," clothed with a long garment. That garment was a special article of clothing chosen by God for the high priest and the judge. Why did Jesus appear wearing such a garment? Because He is the high priest for His believers. The high priest of Israel prayed to God for the people to be blessed and forgiven for their sins. Jesus is our high priest, offering prayers that we may be forgiven of our sins and receive God's blessing.

To those who don't believe in the Lord, however, His garment becomes the special garb of a judge. Thus, our source of great blessing is a source of condemnation to unbelievers.

Second, the Scriptures tell us Jesus was "girded across His breast with a golden girdle" (v. 13). In olden times a golden girdle was worn only by the king. So the girdle around Jesus' chest symbolizes His position as the King of kings.

Third, "His head and His hair were white like white wool, like snow" (v. 14). That means Jesus is not only pure, but also omniscient. White hair usually means one has reached the highest point of wisdom after the springs and autumns of life. However, I have observed that the younger generation today does not seem to show proper respect for the aged. And that is wrong. The Bible says, "A gray head is a crown of glory," a symbol of wisdom (Prov. 16:31). Consulting with aged people, therefore, generally provides wisdom for all.

Fourth, Jesus' "eyes were like a flame of fire" (v. 14). Our hearts palpitate when a person with a pure heart, who prays a lot, looks into our eyes. Why? Because such eyes are able to penetrate the corrupt thinking we may have in our minds. How much more our hearts would palpitate if Jesus were to gaze at us with eyes like a flame of fire! His discerning eyes know and judge all hidden things.

Fifth, Jesus was standing erect, and "His feet were like burnished bronze, when it has been caused to glow in a furnace" (v. 15). Brass is made from copper, which throughout the Bible implies judgment. In Old Testament times the altar and fleshhooks used in sacrifices were all made from brass. Our Lord says He will judge severely those who commit sin.

Sixth, the voice of our Lord is like "the sound of many waters" (v. 15). That's the voice of none other than the Creator, who speaks to us, His creation, with the same voice He used in the days of creation.

Seventh, "He held seven stars" (v. 16). The seven stars signify the pastors of the seven churches in Asia Minor. From this verse we can understand how close pastors are to the heart of Jesus Christ. Their position is immensely honorable and high before Him. But pastors who have entered the ministry without a divine calling—perhaps through the influence of their parents, relatives, or neighbors—are not the stars laid upon His palm. They're fallen stars. Those who pastor only for a profession establish numerous churches that follow a secular direction, and innumerable souls are led down a wrong path.

An elder of our denomination once sent me a letter in which he said he was dissatisfied with the pastor of his church and wondered what he should do. Should he drive the pastor out, or should he resist him? As far as I knew, the pastor was God's sincere servant who was carrying out a divine calling. It was true he had lots of character weaknesses, but anyone who resisted him would eventually inflict an injury upon the right hand of Jesus. As a result, that person would receive God's judgment.

In view of this, I told the elder he should choose to do one of the following: support the pastor with prayer, covering his weaknesses, or leave the church. Later I heard he had left the church. It was a wise decision.

Eighth, "out of His mouth came a sharp two-edged sword" (v. 16). The Word that proceeds out of the mouth of Jesus Christ is indeed a sword: "The word of God is living and active and sharper than any two-edged sword, and piercing as far as the division of soul and spirit, of both joints and marrow, and able to judge the thoughts and intentions of the heart" (Heb. 4:12).

The Word is a surgical knife God uses to save our lives. When we hear and receive it, wonderful things happen to us. Our sins and wickedness are laid bare. The devil is cast out. Sickness and disease are healed. Despair and heavy burdens are removed. All these things happen because they are pierced to the dividing by the Word. Therefore it is in vain to try to receive God's blessings of salvation and healing without desiring the Word or hearing it.

Ninth, Jesus' face "was like the sun shining in its strength" (v. 16). When the cold winter passes and the warm spring comes, the sun sheds its light strongly, and everything comes to life. The full strength of sunshine means overflowing vitality. Whoever comes to Jesus will receive the shining light that radiates from His face and will be filled with the joy of the Lord to the fullest.

That same pure, kingly Jesus is here with us right now. Blessed are they who bow their knees to Him, for He will become their Shepherd and lead them down the path of abundant life.

REACTION OF THE APOSTLE JOHN (1:17–18)

JOHN WAS PROBABLY already past eighty years old when he saw the awesome figure of the glorified Jesus. His terror was so intense he fell at His feet as though dead.

I had a similar experience twenty years ago when I was still a lay believer. I was fasting and praying through the night, and at about two o'clock in the morning I saw a vision. Suddenly the room filled with a bright light. Jesus was standing in front of me. When I saw that great sight, I fell down as though I were dead. I felt drained of all energy. The beating of my pulse seemed to stop. That scene remains vivid in my memory. After reading verse 17 against the backdrop of my similar experience, I can fully understand John's reaction.

When John fell, our Lord laid His hand tenderly on him and said, "Do not be afraid; I am the first and the last, and the living One; and I was dead, and behold, I am alive forevermore, and I have the keys of death and of Hades" (vv. 17–18).

Jesus, who died on the cross of Calvary and was resurrected on the third day, has the keys of death and Hades. Therefore anyone who believes in Him does not need to be afraid of anything, because both life and death are under the authority of Jesus.

THE KEY TO OPEN THE REVELATION (1:19–20)

VERSES 19 AND 20 are keys that open John's revelation to our understanding. When misunderstood, however, these verses can cause one to misinterpret the whole book. Unfortunately, that happens frequently.

> Write therefore the things which you have seen, and the things which are, and the things which shall take place after these things. As for the mystery of the seven stars which you saw in My right hand, and the seven golden lampstands: the seven stars are the angels of the seven churches, and the seven lampstands are the seven churches.
>
> —REVELATION 1:19–20

That which the apostle John was told to record falls into three divisions.

The first is "the things which you have seen." That corresponds to the first chapter of the Book of Revelation. The second is "the things which are," which corresponds to the period of the churches in the second and third chapters. The third is "the things which shall take place after these things," which corresponds to the remaining chapters (4–22). They deal with things that will unfold at the end of the church age, such as the Rapture of the church to heaven, the last day of the world, and the unfolding of the new heaven and the new earth.

14

The Church Age

CHRIST'S MESSAGES TO the seven churches in Asia Minor were not only words of exhortation accompanied by praise and rebuke, but also words of prophecy covering the span of church history until the present time. That history falls into seven periods.

Examining the prophecy in light of what has happened, we are thrilled to find that events took place just as foretold and are still being fulfilled. Studying the second and third chapters of Revelation leads to a firm belief that this is truly the last age for the church.

Each letter to the seven churches can be divided into six parts. First, Christ indicates the name of the recipient church. Next comes His spiritual evaluation of the church; third, His commendation; fourth, His rebuke; fifth, His exhortation; and sixth, His promise. In each letter we will see how those things applied prophetically to the church during the past two thousand years.

TO THE CHURCH IN EPHESUS (2:1–7)

DESTINATION

THE FIRST LETTER was addressed to the church at Ephesus, which was a major city in Asia Minor, a seaport, and a commercial and export center. It was also the location of the great temple of Artemis (Diana). This large city was so thoroughly stirred by Paul's message that the silversmiths rioted because they believed their business of making shrines for Diana was threatened (Acts 19:23–41). There were also many people practicing magic arts. As a result of Paul's preaching, a number of those who practiced magic arts believed in Jesus, brought their books together, and burned them (Acts 19:19).

The church at Ephesus was the most privileged among all the churches because it was blessed with the best of that day's pastors. It was successively pastored by the apostle Paul, Apollos, Timothy, and the apostle John. Therefore, this church was the most trained in the Scriptures and doctrinally orthodox.

But as the church greatly expanded, because of its firm standing on the Word of God, it changed into an organization and became systematized. Naturally, little by little, its first love began to wane and grow cold. Prayer and praise ceased too, and the worship service leaned toward form and ritual.

THE DESCRIPTION OF JESUS

MANY CHURCHES TODAY have members who simply attend the services. They listen to the pastor's sermon. They're interested in things that are scientific and philosophical and in the church ministry. But they forget the Jesus who is present. *He* is the reason for our attending and our worship. These churches typically do not lead people to feel their need to be saved, encourage them to be baptized with the Holy Spirit, or pray for the sick. Therefore, nobody repents. Nobody receives the Holy Spirit. And nobody is healed miraculously from disease. The works of God disappear and are replaced by human efforts. The service turns into a humanistic meeting, void of spiritual nourishment and blessing.

The church at Ephesus had become like that. At first it was a God-centered church, full of the Word and the Holy Spirit. But then the church degenerated into a humanistic body that leaned toward activity and organization. Jesus showed His insight into the church with His rebuke: "Look! I'm still walking in the midst of the seven candlesticks holding the seven stars in My right hand, but you have forgotten" (my paraphrase).

COMMENDATION

THE METHOD OF discipline our Lord used was always to commend first before He rebuked. Our feelings are hurt less that way, and we're more open to reprimand to correct our shortcomings. This approach is also effective in bringing up our children and in all our relationships.

Thus, Jesus commended the Ephesians because their work had been Christ-centered. They also toiled sacrificially, bearing trouble and hardships in much perseverance. He also commended their purity; they would not tolerate those who were evil. Instead, they drove the false apostles out of the church.

According to Jewish tradition, the Nicolaitans referred to in verse 6 were the followers of Nicolas, one of the first seven deacons chosen by the early church. Nicolas, who had fallen from orthodox faith, introduced heretical Greek philosophy into the church. He held the belief that the spirit of man is good and pure, but his body is fundamentally forever evil. The spirit is by no means affected by the body's activities because the spirit is pure and holy forever. Therefore one's spirit is not affected harmfully even though one lives an unrestrained life of indulgence, drinking and eating as one wishes, and living immorally. And Nicholas taught that since the spirit is purified, once a man believes in Jesus, there is no difference in his body even though it commits evil.

Many churches followed the Nicolaitans and went into corruption and licentiousness. Furthermore, the Nicolaitans systematized the church and set up a sinful hierarchy. Understandably, our Lord hated the deeds of the Nicolaitans. The church at Ephesus did too, so He commended them for that as well.

REBUKE

NEXT OUR LORD sharply rebuked the church by declaring, "You have left your first love" (v. 4). It was a grave problem indeed. They had learned the Word well, but while they had been busy with their many activities, including service and sacrifice and bearing hardships, they lost Jesus from their midst. What was left but form and ritual?

The situation was analogous to what can happen in a marriage relationship. When the love is lost, the husband is bound only by the duty of earning bread for his family. The wife is bound only by her duty of rearing the children and running a household. There is not a day of rest from irritation and quarrels in such a home.

The same is true in the church. Once believers' fervent relationship with Jesus has cooled off, they will just attend church on Sundays out of habit. They're going through the motions without joy or enthusiasm. How many churches today are like that? How fervent the early Christians must have been when they first believed in Jesus Christ! Does not the Bible say they were all filled with the Holy Spirit?

Therefore the church cannot please God unless her members maintain a constant, fervent fellowship with Christ.

EXHORTATION

JESUS EXHORTED THE church at Ephesus to "remember . . . from where you have fallen" (v. 5). We so easily forget the blessing of the Lord. We also forget His chastisement. Jesus says, "Remember . . . from where you have fallen." He asks, "What happened that you now possess only a hollow faith?" If we come to our Lord at such times, confessing what we've done and repenting, we can return once again to a fervent faith life. Then we will not repeat the failure of the church at Ephesus.

PROMISE

JESUS PROMISED THAT when the Ephesian church's first love was restored, two blessings would be given (v. 7).

First He promised paradise. This paradise is far better than the one where Adam and Eve lived. The new paradise will be in heaven. Christ will transform our bodies from their former state of dishonor to a glorious new state; from weakness to power; from the natural to the spiritual so that these mortal bodies will put on immortality, and we will live forever with Him. Second, He promised He would give the fruit of the tree of life. That fruit isn't given just for the pleasure of seeing, but also for nourishment.

INTERPRETATION OF THE PROPHECY (A.D. 33–100)

THE LETTER TO the Ephesian church represents the apostolic church in the period from A.D. 33 to 100. The name *Ephesus* means "to relax or let go." Hence, the name implied that love had departed, and only form and rituals were left.

The church of Christ, which had been red-hot with the fire of the Holy Spirit in its initial stages following His ascension, slowly lost its first love. By the year 100 it had turned into a church with nothing more than forms, like the Ephesian church.

What will happen to a church that has lost its first love if it doesn't repent and return to the Lord? God will visit it with chastisement, as we will see in the next letter.

To the Church in Smyrna (2:8–11)

DESTINATION

JESUS' SECOND LETTER was addressed to the church in Smyrna, a seaport forty miles north of Ephesus. This flourishing city was situated on the trade route linking Rome to India through Persia, so commerce developed rapidly. Smyrna was founded by Alexander the Great and had temples erected to the sun god, Zeus. It was also the center of emperor worship and had temples honoring Roman rule.

THE DESCRIPTION OF JESUS

JESUS APPEARED TO the church at Smyrna as the One who was the first and the last; who had been dead and was now alive. He said (paraphrase), "You shall also suffer death and affliction." But He added, "I am the first and the last, so leave everything to Me. As I was dead and am now alive, so you shall be alive even though you die, if you believe in Me." Through this saying Jesus was foretelling the severe persecution that would come to the church at Smyrna.

COMMENDATION

OUR LORD ALWAYS commends the church under persecution. His saying can be paraphrased thus: "Though outwardly you look very poor because you're under persecution, actually you are not so. The truth is that you're rich." Tribulation and affliction always purify our faith.

The following testimony of deliverance from the much-feared Soviet army has a surprising, miraculous ending.

In the former U.S.S.R., Christianity was under such severe persecution that believers worshiped in secret places like warehouses or underground rooms. One day while the Christians were holding a secret service in a warehouse, several soldiers of the Soviet army, armed with submachine guns, kicked the door open and raided the place in the middle of a service. All the Christians held up their hands at gunpoint. In the Soviet Union, those who were discovered holding worship services were sent to Siberia, a place of endless suffering and agony.

Then the soldiers said, "You shall be tried summarily at an appointed place. If any of you want to disown Jesus Christ, step forward. Now is your chance to avoid persecution."

Some people stood up and went out. Most of the people, however, turned pale but stood still. They had to decide whether to die for Jesus' sake or to flee like the others. The silence was deadening as the soldiers waited.

Once more the soldiers shouted, "We will give you one more chance. If any of you want to live, come out quickly. Those of you who still 'stick to Jesus,' prepare yourself now for death!"

Nobody moved a muscle. Then the believers all lowered their hands and began to pray, readying themselves to die.

At that point, the soldiers bolted the doors of the warehouse and turned around. Throwing their rifles to the floor, they said, "Brothers, we are Christians, too! We have come here to attend the worship service. We had to behave like that because we were afraid there might be some false Christians among you. Since the false believers have all fled, we do not need to worry about detection. Now let's continue the service!"

Hallelujah! As you can see from that story, you can always distinguish sham from the genuine. And when Christ said to the church at Smyrna, which was under persecution, "You are rich," He meant spiritual richness.

The Lord also commended the Christians at Smyrna for overcoming the blasphemy they received from the Jews. Since Smyrna was a center of emperor worship, anybody who would not bow down and worship the emperor was in danger of death. Many Jews were executed for their monotheistic faith, and while being pulled to death they dragged the Christians to the same death out of hatred. Thus were many Christians at Smyrna executed. Jesus said it was not the Jews but Satan who worked behind them.

REBUKE

LIKE THE CHURCH at Philadelphia, the church at Smyrna received no rebuke, as Smyrna's sufferings had helped to keep the believers pure in faith and life.

EXHORTATION

THE LORD EXHORTED the church at Smyrna to be faithful unto death. Jesus said He would be their guarantor and give them a crown of life. Since we are also guaranteed by the Lord Jesus Christ, we shall also be taken care of if we have been faithful to the Lord, whether we live or die.

PROMISE

THE LORD PROMISED the church at Smyrna that it would not be hurt at the second death. The first death is the death of the body, and the second is the death of the soul. The first death comes to every being on this earth, but the second death, signifying the death of the wicked in the next world, is identified as everlasting torment of the soul in the lake of fire burning with brimstone. That has no power over the faithful. This promise means that even though the church at Smyrna was being put to death by the Roman persecutors, the Lord guaranteed it would avoid the second death and be translated to heaven.

INTERPRETATION OF THE PROPHECY (A.D. 100–312)

THE CHURCH AT Smyrna characterizes the church from A.D. 100 to 312, when Christianity was officially recognized by Constantine the Great. The church of this period was under severe persecution.

The name *Smyrna* means "crushed myrrh." Imagine! Myrrh is a bitter-tasting preservative, so wouldn't crushed myrrh taste even more bitter? It was a prophetic name that foretold how terrible the persecution would be for the church there.

The church at Smyrna follows the church at Ephesus. Don't forget that when love waned at the Ephesian church, the judgment of God followed. Through persecution and tribulation God restores the pure first love to the church.

The Bible says the church at Smyrna would have tribulation for ten days (v. 10). This signified that ten Roman emperors would persecute the church.

The first was the notorious Nero, who reigned in Rome from A.D. 37 to 68. He was sixteen years old when he ascended the throne, and he killed his wife, Octavia, and his mother and put all his brothers to death. Tradition says that after he committed those horrible crimes, he wanted to write a poem. However, when no poetic inspiration came into his mind, he was suddenly possessed with a wild desire to see the city of Rome aflame, and he ordered it set on fire.

The entire city was engulfed in flames, and the citizens were dying with agonizing cries. Nevertheless, in the midst of this hellish conflagration Nero was enjoying himself by writing a poem. The truth began to circulate that the fire had been started by the emperor, so he concocted a false rumor that the Christians were responsible and ordered their arrests.

Many Christians were imprisoned and executed because of this. In A.D. 67 Peter, the chief of the disciples and a pillar of the early church, was arrested and died a martyr's death. It is said he was crucified upside down at his own request because he felt himself unworthy to be put to death in the same manner as his Master.

In A.D. 68, the year following Peter's martyrdom, Paul also became a martyr. According to tradition, Paul was beheaded.

Thus, during the persecution of Nero, the two most prominent figures of the early church died.

The second persecution occurred from A.D. 81 to 96 during the reign of Domitian. He ordered the people to worship him as the god Jupiter. Under his persecution the apostle John was exiled to the Isle of Patmos, where he wrote the Book of Revelation.

The third persecution arose during the reign of Trajan. He outlawed the Christian faith and persecuted the church from A.D. 98 to 117. During this period, tradition says that Ignatius, the chief disciple of Peter, was thrown into a den of lions, where he was torn into pieces.

Church tradition says that a judge urged Ignatius to betray Jesus, but the disciple, who was more than eighty years old, refused.

He answered, "I have believed in Jesus from my youth until today. He has never betrayed me even once. How can I betray Him now?"

When such heroic martyrdom occurred in the amphitheater, the grace of Jesus Christ touched the hearts of the onlookers. They were so greatly moved that they were converted. This also showed, as when the early church was persecuted in Jerusalem, that Christianity is like a burning bonfire. The more you strike it with a stick, the more sparks will fly in all directions, starting thousands of new fires.

The fourth persecution occurred during the reign of Marcus Aurelius, who was on the throne from A.D. 161 to 180. He was a philosopher who tried to restore the Roman ideal of self-reliant, stoic virtue and the old state religion. The emperor martyred (among many others) Polycarp and Justin.

The fifth persecutor was Septimus Severus, who reigned from A.D. 202 to 211. He enacted a rigid law against the spread of Christianity. As a result, the father of Origen, North Africa's renowned theologian, was beheaded.

The sixth persecutor was Maximum, who reigned from A.D. 235 to 237. He was a rude barbarian who massacred the Christians and had their bodies buried together in lots of fifty and sixty.

Emperor Decius reigned from A.D. 249 to 253 and persecuted the church fiercely, intending to destroy it. Fortunately, God caused him to die at an early age.

The next ruler to persecute the church was Valerian, who reigned from A.D. 257 to 260. During his persecution Cyprian, the bishop of Carthage and a renowned Christian author, died a martyr's death.

The ninth persecutor was Aurelian, who reigned from A.D. 270 to 275.

The last persecutor was Diocletian, who ruled from A.D. 303 to 312. He issued edicts causing the Christian churches to be destroyed and all copies of the Bible to be burned. His persecution was so extensive and violent throughout the entire Roman Empire that Diocletian erected a monument commemorating the termination of Christianity. Twenty-five years after his death, however, Christianity became the state religion of Rome.

Thus, ten persecutors tried in vain to destroy Christianity throughout the years from 100 to 312. Christianity never did die completely, and the prophecy "you will have tribulation ten days" was fulfilled.

During that period the church went underground to avoid capture. The underground galleries called catacombs still remain in Rome. I once entered a catacomb, following a guide. It seemed like a maze with long, winding tunnels. It seemed to me that there would be no possible way out.

The catacombs had enough space for places of worship. Additionally, their perpendicular walls contained small compartments that had been cut out to bury the dead. On the walls of these tombs, pictures were drawn of a bird and the face of Jesus with the following inscription: "Our beloved resurrects and goes to the presence of the Lord. Wait for the coming of the Lord." The symbolism meant that the soul flies away like a bird and goes to the throne of Jesus Christ.

I was greatly moved to see the joy and hope in the epitaphs and pictures the Christians left behind rather than the shadow of sorrow. For more than two centuries numerous Christians were born in those dark catacombs. But they never gave up the staunch hope they cherished in their hearts for a bright tomorrow.

To those spiritual warriors who kept their faith under persecution and handed it down to us, we owe our freedom to hear and read and preach the gospel. Sometimes we're frustrated and prone to complain at small hardships and afflictions. I pray in the name of the Lord Jesus, however, that you and I will look at those heroes of the faith and become victorious warriors ourselves by overcoming tribulation and persecution with boldness.

TO THE CHURCH IN PERGAMUM (2:12–17)

DESTINATION

JESUS' THIRD LETTER was addressed to the church in Pergamum. In those days Pergamum was the capital of Asia Minor and a flourishing center of politics, power, heathen worship, and learning. It had temples to Zeus and altars offered to Aesculapius, its guardian idol. The people put serpents on their altars and worshiped them. Moreover, the cult of emperor worship flourished here, too. It was the duty of every citizen to burn incense once a year to his deified image.

THE DESCRIPTION OF JESUS

THE LORD APPEARED to the church in Pergamum as "the One who has the sharp two-edged sword" (v. 12). Because this church "[has] there some who hold the teaching of Balaam . . . to eat things sacrificed to idols, and to commit acts of immorality" (v. 14), it needed to repent, or He would come in judgment. With the sword of the Word, the Lord will reveal and sever false doctrine.

COMMENDATION

JESUS COMMENDED THE church in Pergamum for keeping its pure faith and not compromising with heresies. He especially pointed out a man named Antipas. Tradition relates this concerning the martyrdom of Antipas:

> At that time emperor worship was in full force. One day a Roman official took Antipas before the image of the emperor and said, "Antipas, worship the image."
>
> Antipas answered, "The King of kings and the Lord of lords is Jesus Christ only, so I will not worship any other god. Only Jesus."
>
> The Roman official was infuriated and shouted, "Antipas, don't you know that all the world is against you?"
>
> Antipas responded, "Then I, Antipas, acknowledge Jesus as the Lord of lords against all in the world."
>
> Enraged at this answer, the official ordered some men to heat up a brazen bull, and Antipas was put into it. There he was slowly roasted to death. Yet he never denied Jesus.

REBUKE

JESUS ALSO REBUKED the church in Pergamum, saying, "You have there some who hold the teaching of Balaam" (v. 14). When the children of Israel came out of Egypt and entered the land of Canaan, Balak, king of Moab, called Balaam, the prophet, and asked him to curse Israel. Balaam, whose eyes were darkened by power and money, advised Balak that if the Moabites tempted the Israelites with fornication, God would destroy them (Num. 25:1–9; 31:16). So Balak had beautiful Moabite women dance lewdly on the altars of the idol, and the men of Israel committed fornication with the women of Moab and worshiped the idol. As a result, God's judgment came upon them, and thousands of people died in a single day.

The church in Pergamum harbored fornicators, and the Christian church of that day committed spiritual fornication by joining itself with the Babylonian religion.

The Lord also rebuked the church in Pergamum for including some who held the doctrine of the Nicolaitans. As previously explained, the Nicolaitans were the followers of Satan. They introduced Greek philosophy into the church and also caused it to commit fornication and adultery.

EXHORTATION

JESUS EXHORTED THE church, "Repent therefore; or else I am coming to you quickly, and I will make war against them with the sword of My mouth" (v. 16). From this we know how indignant He was. The church He bought with His own blood was tainted with heresy and immorality.

PROMISE

HE PROMISED, however, that He would give the hidden manna to the person who repented and overcame temptation. This hidden manna is heavenly, spiritual food—Jesus Himself.

Jesus also promised that He would give a white stone to those who overcame. This refers to the stone the court of that day gave as a token to accused criminals when they were found not guilty. (If they were found guilty, they were given a black stone.) Therefore, Jesus was promising that when people repented, He would forgive their sins and make them righteous. The promise extends to us as well. Hallelujah!

INTERPRETATION OF THE PROPHECY (A.D. 312–590)

PROPHETICALLY, THE church in Pergamum refers to the church period from A.D. 312, when Constantine the Great proclaimed Christianity as Rome's state religion, until the year 590.

Pergamum means "marriage." While Constantine made Christianity the state religion, he also took advantage of it politically. He used the marriage of state and church (including the incorporation of the Babylonian religion's heresy) to consolidate the empire's unity. Accordingly, in the annals of church history the church in Pergamum represents the adulterous church that compromises with the world. When suffering persecution, the early church became pure. But when they received blessings and political approval, they compromised with the world, turning into the Pergamum church and falling to depravity in pursuit of worldly pleasure.

TO THE CHURCH IN THYATIRA (2:18–29)

DESTINATION

THE FOURTH LETTER is addressed to the church in Thyatira, a little city in Asia Minor. The chief industry of this city was fabric dyeing. Fortune-telling was also prevalent, and numerous people would gather for this purpose in a large temple.

THE DESCRIPTION OF JESUS

JESUS WAS DESCRIBED to the church in Thyatira as having "eyes like a flame of fire, and His feet are like burnished bronze" (v. 18). He penetrates reality with those eyes and judges the church with those feet.

COMMENDATION

THE LORD COMMENDED the works, love, service, faith, and patient endurance of the church in Thyatira (v. 19).

REBUKE

IN VERSE 20, however, the Lord also issued a severe rebuke citing the church's tolerance of Jezebel, the false prophetess. Jesus was referring to a woman fortuneteller in Thyatira, who even went into the church to practice her evil. But He was symbolically referring to the Jezebel of the Old Testament. She was the daughter of Ethbaal, king of the Zidonians. Ahab, king of Israel, took her to be his wife (1 Kings 16:29–33). She brought the worship of Baal into Israel and had the altars of the Lord God demolished.

In Seoul, Korea, alone, more than six hundred pseudo-churches practice fortunetelling. What they have received is not the Holy Spirit but the spirit of a mountain god, a demon. Jesus rebukes this.

Jesus also rebuked the spiritual adultery of this church that followed Jezebel, mixing faith and divination.

EXHORTATION

THE LORD GAVE the church in Thyatira the exhortation that it should not compromise with the shamanistic faith but stand firm on the Word (vv. 24–25). Our faith also should be based firmly on the Word. Extravagant fondness for prophecy—an obsession with details not revealed in the Bible—might lead your faith astray just as in the case of the church in Thyatira.

PROMISE

JESUS PROMISED HE would give power over the nations and the morning star to him who overcomes temptation (vv. 26–28). The morning star signifies the Second Coming of Jesus Christ. If we stand firm on the Word with pure faith, we will have the privilege of taking part in the Second Coming of Christ.

INTERPRETATION OF THE PROPHECY (A.D. 590–1517)

THYATIRA MEANS "continued sacrifice," which the Catholic mass is all about. In terms of church history, Thyatira signified the Dark Ages of the church from A.D. 590 to 1517 when Martin Luther began the Reformation. After Christianity became the state religion of the Roman Empire, the church grew steadily more worldly. It left the true nature of the faith—the religion of the Word, praise, and prayer. Lay people attending services only watched what was going on, the priests offering sacrifices. Consequently, the faith of the laity atrophied into little more than spectating at rituals.

One of the abominable practices adopted by the church was the selling of indulgences to collect contributions from the believers. It was a last unbiblical resort to finance the building of a new church for Saint Peter in Rome. Buying an indulgence was a commercial transaction; it was like buying a ticket to heaven, and it was advertised as such. However grave a person's sin may have been, it was immediately forgiven the moment he bought this indulgence. Even a person who was already dead and whose soul was thought to be in purgatory could get to heaven if his offspring bought indulgences for him.

Johann Tetzel, a priest who was commissioned to sell indulgences, beguiled believers, playing on their sympathies for departed relatives and friends whom they might release from their sufferings in purgatory "as soon as the penny tinkles in the box." Thus, God's spiritual gift of salvation was corrupted into a commodity to be bought like a sack of wheat. In this manner the church of that day, like the church in Thyatira, became depraved.

In verses 21–23 Jesus said He would cast the church that did not repent of fornication into a bed and kill her children. Therefore, which church we choose to attend is a question of spiritual life or death.

Verse 21 reads, "I gave her time to repent." Several times Jesus gave opportunities for the church to repent in the dark period of the Middle Ages. Various movements arose and challenged the church to repent and reform.

One of the first was the Albigenses, which arose around 1170 in southern France. Rejecting the rites of the church, it put its effort into distributing copies of the New Testament. In those days the church forbade lay believers to read the Bible. Every local church had only one copy, and even that was chained to the pulpit so no one had access to it.

When this reform movement became strong, Pope Innocent III sent crusaders and annihilated the Albigenses.

Another opportunity for repentance came with the Waldense movement in 1170. Peter Waldo, a merchant of Lyon, France, was their leader. The Waldense disguised themselves as tradesmen and peddled wares, distributing copies of the New Testament and preaching the pure gospel as they traveled. However, this movement also came to a halt through persecution.

Yet another opportunity for repentance appeared with the reform movement led by John Wycliffe. An Englishman, he translated the Latin Bible into English and launched a campaign of spreading the Bible throughout the world.

Jan Hus, who was influenced by Wycliffe, became the rector of a university in Bohemia. He cried for reform in 1369, demanding that the church return to pure faith. In 1416 he was excommunicated by the pope and was finally burned to death in France.

On the day Hus was executed, the public square was filled with a large crowd. An effigy of a demon was bound to his body, which in turn was bound to a stake by a chain. Wood was heaped around his body up to his chin, then set on fire. Historians note that Hus sang hymns as the fire was ignited and began to burn his body. Numerous people witnessing the scene were moved to tears and became followers of the reform movement.

Another reform leader was Jerome Savonarola of Italy. He was filled with the Holy Spirit while praying. Whenever he preached in Florence, great crowds thronged the city. He also preached the restoration of a pure faith, shaking off the sacrificial rites. But like his predecessors, he was arrested, excommunicated, and publicly executed.

Because the Thyratira church refused to repent of her spiritual fornication, she had to be "cast . . . upon a bed" (v. 22). That bed was the Protestant Reformation led by Martin Luther, which supplanted the Roman church as God's most faithful witness on earth.

To the Church in Sardis (3:1–6)

DESTINATION

THIS LETTER WAS addressed to the church in Sardis, a city that flourished some five hundred years before John was born. Later the city was conquered by Cyrus of Persia, then by Alexander the Great. Through those conquests Sardis was reduced to ruins. In A.D. 17 a great earthquake turned the rebuilt city into a heap of refuse. However, Emperor Tiberius of Rome gave it new life. This city worshiped the goddess Cybele.

THE DESCRIPTION OF JESUS

JESUS APPEARED TO the church in Sardis as One who had the seven Spirits of God and the seven stars. The seven stars signify the servants of God, and the seven Spirits of God signify that God gives the fullness of the Holy Spirit to the servants whom He has restored.

In the light of church history, the church in Sardis refers to the Protestant church founded by Luther on the biblical principle that we are justified by faith alone, not by good works and adherence to tradition.

COMMENDATION

JESUS COMMENDED the few clothed in white robes in the church of Sardis. They were the ones who were justified before God by their faith, as were the leaders of the Reformation, who also retained pure faith. Because they believed in the precious blood of Jesus and His grace, He washed them clean and clothed them with white robes.

REBUKE

JESUS ALSO REBUKED the church in Sardis, saying, "You have a name that you are alive, and you are dead" (3:1). He meant that in the past the church had been growing and was alive, but little by little their enthusiasm disappeared and their faith became cold. Only a memory of the past was left.

Historically, the church of this period launched the Reformation, breaking with sacrifices and rituals of the Roman church. Since the reform was linked with many political motives, however, it was not completely changed.

EXHORTATION

JESUS EXHORTED THE church in Sardis to be awakened to life from its dead state, to remember His graces received, to hold fast to the faith and repent.

PROMISE

JESUS PROMISED THAT He would clothe with white robes those who were thus quickened to life and record their names in the Book of Life, that they might live forever (v. 5). He would also vouch for those names before God and His angels.

INTERPRETATION OF THE PROPHECY (A.D. 1517–1750)

IN TERMS OF church history, the church in Sardis signifies the period from 1517 to 1750. The name *Sardis* means "those escaping"—the people who left what became the Roman Catholic church. The most prominent figure of this period was Martin Luther, a priest who led the Reformation beginning in 1517. Through much fasting and prayer, he tried to obtain assurance of his salvation, but he was unable to do so. Therefore he was in agony.

On one occasion Luther ascended the same stairs that tradition said Jesus had walked up to be tried before Pilate. Each step was strewn with pieces of broken glass, and pilgrims would go up on their knees to participate in the same sufferings as Jesus. Also, a superstition held that if people ascended the stairs on their knees, they would receive remission for their sins.

In the middle of climbing the stairs, however, Luther received a clear revelation from God: "The just shall live by faith" (Heb. 10:38, KJV). Hearing these words in his heart and suddenly realizing forgiveness comes not by deeds but by faith, he rose to his feet and descended the steps. It was considered sacrilegious to come down from the middle of those stairs, but Luther's heart was filled with the assurance of a firm biblical belief.

Returning from Rome, Luther posted a written protest of ninety-five articles on the church gate in Wittenberg, Germany, that firmly declared that indulgences were unbiblical. That written protest launched the Reformation, which freed the church from its dead state. Luther underwent numerous persecutions and was excommunicated, and his life was under constant threat. Fortunately, however, the king and the feudal lords of Germany protected him and saved his life. They had been struggling to free themselves from the rule of the pope and took advantage of the Reformation to revolt against Rome.

The result was that even though the Reformation was achieved, it had political as well as spiritual motives behind it. The church was still bound by form and ritual. And the church was actually still in the state of death, even though it had the appearance of being alive.

TO THE CHURCH IN PHILADELPHIA (3:7–13)

DESTINATION

THE DESTINATION OF our Lord's sixth letter was to the believers in the church at Philadelphia. Located thirty miles southeast of Sardis, Philadelphia was also destroyed by the great earthquake of A.D. 17 and rebuilt by Tiberius. It was known for its wine, and drinking was a major problem.

THE DESCRIPTION OF JESUS

THE LORD APPEARED to the church in Philadelphia as the One who had the key of David. When He opens, no one can shut, and when He shuts, no one can open. This signified that the Lord would cause a great revival in the Philadelphian church.

COMMENDATION

JESUS COMMENDED the Philadelphian church for doing many activities with little ability and behaving sincerely, causing no shame to His name.

REBUKE

THE LORD DID not rebuke the Philadelphian church, a missionary church where a great revival took place (as it did in the church of Smyrna). He never rebukes a gospel-proclaiming, mission-sending church.

EXHORTATION

JESUS EXHORTED THE Philadelphian church, which fulfilled its missionary role with little ability, to "hold fast what you have" (v. 11). He didn't demand more than that, but urged the church to preserve its enthusiasm for missions and service and to develop them more.

The Church Age

PROMISE

JESUS PROMISED THE Philadelphian church that if it kept the word of patience, continuing its mission work, He would keep it from the hour of temptation, when God will judge all the people who have lived on the earth.

To him who overcame, holding fast what he had, Jesus also gave the promise that He would "make him a pillar in the temple of My God" (v. 12). What does that mean? The pillar of the temple supports the house where God dwells. The blessed promise is that Jesus will make this church live forever with God.

Jesus also promised He would give the church a new name (v. 12). Saying He would write the name of God, the name of New Jerusalem, and His own new name means He would bless him who overcomes, that he may live forever in the New Jerusalem with the triune God.

INTERPRETATION OF THE PROPHECY (A.D. 1750–1905)

THE CHURCH IN Philadelphia foretold the church age between 1750 and 1905. *Philadelphia* means "brotherly love," and the church there preached the gospel with such love. Indeed, proclaiming the gospel is impossible unless we have compassion for our fellow men and women. When we do, Jesus opens the door of revival.

For a century and a half, from 1750 to 1905, churches experienced wonderful revival movements, and the fire spread to various parts of the world. A Society for China Inland Mission was formed in Great Britain, and through its efforts the gospel was preached to the inner parts of China. The Student Volunteer Movement, also arising in Great Britain, became a great mission society.

Also during this period, the Methodist movement, The Salvation Army, and the Holiness church arose. George Whitefield shook England, America, and Europe with the gospel. Following him, numerous evangelical revivalists such as Jonathan Edwards, Charles Finney, Charles Spurgeon, and Dwight Moody set America and Europe on fire.

As a result of the worldwide revival, a large number of missionaries went out inflamed with zeal. Leading figures among them were William Carey, who went to India; Robert Moffat, who went to Africa; and David Hill, who went to China. The revival and brisk mission activities continued until just before World War I.

Jesus' prophecy came true during the church age of Philadelphia. He also forewarned the church of the coming of great tribulation, but He promised He would cause the church to miss that tribulation.

To the Church in Laodicea (3:14–22)

DESTINATION

THIS LETTER WAS sent to Laodicea, forty miles north of Ephesus. In this city was a famous medical school, and eye salve made here became known for its healing power. Being a center of finance, Laodicea was extremely rich and one of the largest cities in Asia Minor.

Moreover, it was a city of entertainment, where all the citizens sought continual pleasure. Since the church had compromised with the world, it became neither cold nor hot.

THE DESCRIPTION OF JESUS

JESUS APPEARED TO the church in Laodicea as One who was "the Amen, the faithful and true Witness, the Beginning of the creation of God" (v. 14). Accepting the Word of God with "amen" expresses our sincere loyalty to the Lord. Mankind was originally created that we might love God and give Him glory. Therefore when we bring glory to God by our faithful service, His original purpose for us is fulfilled.

The Laodicean church, however, had lost its loyalty to Christ, its true witness, and the original purpose of creation. So Jesus pointed out its hypocrisy and lifeless faith and urged it to repent.

COMMENDATION

UNTIL NOW, THE six churches we have seen so far, all received a commendation. The Laodicean church, however, did not. They received only rebuke. This church represents the church age in which we now live.

REBUKE

JESUS CONDEMNED the lukewarm faith of the Laodicean church: "So because you are lukewarm, and neither hot nor cold, I will spit you out of My mouth" (v. 16).

Those are dreadful words. But I'm afraid many churches today have a Laodicean philosophy. Their people are either believers or unbelievers. They attend church when they want to and stay home when they don't. They can accept the Bible as the Word of God or not. Sometimes the Scripture seems to have relevance to them, but sometimes not. Jesus hates the Laodicean church's lukewarm faith.

If faith is cold, Jesus can move a person toward repentance. On the other hand, people who vehemently oppose Jesus can easily be converted when their egos are crushed and they become hot with conviction. However, those people who go to church and give agreeable answers but whose hearts are not in it are the last kind to be converted.

Why was the church in Laodicea lukewarm in its faith? They had a wrong understanding of themselves. They said, "I am rich, and have become wealthy, and have need of nothing" (v. 17). You can just imagine some of the leaders' thinking: *The chapel building program is completed. Contributions continue to flow in. We're well-educated. Everything is so rich and fine. Therefore let's have fun in our faith life.*

Today many American churches also allow their meetings to degenerate into social gatherings. On Sundays they have a short worship service, and then they enjoy eating and drinking under the false name of Christian fellowship.

"The kingdom of God is not eating and drinking, but righteousness and peace and joy in the Holy Spirit" (Rom. 14:17). One time when I was in the United States conducting a crusade, I strongly rebuked some American churches for putting social activities ahead of God's work. They responded beautifully by sending money to poor Korean ministers.

While the Laodicean church thought itself rich, Jesus rebuked its spiritual poverty: "You do not know that you are wretched and miserable and poor and blind and naked" (v. 17).

EXHORTATION

JESUS FIRST EXHORTED the Laodicean church to seek true richness—spiritual richness that can be obtained only from Jesus through faith (v. 18).

Then Jesus said the church should seek from Him a white raiment (v. 18). This is the robe Jesus clothes us with, signifying our righteousness through His precious shed blood.

Finally, Jesus exhorted the Laodicean church to buy eye salve and anoint its eyes that it might see (v. 18). This is the eye salve of the Holy

Spirit, who opens spiritual eyes. In other words, the church should look at its
material and educational wealth through eyes of right self-understanding.
Then it would realize that the wealth of the world in which it put so much
trust is only transient.

PROMISE

JESUS PROMISED THE Laodicean church, "He who overcomes, I will grant to
him to sit down with Me on My throne, as I also overcame and sat down
with My Father on His throne" (v. 21). There is no other place to go except
the throne of God. This is a wonderful saying, for when we go to the
throne of God, the world ends.

INTERPRETATION OF THE PROPHECY (A.D. 1905 TO THE BEGINNING OF THE GREAT TRIBULATION)

IN TERMS OF church history, the Laodicean church signifies the age from
the 1900s to the time of the Great Tribulation. *Laodicea* means "the right
of laity," namely the church of people's rights. This is a time when the
laity have become more "enlightened" than the ministers and when their
power is such that they can even hire and fire a pastor at will. Hence, it is
a spiritually corrupt age.

From the beginning of the Laodicean age in 1905, theology began to
criticize the Bible historically, scientifically, and philosophically by intro-
ducing rationalism and higher criticism. This started in Germany. But the
Scripture cannot be subjected to higher criticism through science and reasoning, because it was written by divine revelation. Nevertheless, the
liberal new theology asserted that the Bible is neither scientifically or historically correct. The "new" theology states the Bible's accounts are
mostly myth. Therefore, all the miracles in it must be removed.

This new theological thinking began to gain ground in America in the
1920s. It contaminated the pulpits and people, killing many churches just
as it had done in Europe. Younger generations left the church, and only
the older people remained in them.

Once I heard of a liberal church whose pastor said to the congregation,
"Brothers and sisters, the Pentateuch of Moses is the five books of the
Bible from Genesis to Deuteronomy; it records the history of Israel in a
mythical and instructive way." The members who heard that reasoned,
"Why then should we carry these heavy books that are merely the mythical

130

history of Israel?" So they removed the Pentateuch from their Bibles.

The next time they attended a service the pastor said, "All the prophetic books in the Bible were written by those who dreamed strange dreams." So the members decided, "We now know why they're so complicated," and they cut those parts out of their Bibles.

The next Sunday the pastor said, "The four Gospels of the New Testament are books the disciples of Jesus made up out of extensive delusion to create a new religion with Jesus as its center." So the members removed the Gospels from their Bibles.

When the pastor said, "All the epistles of the New Testament are the personal letters of the apostles that were sent to the churches to revive them," the members also removed those parts from their Bibles.

Finally, when the pastor said the Revelation of John was written while the apostle John was in a state of delusion, the members tore *those* pages from their Bibles, too.

After all the section tearing, all that remained was the black leather cover that had bound the pages of the Bible together. So the members left the church, concluding there was nothing believable in God's Word.

Liberal theology leads inevitably to a single conclusion: the death-of-God theory proposed by a theologian named Thomas Altizer. He asserted that since God is dead, humanity should rebuild the church without Him.

Therefore, Jesus did not commend the Laodicean church, the church of today, for there was nothing commendable about it. The church has economic strength, many theological schools, and much knowledge. However, those don't make it commendable. Rather, liberal churches should buy the eye salve of the Holy Spirit and apply it to their eyes so they can see their spiritual wretchedness, misery, poverty, blindness, nakedness, and shame.

God is using the Full Gospel movement to help the church regain its faith by opening its eyes. All believers need to return to the pure gospel by purchasing gold tried in fire, putting on the white raiment of righteousness and buying the eye salve that gives spiritual understanding. All the words in the Bible from Genesis through Revelation are true, and in them we find God's plan of salvation that brings us to heaven. Those people who keep their faith in this lukewarm age will be taken to the very throne of Christ (v. 21). Hallelujah!

The word *church* appears seven times in the second and third chapters of Revelation, but it doesn't appear even once in chapters 4–19. Why? Because, as we will see in chapter 4, Jesus is going to take the church away to that throne in heaven.

15

The Rapture of the Church

I N REVELATION 1:19 John was told to write three things: "the things
which you have seen, and the things which are, and the things which
shall take place after these things." So far we've looked at the first two of
those in chapters thirteen and fourteen of this book. Now, beginning with
Revelation 4, we consider the third, which involves the Rapture of the
church from earth to heaven into the very presence of the throne of God.

A DOOR THAT WAS OPENED IN HEAVEN (4:1)

> After these things I looked, and behold, a door standing open in
> heaven, and the first voice which I had heard, like the sound of a
> trumpet speaking with me, said, "Come up here, and I will show you
> what must take place after these things."
>
> —REVELATION 4:1

The panorama John now viewed had changed from earth to heaven.

133

Only a short time before, Jesus stood in the midst of the golden candlesticks and spoke to the seven churches. That scene disappeared, and when an awesome gate of heaven was flung open, a voice like a trumpet said, "Come up here." God will likewise use a trumpet sound when He calls the church to meet Him in the air. We read:

> For the Lord Himself will descend from heaven with a shout, with the voice of the archangel, and with the trumpet of God; and the dead in Christ shall rise first. Then we who are alive and remain shall be caught up together with them in the clouds to meet the Lord in the air, and thus we shall always be with the Lord.
> —1 THESSALONIANS 4:16–17

John was the last surviving apostle. His ascending to heaven pictures the church that has prepared oil at the end of the age—being filled with the Holy Spirit—that will be taken up into heaven as the bride of Christ (Matt. 25:1–13). It will not be long before that same voice will be heard by your ears and mine, and we also shall be taken up to heaven. As a door opened when John looked up, so a door in heaven will open for us, and we shall also ascend. Those people who have not been born again by the Holy Spirit, but simply go to church for form and religious ceremony, will not be taken up into heaven. For this reason Jesus said, "Unless one is born of water and the Spirit, he cannot enter into the kingdom of God" (John 3:5).

The Holy Spirit began the church on earth. So when Jesus calls the church in the Spirit to come, the Holy Spirit will take responsibility for that church, taking it to heaven in His bosom.

Nevertheless, many Christians still ask, "Shall we ascend *before* the Tribulation, or will we have to pass through it?"

That is a serious question. Some theologians answer that the church will ascend in the *middle* of the Tribulation; others say the church will undergo the Tribulation. Both those answers are wrong, I believe, ignoring the fact that there are two comings of Christ.

CHRIST'S TWO COMINGS

CHRIST'S COMING IN THE AIR

THE FIRST COMING of Christ is His coming in the air as described in

1 Thessalonians 4. This coming is not for the people who belong to the world but for those who have looked forward to this event and prepared for it. The day and the hour of Christ's coming in the air is known to no one (Luke 12:40). Jesus, our bridegroom, will come and take away His bride. This coming is not one of judgment, but to receive and take His bride away.

Jesus' feet do not touch the earth at this coming; the Bible says clearly that He will receive us in the air (1 Thess. 4:17). The dead in Christ will rise all at once and meet Him with resurrected bodies, and we who are living will be changed in a moment. Thus, all will ascend into heaven as dew goes up into the sky in the heat of the morning sun.

This coming of Christ in the air will be wonderful. Those who do not participate in it must go through the Tribulation, but many of them will also be saved as we will see later in Revelation.

CHRIST'S COMING TO EARTH

REVELATION 19–20 tells us that when the last day of the earth comes near, after the battle of Armageddon, Jesus will come down to earth accompanied by a multitude of His saints. That is His coming to earth. During that time Jesus will destroy all His enemies with a sword that comes out of His mouth. He will take the Antichrist and cast him into the lake of fire that burns with brimstone. He will lay hold of the devil and cast him into the bottomless pit. Then He will reign with the saints for a thousand years. This coming of Christ to earth will be visible to everyone, as recorded in Revelation 1:7.

Regrettably, even though the Bible makes a clear distinction between the two comings of Christ, some people are still mistaken in interpreting what will happen. When they teach that the church will also go through the Tribulation, they not only hurt themselves but also lead others astray.

BIBLICAL PROOFS OF A PRE-TRIBULATION RAPTURE OF THE CHURCH

THERE ARE SEVERAL proofs that the church will not pass through the Tribulation. First, because we are in Christ, we cannot be judged a second time. Our sins were judged at the cross of Calvary, borne by the sinless Savior. By offering His own body as a sacrifice, He made all who believe in Him justified and perfect before God.

The Tribulation is a seven-year period of the most dreadful nature that will come to those wicked people who rebelled against God and forsook the path of faith. If the church were to pass through it, we would undergo a second judgment, as if Jesus' sacrifice were not sufficient to justify us, and that is impossible. Therefore the Holy Spirit will translate the church before the Tribulation.

Second, we see a pattern of what will happen in the stories of Noah and Sodom and Gomorrah. Let's look first at the time of Noah (Gen. 6–8).

Following Noah's repeated cry that God would judge the world, the flood finally came and lasted forty days and forty nights. Just before that, however, He caused the eight members of Noah's family to enter the ark and escape the flood. *Then* God judged. Jesus said, "For the coming of the Son of Man will be just like the days of Noah" (Matt. 24:37).

God let Noah and his family escape the flood by taking refuge in the ark before He judged the world. How much more will He make a way of escape from the Tribulation for those whom Jesus Christ bought with the price of His own blood and sealed with the Holy Spirit? It would be contrary to God's nature for Him to make no distinction between His saints and the rest of the world, judging us the same as He judges them.

Consider also Sodom and Gomorrah. Though Lot lived there by his own free will, yet God, knowing him to be a righteous man, spared the lives of Lot and his family when He rained down judgment. Not until angels had led them safely away did He loose the fire and brimstone (Gen. 19:15–29).

Thus, God rescues those whom He has chosen and who have trusted in Him by faith. And so shall we who have been justified by the precious blood of Jesus escape the Tribulation.

Third, the fact that the church is mentioned often in Revelation 1–3, but not once in chapters 4–19, also suggests it will not pass through the Tribulation. If we *were* going to endure it, we would surely find references to the church in those chapters.

The word *saint* is used often, however, in those chapters. It may refer to people who become Christians after the Rapture. So at least by its silence, then, this portion of Revelation strongly suggests the church will not pass through the Tribulation.

Fourth, Jesus indicated the church will not pass through the Tribulation:

> Be on guard, that your hearts may not be weighted down with dissipation and drunkenness and the worries of life, and that day come on

> you suddenly like a trap; for it will come upon all those who dwell
> on the face of all the earth. But keep on the alert at all times, praying
> in order that you may have strength to escape all these things that are
> about to take place, and to stand before the Son of Man.
>
> —LUKE 21:34–36

Did Jesus say we should make preparations to pass through all the things that will happen to us? No. He said we must watch and pray so that we may escape all the things that will happen and so stand before Him.

First Thessalonians 1:10 also tells us to "wait for His Son from heaven, whom He raised from the dead, that is Jesus, who delivers us from the wrath to come." If He delivered us from the wrath to come, how could He also make us go through it? In Revelation 3:10 Jesus also said to the Philadelphian church, "Because you have kept the word of My perseverance, *I also will keep you from the hour of testing,* that hour which is about to come upon the whole world, to test those who dwell upon the earth" (emphasis added).

When we take into account all these scriptures and teachings of Jesus, we can conclude with certainty that Jesus will not bring the Tribulation of judgment to this world until He completely translates His church at His first coming in the air.

My purpose in writing this book is not to teach you how to pass skillfully through the Tribulation, nor is it to teach you with what resolution you should pass through. Rather, I want to stimulate you to watch and pray by showing you sure proof that you will be caught up in the air before the Tribulation.

A THRONE IN HEAVEN (4:2–11)

ONE WHO WAS SITTING ON THE THRONE

As JOHN LOOKED into heaven, he first saw someone sitting on a throne (v. 2). The center of heaven is the throne of God, and on it are the Father, the Son, and the Spirit. John thus described the figure of God the Father on the throne: "And He who was sitting was like a jasper stone and a sardius in appearance; and there was a rainbow around the throne, like an emerald in appearance" (v. 3). Jasper signifies the inscrutable divinity and holiness of God. A jasper is a precious, sometimes blue stone—blue like the sky. The sky signifies infinite divinity and holiness.

The ruby-colored sardius stone signifies righteous judgment. When John first saw God, he felt not only the infinite divinity and holiness of God but also His sternness of righteous judgment. John's heart might well have trembled with awesome fear.

The rainbow around the throne resembled an emerald. When we see a rainbow from the earth, it looks like a half circle. But when we see it from an airplane in the sky, it looks like a complete circle. The sight must have filled John's trembling heart with joy.

The origin of the rainbow goes back to the days of Noah. When Noah sacrificed animals after the flood, God made a covenant with him, saying He would not judge the world again with a flood. As a sign of this covenant, God made a rainbow to appear in the clouds. (See Genesis 9:13.)

Thus, a rainbow resembling an emerald and surrounding the throne means that God, in spite of His infinite divinity and holiness, has already accepted a sacrifice for our sins. That offering is Jesus Christ, the Lamb of God, who died on the cross of Calvary.

By accepting Jesus' sacrifice, God made another covenant between Himself and mankind: "Whoever believes in Him [the only begotten Son of God] should not perish, but have eternal life" (John 3:16).

TWENTY-FOUR ELDERS AROUND THE THRONE

AFTER JOHN SAW Him who sat on the throne, he also saw twenty-four seats surrounding the throne. Twenty-four elders, with crowns of gold on their heads, sat on those seats. Jesus promised the Laodicean church, "He who overcomes, I will grant to him to sit down with Me on My throne, as I also overcame and sat down with My Father on His throne" (3:21). Those who overcome will ascend to heaven and sit on the throne that even angels cannot come near.

What do the twenty-four seats in verse 4 signify? I believe they represent the twelve tribes of Israel in the Old Testament and the twelve disciples of Jesus in the New Testament. Altogether the twenty-four seats represent the saints who were saved in both Old and New Testament times.

The twenty-four elders were human beings. Angels cannot have an office such as elder, neither does God give them golden crowns. Such crowns are given only to those who have been saved by the precious blood of Jesus Christ.

Imagine in your mind a picture in which you are praising God and wearing a golden crown at His throne. How glorious it will be!

THE THRONE

JOHN ALSO SAW "flashes of lightning and sounds and peals of thunder" proceed out of the throne (v. 5). What comes after a flash of lightning and peals of thunder in a summer storm? A shower. God is ready to rain judgment upon this earth like a summer shower. But He is postponing His judgment until His children are taken away to heaven and seated with Him.

Do you know how much God loves you? The love of God toward us is the same sort of love that parents have toward their children, only much stronger. During one overseas trip, a member of my company told me, "Pastor, at this moment I am married and have children, but it seems to me I could not dare sacrifice my life for my parents or my wife. However, for the sake of my children I could do it." Because of that kind of love, the holy Son Jesus died on the cross, so now God will not judge the world until He translates all His children to His throne.

"There were seven lamps of fire burning before the throne, which are the seven Spirits of God" (v. 5). This image shows the Holy Spirit on the throne in heaven, having returned there with the church.

In front of the throne was a sea of glass. The sea can be interpreted to mean either mankind or the world. This world, which we call "the troubled sea" because of its many cares and worries will then be changed into a sea of glass, calm and serene. That means all our tears, cares, and troubles will no longer exist.

THE FOUR BEASTS

NEXT JOHN SAW four beasts around the throne of God and the thrones of the elders (vv. 6–8). The first was like a lion; the second like a calf; the third had a face like a man; and the fourth was like an eagle. They were praising the Lord God Almighty, saying, "Holy, holy, holy."

Isaiah saw a similar vision. He wrote of seraphim standing above the throne:

> Each having six wings; with two he covered his face, and with two he covered his feet, and with two he flew. And one called out to another and said, "Holy, Holy, Holy, is the LORD of hosts."
> —ISAIAH 6:2–3

Ezekiel also saw four living creatures in his vision. Each had four faces that looked like this: "Each had the face of a man, all four had the face of a lion on the right and the face of a bull on the left, and all four had the face of an eagle. . . . And each went straight forward" (Ezek. 1:10, 12).

What were the four living creatures in Revelation 4? They were cherubim, the angels that guard the holiness of God at His throne. The first was like a lion. That symbolizes Jesus' coming as the King of the Jews, as Matthew's Gospel describes Him. The second creature was like an ox [bull], which signifies Jesus who works, as Mark's Gospel emphasizes. The third creature was like a man, and Luke's Gospel describes Jesus as the Son of man. He had a complete human nature, being born of the virgin Mary. The fourth creature was like an eagle, and the eagle represents the divinity of God. John's Gospel emphasizes that Jesus was the divine Son of God.

Thus, the four living creatures standing around the throne all symbolize the person of Jesus.

WORSHIP

WHAT COMES NEXT is a scene of worship. First the four living creatures worship God day and night, never resting. They ceaselessly say, "Holy, holy, holy, is the Lord God, the Almighty, who was and who is and who is to come" (v. 8).

And when the living creatures give glory to God, the twenty-four elders also fall down and worship Him. They lay their crowns before the throne and say, "Worthy art Thou, our Lord and our God, to receive glory and honor and power; for Thou didst create all things, and because of Thy will they existed, and were created" (v. 11).

This is the scene of heavenly worship in Revelation 4.

16

The Seven-Sealed Book

I N Revelation 5 the scene changes from heavenly worship to preparation for the Great Tribulation and judgment.

THE SEVEN-SEALED SCROLL (5:1)

> And I saw in the right hand of Him who sat on the throne a book written inside and on the back, sealed up with seven seals. And I saw a strong angel proclaiming with a loud voice, "Who is worthy to open the book and to break its seals?" And no one in heaven or on the earth was able to open the book, or to look into it.
>
> —Revelation 5:1–3

John wept bitterly, for there was no one worthy to open the sealed book.

A REDEMPTION FOR THE LAND

WHAT IS THIS book? Again we must be cautious, for if we wrongly interpret this passage we will miss the whole meaning of the Book of Revelation. We can guess the importance of the sealed book from the way its need to be opened was proclaimed and from John's weeping because there was no one worthy to do the job.

This scroll was a title deed. In Old Testament times God gave this commandment to the Israelites concerning the land they would possess in Canaan:

> The land, moreover, shall be not sold permanently, for the land is Mine; for you are but aliens and sojourners with Me. Thus for every piece of your property, you are to provide for the redemption of the land. If a fellow-countryman of yours becomes so poor he has to sell part of his property, then his nearest kinsman is to come and buy back what his relative has sold.
>
> —LEVITICUS 25:23–25

If a person bought a piece of land from his neighbor, that land became his possession. However, if the closest relative of the original owner came and wanted to repurchase the land, the present owner had to accept that claim no matter how much he desired to keep the land. This law was called "the redemption of the land."

The contract recording a sale of property was a title deed. After the first article was written, the scroll was rolled and sealed with wax and a stamp. Then the second article was recorded, the same sealing procedure was followed, and so on through every new article. The purpose was to protect the contract from counterfeits. Finally, the sealed original was taken to the temple and kept in its archives. A copy of the contract was laid open on a document inspection stand in the temple.

If a kinsman of the original owner read the conditions of such a contract and wanted to buy the land back, he could approach the present owner. If he produced proof that he was a close relative of the original owner and asked to repurchase the land, the present owner had to cooperate. First the kinsman gave the amount of silver and gold specified in the contract to the present owner. Then he went to the temple archives, found the scroll of the contract, and opened its seals. Opening one seal, he made sure the conditions of the contract were being met. Then he opened another seal and checked again. During this time he would have several leading people of his village there as witnesses.

After the satisfaction of the contract terms had been thus confirmed before the witnesses and the former and new owners of the land, the change of ownership was declared, and the scroll was burned. With that the transfer of the land was complete.

A SCROLL WITH SEVEN SEALS IN THE HAND OF GOD

WHAT KIND OF title deed was the scroll in the hand of God? It was the title to ownership of this earth. Before Adam fell into sin, God had given him dominion over, or control of, the earth. When sin came in, however, the earth was corrupted and became the domain of the evil one. Satan was making a valid offer to Jesus:

> And he led led Him up and showed Him all the kingdoms of the world in a moment of time. And the devil said to Him, "I will give You all this domain and its glory; for it has been handed over to me, and I will give it to whomever I wish. Therefore if You worship before me, it shall all be Yours."
>
> —LUKE 4:5–7

Adam had forfeited his dominion over the world to Satan, in effect making a title deed of this world before God. And how has the devil used his power? He instigates bloody wars; he foments robbery, abuse, and murder. For this reason Paul said, "For we know that the whole creation groans and suffers the pains of childbirth together until now. And not only this, but also we ourselves, having the first fruits of the Spirit, even we ourselves groan within ourselves, waiting eagerly our adoption as sons, the redemption of our body" (Rom. 8:22–23).

Therefore if humanity was to have any hope, someone had to repurchase this earth.

NO MAN ABLE TO OPEN THE SEALED SCROLL (5:2–4)

QUALIFICATIONS

THE ONE WHO could open the scroll had to be a close kinsman to the original "owner" of the world. Thus, the one who would redeem the earth from the devil had to be a human being. But how could sinful people, descendants of Adam, be qualified for this job? In addition, whoever would redeem the earth would have to want to do it enough to pay the price.

143

Who then would have all these four qualifications: 1) a kinsman to human beings; 2) not a descendant of Adam; 3) able to redeem the earth; and 4) willing to pay the price? The person could not be found in heaven, for the angels are not close kinsmen to us. Nor could the person be found among ordinary, sinful mortals. And the person certainly could not be found under the earth, where devils and evil spirits are, for they would be the last to desire to redeem the earth.

THE WAILING OF JOHN

THUS, THERE WAS no one able to open the book and look at it, and John wept bitterly as he realized there was no hope for human beings on the earth. He also wept over his own incompetence in that situation, because he, too, was a member of the fallen human race.

THE LION OF THE TRIBE OF JUDAH, THE ROOT OF DAVID (5:5–14)

A LAMB THAT WAS SLAIN

WHILE JOHN WAS thus weeping, one of the elders said to him, "Stop weeping; behold, the Lion that is from the tribe of Judah, the Root of David, has overcome so as to open the book and its seven seals" (v. 5).

Then John saw that in the midst of the throne, the four beasts, and the elders, stood a Lamb. Jesus appeared, not as the Son of God, but as a Lamb, the sacrifice for sin. The Greek word for this lamb is *arnion,* a lovely little lamb.

On the night before the Israelites left Egypt, they slaughtered Passover lambs and put the blood on the sides and tops of their door frames before eating the meat. Those lambs may have been like family pets, making it painful for everyone when the day came to take a knife and slaughter them.

Jesus Christ was such a lovely little lamb in the sight of God. How pained was the Father's heart when He delivered His Son to be killed, the Son who was the brightness of His glory and the express image of His Person!

Therefore, when God commanded the Israelites to kill the Passover lamb, He was foreshadowing the sacrificial death of Christ and the pain He would bear.

144

Moreover, verse 6 describes Jesus as "a Lamb standing, as if slain." Our Lord forever bears the marks of the death He tasted for our sake—the mark of the nails in His hands and feet, of the thorns on His head, and of the spear in His side. Whenever we see those marks, we will worship and give thanks to Him for His abounding grace.

SEVEN HORNS AND SEVEN EYES

WHEN JOHN SAW this lovely, scarred Lamb come to the throne of almighty God and take the scroll, he noticed the Lamb had seven horns (v. 6). Since horns symbolize strength, the seven horns represent the authority and strength of a ruler; Jesus has all the power and authority of heaven and earth. The Lamb also had seven all-seeing eyes, which symbolize the Holy Spirit.

THE LION OF THE TRIBE OF JUDAH

ALSO DESCRIBED IN verse 5 as the Lion of the tribe of Judah, Jesus met all four conditions for redeeming the earth.

First, to be a close kinsman of human beings—one of us—Jesus left His throne in heaven and became a man, born of the young woman Mary in Bethlehem.

Second, to not be a sin-tainted descendant of Adam, He was supernaturally conceived and born of a virgin. The Bible clearly says in Isaiah 7:14, "Behold, a virgin will be with child and bear a son, and she will call His name Immanuel." The angel told Mary, "The Holy Spirit will come upon you, and the power of the Most High will overshadow you; and for that reason the holy offspring shall be called the Son of God" (Luke 1:35). Therefore Jesus was free from the original sin of Adam and lived a perfect life.

Therefore, since Jesus is God who came in the flesh, only He could meet the third condition, the ability to redeem the earth by virtue of His sinlessness. It freed Him to take the punishment we deserved for our sins upon Himself (Rom. 5).

Fourth, Jesus *wanted* to redeem the earth. For all His ability, if Jesus had not wanted to redeem us enough to go to the cross, we would have remained in sin. Yet He voluntarily gave up His life for us. And thus did He rightfully take the title deed of the earth from the hand of God.

When Jesus received the scroll, His identification as the Lion of the tribe of Judah symbolized His reign as the King of kings. And when our Lord receives the scroll from the Father and tears it open, judgment will have already started. The final work of redeeming the earth will have begun. But the devil will resist with all his might for seven years, knowing the lake of fire awaits him if he loses. At the end of the Tribulation, however, Satan will indeed be driven from the earth.

In a sense, Jesus has already taken the scroll, paying for it with His blood. And we don't know the time or season when He will come to claim His purchase; neither do we know when the Great Tribulation will begin.

One thing is certain, however: When the sound of the trumpet is heard, the saints who have been saved by Jesus' blood will not be on this earth. They will have already been taken up into heaven to attend the marriage supper of the Lamb!

Those who are saved during the Tribulation will have suffered great misery. But those who still remain on the earth at the end of the Tribulation will be even more miserable. They will weep bitterly when Jesus comes down to this earth with His saints to reign in the millennial kingdom.

THE SONG OF THE LIVING CREATURES AND OF THE ELDERS (5:9–10) (THE SONG OF THE REDEEMED SAINTS IN HEAVEN)

THE SAINTS WILL sing a song when Jesus takes the scroll with the seven seals from the hand of God:

> You are worthy to take the scroll and to open its seals, because you were slain, and with your blood you purchased men for God from every tribe and language and people and nation. You have made them to be a kingdom and priests to serve our God, and they will reign on the earth.
>
> —REVELATION 5:9–10, NIV

Angels are not able to sing such a song. Only the saints can sing this song, because we are the ones Jesus bought with His own blood. And what a wonderful position He has given us as His kingdom and priests—we who have been purchased from every tribe and nation! One day we will also reign with Him.

THE SONG OF THE ANGELS (5:11–12)

NEXT COMES THE song of the angels. First notice their position: "And I looked, and I heard the voice of many angels around the throne and the living creatures and the elders; and the number of them was myriads of myriads, and thousands of thousands" (v. 11).

The redeemed saints are sitting on the throne; the hosts of angels are standing. As we have learned, the twenty-four elders signify the twelve tribes of Israel and the twelve apostles, which in turn represent all the redeemed saints. As angels were created to serve the redeemed saints (Heb. 1:14), there is a distinction between the two. They praised Jesus thus: "Worthy is the Lamb that was slain to receive power and riches and wisdom and might and honor and glory and blessing" (v. 12).

Since the angels have never fallen and were made for a different purpose, their song does not refer to precious blood being purchased or to becoming priests. It is simply a song of praise.

THE SONG OF ALL CREATURES (5:13–14)

FOLLOWING THE SONG of the angels, all creatures sing thus: "To Him who sits on the throne, and to the Lamb, be blessing and honor and glory and dominion forever and ever" (v. 13).

When all these hymns are ended, the four living creatures respond with *amen,* and the twenty-four elders bow down and worship.

It seems to me that the most beautiful song of the three is the song of the redeemed saints. Isn't God's divine grace wonderful? We are the ones who rebelled against Him and consequently received the greatest love and destiny from God. Part of our response should be beautiful songs of praise to God, and He wants to hear them.

Thus, the preparation for God to reclaim the earth will be completed. As soon as our Lord opens the seals of the scroll, the curtain on the stage of the Great Tribulation will finally be drawn up.

17

The Great Tribulation:
Part One

ONCE AGAIN, Revelation 1:19 reads, "Write therefore the things which you have seen, and the things which are, and the things which shall take place after these things."

We have already considered "the things which you have seen" (Rev. 1), "the things which are" (Rev. 2–3) and the first part of "the things which shall take place after these things" (Rev. 4–5). Now the Great Tribulation starts in Revelation 6, where our Lord opens the first seal in the book that has seven seals.

How do we know the period of the Great Tribulation will be seven years?

Where in the Bible do we see that time frame given, inasmuch as the exact words *seven years* are not found anywhere in Scripture?

The answer, as we have already learned, is found in the Book of Daniel, to which the Book of Revelation is closely related. This is why I have combined the two books. A deeper and clearer understanding can be found by interpreting them together.

149

Daniel's Seventy Weeks (Dan. 9:24–27)

WE HAVE ALREADY studied this portion of Daniel in the first section of this book. But now we must look at his words again to make Daniel's New Testament connection. Daniel was one of the Jews taken captive to Babylon when the kingdom of Judah fell in 605 B.C. While reading the Book of Jeremiah there, he came across the prophecy that said that Israel would return home after seventy years. To know exactly when that would happen, he prayed earnestly to God. Then an angel of the Lord appeared to him and showed him in detail not only the return of Israel to its land, but also what would happen from then to the end of the world. The following is what the angel told Daniel:

> Seventy weeks have been decreed for your people and your holy city, to finish the transgression, to make an end of sin, to make atonement for iniquity, to bring in everlasting righteousness, to seal up vision and prophecy, and to anoint the most holy place. So you are to know and discern that from the issuing of a decree to restore and rebuild Jerusalem until Messiah the Prince there will be seven weeks and sixty-two weeks; it will be built again, with plaza and moat, even in times of distress. Then after the sixty-two weeks the Messiah will be cut off and have nothing, and the people of the prince who is to come will destroy the city and the sanctuary. And its end will come with a flood; even to the end there will be war; desolations are determined. And he will make a firm covenant with the many for one week, but in the middle of the week he will put a stop to sacrifice and grain offerings; and on the wing of abominations will come one who makes desolate, even until a complete destruction, one that is decreed, is poured out on the one who makes desolate.
>
> —DANIEL 9:24–27

The angel Gabriel told Daniel that seventy weeks would be determined upon "thy people," the people of Judah, and "thy holy city," Jerusalem. Since one week in the Bible signifies seven years, seventy weeks is four hundred ninety years.

Therefore the prophecy meant that after four hundred ninety years had passed, the transgression would be finished, sins would end, reconciliation for iniquity would be made forever, everlasting righteousness would be brought in, all the visions and prophecies would come to pass, and the most Holy—the Messiah, our Lord Jesus Christ—would come to this world to redeem the world.

The angel even predicted the exact time of Jesus' entering Jerusalem, riding on a donkey from the Mount of Olives. The Messiah in verse 25 refers to Jesus Christ. Gabriel said that from the going forth of the commandment to restore and rebuild Jerusalem until the Messiah, the Prince, would be seven weeks and sixty-two weeks, or a total of sixty-nine weeks. And on March 14, four hundred forty-five years before Jesus was born, King Artaxerxes of Persia gave an order to restore Jerusalem.

As a result, some of the Israelites who had been carried away to Babylon as captives returned home. On April 6, A.D. 32, sixty-nine weeks (four hundred eighty-three years) after that, Jesus entered Jerusalem on a donkey, so the prophecy was fulfilled precisely. (This includes leap years.)

Out of the seventy weeks in Daniel 9:24, sixty-nine have already passed. In verse 27 we have the record of just one week. Again, one week signifies seven years. The "he" mentioned in verse 27 refers to a Roman emperor who will appear at the end of the world (the Antichrist). He will confirm the covenant with many Jews for seven years. However, in the middle of that period, after three and one-half years, he will break the covenant and cause the worship of the Jews to cease. Thus, during the first part of the Great Tribulation the persecution will be less intense.

During the second three and one-half years, the Antichrist will completely break the covenant with the Jews. He will enter the temple and claim to be the king. This will be the period of severe tribulation, but "that determined" (God's wrath) will be poured upon "the desolate" (the Antichrist).

In Daniel 9:26 is a prophecy about what would happen during the church age after the Resurrection of Jesus. A Roman general named Titus came with his army and destroyed Jerusalem in A.D. 70, fulfilling the part of the prophecy saying "the people of the prince who is to come will destroy the city and the sanctuary." At the end of the church age, which has so far lasted two thousand years, the Antichrist will appear and begin the Great Tribulation.

Daniel 9 has deeper theological implications that go beyond the scope of this book, but I trust you can see now why scholars conclude the Great Tribulation will be seven years long. It will be the last period in which God exhorts the Jews, His chosen people, to repent. For the Gentiles it will be a period in which they betray Jesus Christ and go through torment and destruction to the end. Let's look now at what will happen during the Great Tribulation.

OPENING OF THE SEALS (6:1–17)

THE FIRST SEAL, AND THE MAN WHO RODE ON THE WHITE HORSE (6:1–2)

As JOHN IN the Spirit watched these future events unfold, Jesus opened the first of the seven seals on the scroll. Then one of the four living creatures, with a voice like thunder, said to John, "Come."

John looked and saw "a white horse, and he who sat on it had a bow; and a crown was given to him; and he went out conquering, and to conquer" (v. 2).

THE MAN WHO RODE ON THE WHITE HORSE IS NOT JESUS

IT'S EASY TO make the mistake of interpreting this figure riding on a white horse to be Jesus. The Great Tribulation had already begun, however, and Jesus was in heaven, opening the first seal. Therefore to suppose that Jesus rode on a white horse and "went forth conquering, and to conquer" does not fit the time sequence, nor is it acceptable from a logical point of view. There are several reasons this must take place at the outset of the Great Tribulation.

First, the church has already been carried into heaven. Jesus works through the church and the Holy Spirit, but as we saw in Revelation 4, the church has already gone through the open door of heaven, accompanied by the Holy Spirit. Hence, the age of grace, the church age, has ended. Therefore, to interpret 6:2 as saying Jesus appears again, riding on a white horse and preaching the gospel ("conquering, and to conquer"), at the beginning of the Tribulation is not reasonable chronologically.

Second, the man on a white horse goes forth conquering with a bow, but Jesus is clearly identified in Revelation 19 as fighting with a sword that comes out of His mouth (19:15). As that passage shows, such a weapon is enough.

Third, Revelation 19:12 says that on the head of Jesus, the King of kings, were many crowns. The man who rides on a white horse wears only one crown.

Fourth, Jesus has already won the victory and will come next to the earth to judge. He has no need to fight belatedly, "conquering, and to conquer." He wrote to the church in Laodicea, "He who overcomes, I will grant to him to sit down with Me on My throne, as I also overcame and sat down with My Father on His throne" (3:21). Therefore he who rode on a white horse is not Jesus.

HE WHO RODE ON A WHITE HORSE IS THE ANTICHRIST

WHO THEN IS riding on a white horse? None other than the Antichrist, disguising himself as Jesus Christ, falsely claiming he is the messiah who will bring peace and prosperity to the world. The title "Antichrist" is put on him because he pretends to be Christ. For that purpose he rides a white horse (which symbolizes purity and victory), wears a crown, and has a bow in his hand to conquer. Figuratively speaking, this is the same as a spy who, having infiltrated enemy territory, pretends to be a citizen of the foreign land by imitating the language and customs of the people and by wearing their clothes.

Thus, the Antichrist will come as a self-styled messiah, and the whole world will exalt and welcome him.

I believe this Antichrist has already been born. Perhaps he was born somewhere in Europe or in the Middle East and is now attending a university, or perhaps he has already started his career as a politician. And if he is indeed already in this world, the day of our going to heaven is nearer than we may think.

One thing we should notice in Revelation 6:2 is that there is no mention of arrows with his bow. The Antichrist will take possession of the white horse of victory and the crown of glory—the position of a top leader—not by the means of war, but by his subtle political and diplomatic ability.

By using some trick, he will put all the countries in a united Europe under his control. As we have already seen in Daniel, and will look at again in coming Revelation chapters, at first he will have only three countries in his hand by taking them out by their roots. Then the rest of the seven countries will surrender to him. In this way he will unify the ten European countries in the former territory of Rome.

When Europe comes under the banner of one union, it will possess enormous economic and military power, and the whole world will kneel down to it. When the Antichrist appears, however, he will make a covenant with Israel for seven years, as we saw in Daniel 9:24–27. Accordingly, the day when the united nations of Europe and Israel ratify a seven-year contract is the very day when the first seal of the Tribulation will be opened.

If people read in the morning newspaper one day that the president of the united nations of Europe has concluded a seven-year treaty of friend-ship and prosperity with Israel, they will be sorry, because they were not caught up into heaven. I pray in the name of our Lord that you will not be among them.

Is the world situation really going in the direction of producing the seven-year treaty between Europe and Israel? First, let's consider Israel's perspective. The Jews, who had wandered for two thousand years, mirac-ulously regained their state of Israel on May 14, 1948. That was a miracle of miracles indeed.

Can you imagine the difficulty a nation would face in regaining its lost territory after two thousand years? Try to imagine your feelings in such a situation. In Korean history, Ko-gu-ryu, an old kingdom of our ancestors located in the northern part of the Korean Peninsula, once possessed the territory reaching to Manchuria. With the fall of the kingdom in 668, however, Ko-gu-ryu lost her vast domain to the kingdoms of Silla and Tiang. Since then, Korea has never regained that territory in Manchuria. If we should now ask Communist China to return that territory thirteen hundred years later, do you think she would accede to our request? Would such a thing even be possible?

Nevertheless, Israel regained her land after two thousand years. If that's not a miracle of God, what is? He granted it in order to accomplish His preordained will, gathering dispersed Jews from all over the world.

God has also preserved Israel through several wars in which Arab states, with a collective population of over two hundred million, strug-gled to swallow the tiny nation of Israel, which had a mere three million people. These, too, were miracles. Though the enormous group of Arab nations, like a lion, has tried to devour Israel, which is like a mouse by comparison, every time the lion has been beaten by the mouse.

Europeans began to be concerned when World War II ended and they found themselves sandwiched between the mighty military and economic strength of the United States and the U.S.S.R. To enhance their position, their leaders concluded that all the nations in Europe (the former territory of Rome) should work together at various levels.

In 1958, ten years after Israel became an independent nation, the European Economic Community was formed, with its capital in Brussels, Belgium. Since that time, progress in economic cooperation has given rise to plans for military and political unity as well. In 1991, their "Treaty of European Union" set guidelines for political and economic union by the end of the decade.

When this unification is complete, the people of the countries belonging to the EEC will not need passports when traveling to other countries within the bloc. They will cross the borders freely and hold the jobs they want in other countries.

Thus, Europe is currently achieving this prophesied economic unification through the EEC, with a degree of military cooperation from the North Atlantic Treaty Organization. Now, when they achieve political unification, the so-called United Nations of Europe will be complete.

The establishment of a Jewish state has been accomplished. The unification of Europe is progressing steadily. Since everything thus proceeds according to the prophecy of the Bible, we can conclude that the coming of our Lord is at hand.

When Europe is unified politically and the Antichrist takes over, he will make the treaty with Israel for whatever reason—perhaps with the intention of betraying the Jews from the start. Why would Israel make such a treaty? Maybe its leaders will think a strong Europe can help it rebuild the temple in Jerusalem. Many Jews are eager to resurrect Solomon's temple, which was destroyed and replaced by a Muslim mosque (the Dome of the Rock). Those Jews want to pull down the mosque and build their own temple there. If they try to do that, however, the two billion Muslims all over the world will rise to protest, and war will inevitably break out. The power and influence of the Antichrist may be so great, however, that the Jews will think he can help them fulfill their dream.

Whatever their exact reasoning at the time, both parties will find usefulness in each other and so agree to help one another. That treaty will mark the beginning of the end.

THE SECOND SEAL AND THE RED HORSE (6:3–4)

WHEN THE LAMB of God opened the second seal, John saw a red horse coming. "To him who sat on it, it was granted to take peace from the earth, and that men should slay one another; and a great sword was given to him" (v. 4). That red horse symbolizes war and blood. A horrible carnage now takes place.

In the day Israel tries to pull down the Dome of the Rock in Jerusalem and rebuild Solomon's temple in its place, the entire Arab world will launch an all-out offensive against Israel. That mosque is the second most sacred place of the Muslims, so how could they stand by idly while an attempt was being made to demolish it? Following their lead, Russia will also attack Israel.

This has been foretold in Ezekiel 38. According to that prophecy, Russia will invade like the surge of a sea and fight against Israel, but it will be defeated miserably in the end. Then Israel will freely build its temple. Hence, the bloody war that will break out with the opening of the second seal is a war between Israel and the Arabs and Russia. A great number of people will be killed. It is also prophesied in Daniel 9:27 that Israel will rise to be a powerful country and will cooperate with the unified Europe for three and one-half years:

> And he will make a firm covenant with the many for one week, but in the middle of the week he will put a stop to sacrifice and grain offering; and on the wing of abominations will come one who makes desolate, even until a complete destruction, one that is decreed, is poured out on the one who makes desolate.
>
> —DANIEL 9:27

I believe the red horse also signifies Communism, which is symbolized by the color red.

THE THIRD SEAL AND THE BLACK HORSE (6:5–6)

WHEN THE THIRD seal was opened, John saw a black horse, and its rider had a balance in his hands. This is a time of great famine. The shortage of food is so severe that its sale will be rationed by being weighed in the balance, "a quart of wheat for a denarius, and three quarts of barley for a denarius, and do not harm the oil and the wine" (v. 6).

Famine and economic ruin are always in the aftermath of war. During the war, resources are consumed by the war effort, as are available workers, and industrial facilities are destroyed.

The rider of the black horse is forbidden, however, to harm cooking oil and wine. Why? I believe it's because olive oil and wine are precious things used for sacrifices to God. But apart from them there will be a dreadful famine and economic devastation.

Even today, when there is no major war, many parts of the world face a severe food shortage. Experts say a worldwide famine would cost fifty million lives a year. I sincerely pray that all of you who read this book will be in heaven when the famine foretold in verse 6 occurs.

The Great Tribulation: Part One

THE FOURTH SEAL AND THE PALE HORSE (6:7–8)

THE MENTION OF the horse's color makes us shudder. Its rider's name is Death. *Hades,* or hell, means, in this case, "a public cemetery." The war will take many lives, and the famine and epidemics that follow will take even more.

Our Lord said in Matthew 24:7–8, "For nation will rise against nation, and kingdom against kingdom, and in various places there will be famines and earthquakes. But all these are merely the beginning of birth pangs."

We read in Revelation 6:8, "And authority was given to them [Death and Hell] over a fourth of the earth, to kill with sword and with famine and with pestilence, and by the wild beasts of the earth."

Since the population of the world is now 5,852,000,000 people, one-fourth of that is 1,462,000,000 people. During the first three and one-half years of the Great Tribulation, more than one billion people will die on account of war and its aftermath and be buried in public cemeteries.

The present population of China is one billion. Can you imagine what a huge number that is? Therefore the pale horse signifies terrible disasters.

THE FIFTH SEAL AND THE MARTYRS (6:9–11)

THE "SOULS OF those who had been slain because of the word of God, and because of the testimony which they had maintained" (v. 9) are the people who become martyrs during the first three and one-half years of the Great Tribulation. They are said to be "underneath the altar." Since the altar is the place where sacrifices are offered, they are there as a sacrifice offered to God. They weep bitterly and plead to God that He will take His revenge quickly.

If they had earlier believed in Jesus Christ and been caught up into heaven, how much better it would have been for them!

But then Jesus gives them white robes. Those are given to comfort them. And Jesus tells them they should rest yet for a while until their "fellow servants and their brethren who were to be killed even as they had been, should be completed also" (v. 11).

Here we find that God continues His work of salvation even while the Tribulation is going on, like a farmer gleaning ears of grain, because if one more soul can be saved, God wills to do it.

THE SIXTH SEAL AND THE DISASTERS IN NATURE (6:12–17)

As SOON AS the sixth seal is opened, fearful things will happen on the earth and in heaven. A great earthquake will take place, the sky will become pitch black with volcanic ash, and the moon will become red due to the ash and dust (v. 12). The sky will be rolled together like a scroll (v. 14). So severe will the earthquake be that every mountain and island will be moved out of its place, and the stars will fall out of the sky (v. 13).

When such phenomena occur, everyone from kings to slaves will hide themselves in caves and in the rocks of the mountains. They will cry to those mountains and rocks: "Fall on us and hide us from the presence of Him who sits on the throne, and from the wrath of the Lamb; for the great day of their wrath has come; and who is able to stand?" (vv. 16–17).

Notice that in spite of such terrible happenings, those people still do not repent to God but pray to the rocks and stones. People are so foolish! God wants to deliver them, but they will not repent. What a heartbreaking scene that will be!

Six seals have been opened thus far. Between the sixth seal and the seventh, a parenthetical scene appears, and we see God sealing those preachers who will deliver the remaining people on earth during the first half of the Great Tribulation.

PARENTHETIC: SEALING OF GOD'S SERVANTS (7:1–17)

THE ANGELS HOLDING THE WINDS OF THE EARTH (7:1)

IN REVELATION 7:1 John saw "four angels standing at the four corners of the earth, holding back the four winds of the earth, so that no wind should blow on the earth or on the sea or on any tree." The wind signifies war, and God commanded the angels in charge of the war to suspend it until all the preachers of the gospel be sealed on their foreheads (vv. 2–3).

The sealing mentioned here is not the same as the sealing of the Holy Spirit. Our being drawn today to faith in Jesus and to salvation is done by the invisible sealing of the Holy Spirit upon our souls. In that day, however, God's sealing on the foreheads of His servants will be visible to everyone. Later the devil will also seal those who follow the Antichrist with the number 666 on their foreheads or hands.

THE PREACHERS OF THE GOSPEL SEALED DURING THE TRIBULATION (7:2–8)

THUS, THE SEALING of God's servants begins as an angel ascends from the rising of the sun and begins to seal. Some people misinterpret this scene and cause confusion. In Korea, for example, some think it means God will start His sealing with the Korean people, since Korea is located in the East, or toward the rising of the sun. But I do not want to be sealed at that time, because before that happens the Christians will already be in heaven watching events on the earth! The sun symbolizes Jesus Christ. Accordingly, the verse says the angel comes from the throne of Jesus in obedience to His order.

THOSE WHO ARE SEALED ARE ALL JEWS

THOSE SEALED ARE the preachers of the gospel who will deliver the remnants of God during the first half of the Tribulation. Furthermore, verses 4–8 tell us they're all Jews—144,000—out of every tribe of the sons of Israel.

Why was the tribe of Dan omitted and the tribe of Manasseh included instead? There's a definite reason for that.

First Kings 12:25–30 describes how idolatry was committed in the northern kingdom of Israel. Jeroboam, its first king, made two golden calves and set one in Dan and the other in Bethel, the hill country of Ephraim. Both the tribes of Dan and Ephraim worshiped the calves. God had said earlier that He would blot out the names of those who serve other gods from under heaven (Deut. 29:18–20). Therefore, the name of Dan was omitted from the list of the twelve tribes of Israel and replaced by the tribe of Manasseh, who was the firstborn of Joseph.

THE WRONG INTERPRETATION ABOUT THE 144,000

TODAY THERE ARE many heretics who deceive people using the number 144,000. Jehovah's Witnesses maintain that only 144,000 people will go to heaven. If that were true, however, that number would already be there, leaving the rest of us without hope. Park Tae-sun, founder of a Korean cult, also asserted that when the number of the saved reaches 144,000, the end of the world will come. That also was a misinterpretation.

144,000: THE SERVANTS WHO WILL GLEAN THE REMAINING SOULS

THE 144,000 ARE the Jewish servants of God who will glean the remaining souls in the first half of the Tribulation. Why does God choose them for that purpose?

Those who preached the gospel first were Jews. Those who recorded the Bible were also Jews. It is only right that our Lord would again use His chosen people as those who would complete His kingdom.

These 144,000 Jews are like the seven thousand people God preserved during the time of Elijah; they did not bow their knees to Baal but kept their faith in God to the very end. The End-Time Jews will have accepted Jesus Christ as their Savior and entered into salvation. God will seal them for His use as preachers of the gospel, and they will preach it everywhere during the first half of the Tribulation.

A GREAT MULTITUDE OF PEOPLE WHO WILL BE SAVED (7:9–14)

THE 144,000 JEWISH preachers will present the gospel so diligently, even sacrificing their lives, that the people who are saved out of all nations and peoples cannot be numbered. As John saw them, they were "standing before the throne and before the Lamb, clothed in white robes, and palm branches were in their hands" (v. 9).

One of the elders told John, "These are the ones who come out of the great tribulation, and they have washed their robes and made them white in the blood of the Lamb" (v. 14).

Their white robes are proof that they are washed clean by the precious blood of Jesus Christ, and the palm branches they hold are tokens that they overcame the Antichrist and the Tribulation. However, the martyrs, as we saw in Revelation 6, were lying flat under the altar. Therefore this great multitude of people standing around the throne did not pass through martyrdom.

The important point for us is that those who rely on the precious blood of Jesus will be saved even in the midst of the Tribulation. We must witness diligently for Christ. Even if people do not believe now, they may believe and go to heaven when they are exhorted by the 144,000 preachers.

The time is at hand, so let us be faithful to sow the seed of the gospel.

Do not be discouraged if people fail to believe now. Just sow the seed. Jesus will cause it to grow, and many will be saved even after He comes for His church.

WHAT IS IMPLIED BY THE GREAT MULTITUDE WHO ARE SAVED (7:15–17)

THESE PEOPLE WHO come out of the Great Tribulation do not sit on the throne. They stand before it and give praise to God, waving the palm branches in their hands. They do not wear crowns, nor do they receive rewards, because they did not believe early according to faith. The saints who were already saved, however, receive golden crowns as their rewards.

When God dwells among the saints of the Tribulation (v. 15), they shall hunger no more, neither thirst anymore; neither shall the sun light on them, nor any heat (v. 16).

Because those people went through so much hunger and thirst, God will not make them suffer any longer. The Bible also says they will not hurt any longer. From this we can imagine how much pain they suffer from the Antichrist: "For the Lamb in the center of the throne shall be their shepherd, and shall guide them to springs of the water of life; and God shall wipe every tear from their eyes" (v. 17).

THE SEVENTH SEAL AND THE TRUMPETS OF SEVEN ANGELS (8:1–9:21)

THERE ARE MANY symbols in the Book of Revelation. This is because John could not explain what he saw through his experience or words, for he saw things that would happen two thousand years in the future. For example, let us suppose a Korean who lived a century ago were to be resurrected and made to stand at Chongro Square in Seoul. He would not know what to call an automobile. How difficult it would be to explain an automobile if you had never seen one before! You might try to describe it as an iron horse rolling along with four legs, with eyes like flashing lamps.

For this reason, in order to understand Revelation, we must make a thorough study of the meaning of John's symbols. Please bear in mind that most of the words we will study from now on are recorded in symbolic terms.

THE SEVENTH SEAL (8:1–2)

IN THE EIGHTH chapter of Revelation is the opening of the seventh seal, followed immediately by seven trumpets. When the seventh trumpet sounds, seven bowls are introduced. It is like a firework that goes off with a loud bang and breaks into seven smaller fireworks. When the seventh of the smaller fireworks goes off, it explodes into still smaller sparks. The first firework can be compared to the seventh seal; the seven smaller fireworks emanating from it are the seven trumpets; and the sparks emanating from the seventh small firework are the seven bowls.

There is important meaning in the statement "there was silence in heaven for about half an hour" (v. 1). Even while God executes judgment, He still wants human beings to repent and be gleaned into the salvation of eternal life, freed from the snare of the devil. That is why God waits silently for half an hour. It is a chance for people to throw themselves on His mercy and avoid the approaching judgment that will begin with the opening of the seventh seal.

Moreover, this silence of one-half hour is meant to forewarn of a greater coming judgment. You may have felt the same when you scolded your children. When their disobedience is trivial, you quickly scold with a few words. But when the offense is grave, you may just look at them, dumbfounded. When Daddy or Mommy looks into a child's eyes, not saying a word, that is the most awesome and dreadful time for the child, because it means a greater punishment will surely follow. In the same way, the silence of half an hour forewarns of a greater judgment.

AN ANGEL HAVING A GOLDEN CENSER (8:3–5)

AFTER THE SILENCE of one-half hour, seven angels stand, each one holding a trumpet. One angel comes with a golden censer full of incense and offers the incense on the altar of God.

This is the holy of holies. In Old Testament times Solomon's temple contained the holy place and, behind a curtain, the holy of holies. Entrance to the holy place was restricted to the high priest alone. But even he could only enter the holy of holies once a year, and then not without blood. The holy of holies is where God dwells.

John saw there an angel who was about to offer incense. Who is this angel?

Since angels do not have the priesthood, none of them can become the high priest. The priesthood was reserved for Aaron and his descendants. There is another person, however, who has become a priest in the order of Melchizedek. He is Jesus Christ, our high priest (Heb. 7:20–22). Therefore, I believe it is Jesus who offers the incense from the golden censer on the altar of God. The Greek word for angel, *aggelos,* can also mean by implication a pastor. And Jesus is the great shepherd.

The incense Jesus received was offered with the prayers of the saints (vv. 3–4). As our high priest, Jesus still carries out the work of receiving prayers of the saints and offering them on the altar of God. As the high priest who offers sacrifice for us, He also never stops praying for us.

You may be trying to settle in your own mind what is meant by the prayers of the saints, if the saints are already in heaven. One thing you must know for sure is that saints pray not only when they're on the earth, but also when they're in heaven. The Bible clearly calls us "a royal priesthood" (1 Pet. 2:9). And since part of the job of priests is to intercede for others, I believe we will pray all the more while we are in heaven. To those prayers is added the intercessory prayer of Jesus, and thus the golden censer becomes full of the incense of prayers. So I believe the saints from every family in heaven and on earth are given to pray on behalf of God's will. (See Ephesians 3:15.)

Throughout my ministry I have seen a wonderful thing occur. Namely, when Christian parents die leaving non-Christian children behind, the non-Christian children usually accept the faith soon afterward. Even the most stubborn children who used to oppose the evangelism of their parents will usually come to believe in Jesus.

Why does this happen? I believe it is because Christian parents continue to pray fervently in heaven for the souls of their children on earth. Even at this moment the saints who went to heaven before us are praying to Jesus for you and me, asking that the will of the Lord be done on this earth. The prayers turn into incense that is put into the golden censer, and it ascends before the throne of God. Hearing those prayers, God responds by drawing unsaved loved ones to Himself.

The next scene shows that the angel took the censer, filled it with fire from the altar, and hurled it onto the earth, followed by peals of thunder, rumblings, flashes of lightning, and an earthquake. That means Jesus receives our prayers, offers them to God, and, as the high priest who prays for us, receives an answer from the Father and brings it to the world.

From this point God will avenge the martyred saints. Therefore we must not stop praying, for our prayers surely turn into incense as they ascend before His throne. His answers come down and are fulfilled in our lives.

THE TRUMPET OF THE FIRST ANGEL (8:7)

WHEN THE SEVENTH seal is opened, the first angel sounds the trumpet. This scene will unfold in the first half of the Tribulation. With the sound of the trumpet, "there came hail and fire, mixed with blood, and they were thrown to the earth; and a third of the earth was burnt up, and a third of the trees were burnt up, and all the green grass was burnt up."

What does that mean? As I said before, John had to write this way because, in his age, there were no modern weapons—armaments such as the bow and spear were all he knew.

However, we can now speculate that in all probability John was describing the effects of a hydrogen bomb. Today such a weapon can devastate a wide area, burning all the trees and grass in its way. When an atomic bomb was dropped on Hiroshima, Japan, in August 1945, there was a sudden downpour of hail. That happened because the air heated by the explosion went up with the vapor, and as it was cooled in the high altitude of the atmosphere, it turned into hail and fell to the earth. To John, the explosion of numerous nuclear bombs might well have looked like "hail and fire mixed with blood."

I conclude, therefore, that this scripture shows that a devastating nuclear war will occur during the first half of the Tribulation. God will judge this world through human hands. At present, the United States, Russia, France, China, India, and others are all manufacturing and stock-piling nuclear weapons. Other renegade nations in the Middle East are also developing nuclear technology. The day will come when they will use them. We must remember that since human history began, mankind has never made a weapon it did not use. Enough nuclear bombs have already been made to destroy the earth several times. One-quarter of the world's population will die during that time, possibly due to nuclear weapons.

The burning of one-third of the earth's vegetation will also cause food shortages. Moreover, the destruction of one-third of the trees will greatly damage air quality, since trees purify air by turning carbon dioxide into oxygen.

Air pollution is already a major problem in the world today. How much more of a problem will it be then? Such miserable schemes will happen with the sounding of the first trumpet.

THE TRUMPET OF THE SECOND ANGEL (8:8–9)

WHEN THE SECOND angel sounds the trumpet, something like a "great mountain" all ablaze is thrown into the sea.

The fulfillment of that prophecy may relate to something the United States and Russia are developing called the space bus. This device, loaded with atomic and hydrogen warheads, would be put into an earth orbit. When a button is pressed on earth, the bus would explode and fall to the ground like a burning volcano. If ever fully developed, it would split into several hundred or thousand pieces. Accordingly, it could turn a big country into a sea of flames. Some say Russia has already put such a space bus into earth orbit.

When the second angel sounds the trumpet, one-third of the living creatures in the sea die, and one-third of the ships are destroyed. From this scripture we can imagine the following situation.

A space bus is fired toward the place where enemy warships have gathered, and that whole part of the sea turns into havoc. Not only do warships and merchant ships sink, but one-third of the sea's living creatures are killed. That would greatly reduce the earth's transportation capacity and supply of seafood.

THE TRUMPET OF THE THIRD ANGEL (8:10–11)

WHEN THE THIRD angel sounded the trumpet, "a great star fell from from heaven, burning like a torch, and it fell on a third of the rivers and on the springs of waters . . . and a third of the waters became wormwood; and many men died from the waters." John thought it was a great star, but my guess is that it was a biological bomb, because the water was polluted and everyone who drank the water died. This also will happen in the first half of the Tribulation, when the Arab nations, backed by Russia, war against Israel and the league of European nations.

THE TRUMPET OF THE FOURTH ANGEL (8:12)

WHEN THE FOURTH angel sounded the trumpet, one-third of the sun, moon, and stars turned dark. One-third of the day and the night were without light. How could this happen?

If a nuclear war breaks out, the dust arising from the explosions would sweep over the earth, and the earth would become darkened as if an eclipse of the sun or moon were taking place. Scientifically, this is natural. When a volcano bursts into eruption, the sky gets dark even in the daytime. How much more would it be possible in a nuclear war at the end of the world! Thus, the focus of chapter 8 is on the destruction of the natural environment by the first four angels.

THE WARNING OF AN ANGEL (8:13)

BEFORE THE FIFTH angel sounded the trumpet, another angel flew in the midst of the sky, crying, "Woe, woe, woe." It was a warning about the trumpets of the three remaining angels—that is, three dreadful judgments.

THE TRUMPET OF THE FIFTH ANGEL (9:1–11)

WHEN THE FIFTH angel sounded the trumpet, John saw a star fall onto the earth. That star was Lucifer, or Satan. Isaiah 14:12 says, "How you have fallen from heaven, O star of the morning, son of the dawn! You have been cut down to the earth, you who have weakened the nations!"

Satan was given the key of the bottomless pit, where evil spirits are imprisoned. When Jesus cast out demons, they begged Him not to command them to depart into the bottomless pit (Luke 8:31). However, God put those there who attempted to lift themselves up to the throne of God, not keeping their own positions. The Bible says:

> For if God did not spare angels when they sinned, but cast them into hell and committed them to pits of darkness, reserved for judgment . . .
> —2 PETER 2:4

> And angels who did not keep their own domain, but abandoned their proper abode, He has kept in eternal bonds under darkness for the judgment of the great day.
> —JUDE 6

Since human beings will not repent during the first half of the Tribulation, our Lord gives the devil the key to afflict them. When he opens the door to the bottomless pit, there arises a smoke like that from a huge furnace, and the sun is darkened. This may refer to a volcanic eruption.

Out of that dust come hordes of evil spirits that have been shut up there. They had been bound for such a long time that they will be eager to ravage human beings. Perhaps among the loosed demons may be the unclean spirit that afflicted the woman with the issue of blood for twelve years and the demon that had made the man roam naked among the tombs. What great havoc they will wreak on the earth!

The Book of Revelation describes these spirits as locusts, and "power was given them, as the scorpions of the earth have power" (9:3). Scorpions are creatures with an incredibly sharp sting. They're said to have caused Roman soldiers, famous for their bravery, to cry painfully for help. Roman soldiers were so thoroughly trained that when they were beaten by their superiors, they did not break down, even when their bones were broken. How painful it will be for human beings when demons from the bottomless pit hurt them with the power of scorpions!

However, our Lord commanded that they should not hurt the 144,000 Jewish evangelists who will have been sealed on their foreheads. The demons cannot touch those whom God has sealed. This is also true today. When we are sealed and armed by the precious blood of Jesus and by the Holy Spirit, demons can't hurt us.

During the five months when the evil spirits will afflict those who were sealed, their pain will be so severe that they will want to die (v. 6). However, even though they will seek death, God will take it away from them so they will have an opportunity to repent. This is the grace of God, for anyone who dies apart from Christ will be cast into the fire of hell.

At this time, God will have already saved the martyrs who died during the first three and one–half years and were under the altar. After them He will save innumerable people through the testimony of the 144,000 preachers. And He will still continue His saving work beyond that, though the faith of those saved may be tiny like a mustard seed, until there remain only those who absolutely will not believe in Christ. This is the infinite love of God.

This appearance of evil spirits symbolized as locusts is so ghastly that it surpasses our imagination. "Their faces were like the faces of men. And they had hair like the hair of women, and their teeth were like the teeth of lions. And they had breastplates like breastplates of iron; and the sound of their wings was like the sound of chariots, of many horses rushing to battle. And they have tails like scorpions, and stings; and in their tails is their power to hurt men for five months" (vv. 7–10). Their king is identified as

Apollyon in the Greek language, which means "destroyer." They will go everywhere destroying and robbing. But the authority to kill will not be given to them. In Revelation 8 John described natural calamities, but in this chapter the judgment on human beings begins.

THE TRUMPET OF THE SIXTH ANGEL (9:12–21)

WHEN THE SIXTH angel sounded the trumpet, John heard a voice saying, "Release the four angels who are bound at the great river Euphrates" (v. 14), which divided the east from the west. This river basin has been a land of rebellion from the beginning of time.

The Euphrates is a branch of the river originating in the Garden of Eden, where Adam sinned (Gen. 2:14). The first rebellion against God took place there, and it was also the place where Cain, the first murderer, killed his brother, Abel. Moreover, the tower of Babel, that prominent symbol of human rebellion against God, was also built in a place near this river. Idolatrous Babylon was situated along this river. Thus, the valley of the Euphrates has been a place of wicked rebellion against God since the beginning of the world.

God bound four rebellious angels there at some point. When they are loosed during the first half of the Tribulation, they will kill one-third of the world population (v. 15). When the fourth seal is opened, one-fourth of the world population, or more than one billion people, will die. Then when one-third of that remaining population is killed, another one billion will die.

Therefore, during the short period of three and one-half years, more than half the population of the world will die, leaving only about two billion people. Imagine how severe the Tribulation will be! Blessed are the saints who will be caught up into heaven before such a tribulation starts. Hallelujah!

Those four angels cannot kill at any time they choose, however. The hour, the day, the month, and the year have already been fixed (v. 15). Verse 16 says the number of the horsemen is two hundred million. Therefore the four angels will mobilize an army of that size who will cross over the Euphrates. This is the beginning of the battle of Armageddon that will take place during the second half of the Tribulation.

The only country in the world that can mobilize so great an army is China. In 1961 China announced its military strength as being two hundred million (regular forces and militia combined). When John received this revelation, however, the total population of the world was less than that. How amazed John must have been when he heard the number!

In this passage is a picture of modern warfare. In John's day, armies used horses or chariots drawn by horses. Now John saw strange horses and riders with "breastplates the color of fire and of hyacinth and of brimstone; and the heads of the horses are like the heads of lions; and out of their mouths proceed fire and smoke and brimstone" (v. 17). That sounds today like tanks firing their guns, flame-throwers hurling flames, and atomic and hydrogen bombs being dropped from the air. By these weapons one-third of the earth's people will be killed. Nevertheless, many people will not repent of their sins (vv. 20–21). Why does the Bible mention this? It is to show that God is still waiting for their repentance and conversion. If God thought them hopeless, there would be no need to mention it.

PARENTHETICAL (10:1–11)

AFTER SUCH A dreadful second woe following the trumpet of the sixth angel, Revelation 10 reveals parenthetical things that will happen before the judgment of the seven bowls begins with the trumpet of the seventh angel.

THE ANGEL WHO SETS ONE FOOT ON THE SEA AND ONE FOOT ON THE EARTH (10:1–6)

VERSES 1–6 SAY that a mighty angel set his right foot on the sea and his left foot on the earth. Who was this angel? Notice how he is described. He came down from heaven, clothed with a cloud. A rainbow was "upon his head, and his face was like the sun, and his feet like pillars of fire" (v. 1). From that description, it must be Jesus.

When seven thunders sounded, John was about to write, but he heard a voice from heaven saying, "Seal up the things which the seven peals of thunder have spoken, and do not write them" (v. 4). No one knows this secret of the seven thunders. Those things are left for Jesus to reveal in the future.

The angel lifted his hand to heaven and swore by the Creator that there should be "delay no longer," or no more delay. That means the second half of the Tribulation would come without delay, the first half having been completed.

THE MYSTERY OF GOD TO BE FINISHED (10:7)

As SOON AS the seventh angel blows the trumpet, verse 7 says, the judgment of the seven bowls begins, and the world comes to an end. Thus, the mystery of God will be finished as God had declared to His servants the prophets.

As we discovered in earlier Daniel studies, this Old Testament prophet also wrote of a word of mystery:

> Seventy weeks have been decreed for your people and your holy city, to finish the transgression, to make an end of sin, to make atonement for iniquity, to bring in everlasting righteousness, to seal up vision and prophecy, and to anoint the most holy place.
>
> —DANIEL 9:24

There are many mysteries that cannot be understood today! Why did God allow Satan to creep into the Garden of Eden? Why did God allow Adam and Eve to fall? Why did sin enter this world? Since these are mysteries of God, we cannot know them now.

When the seventh angel sounds the trumpet, however, the judgment of the seven bowls will come, leading to the end of the world. Then comes the millennial reign of the Lord, during which He will disclose everything plainly.

THE LITTLE SCROLL (10:8–11)

THE VOICE FROM heaven spoke to John saying, "Go, take the book [scroll] which is open in the hand of the angel who stands on the sea and on the earth" (v. 8). So John went to the angel and asked for the little scroll. He said to John, "Take it, and eat it; and it will make your stomach bitter, but in your mouth it will be sweet as honey" (v. 9).

Some people interpret this little scroll to be the scroll sealed with seven seals, but that is wrong. As we have seen, the seven seals have all been opened. What will happen, then, if that scroll is eaten up? Nothing. So what is this scroll? The answer appears in verse 11: "And they said to me, 'You must prophesy again concerning many peoples and nations and tongues and kings.'"

In other words, this little scroll told the things that will happen during the second three and one-half years. In the Old Testament we find similar cases in which the prophet was told to eat a scroll before he received the word of God (Ezek. 3:1). In the same manner, Jesus told John to eat this scroll that he might prophesy.

When John ate the scroll, it was sweet in his mouth. Since it was the Word of God, it was sweeter than honeycomb (Ps. 19:10). Also, the prophecy included insight into God's millennial kingdom, followed by a new heaven and a new earth. Therefore the Word was very sweet indeed.

However, the prophecy also told of the Antichrist, who will arise in the form of a beast and run around wildly killing innumerable Jews and others who do not kneel down to him. Hence, for John, it was also a moment of bitterness as he thought of the misery and pain that would be suffered by the people who do not repent during this coming.

We turn now to the description of that period in Revelation chapters 11–19. It will be the most tragic and destructive time in human history.

18

The Great Tribulation: Part Two

THE SECOND THREE and one-half years of the Tribulation are covered in Revelation 11–19. To understand this period better, let's take a brief overview before getting into the details.

In chapter 11 the period begins, and the seventh angel sounds the trumpet. Chapter 12 is a parenthetical explanation. Chapter 13 is a description of the two beasts, and chapter 14 is a parenthetical prophecy. Chapters 15 and 16 deal with the last woe, started by the last trumpet sound of the seventh angel that continues through the judgment of the seven bowls.

Since chapters 12, 13, and 14 are parenthetical, we can better understand the events of the Tribulation if we put chapter 15 right after chapter 11.

Chapter 17 deals with the religion of the whore. Chapter 18 describes the downfall of the great city of Babylon. And chapter 19 tells about the advent of Jesus to this earth, bringing the second half of the Tribulation period to an end and ushering in the millennial kingdom.

THE TRUMPET OF THE SEVENTH ANGEL (11:1–19)

MEASURING THE TEMPLE AND ALTAR AND COUNTING THE WORSHIPERS (11:1)

As WE MOVE into the second half of the Tribulation, the first scene we see is of John measuring the Jews' temple and altar and counting the worshipers there (vv. 1–2).

Why such a starting point? In this second part of the Tribulation, the Antichrist will fight his life-and-death struggle with the Jews. During the first three and one-half years he was on peaceful terms with them. He aided them and even built the temple for them. But, in the second half of the Tribulation, Satan, who was driven out of heaven, enters into the heart of the Antichrist. As a result, he breaks the seven-year treaty in the middle and begins a war to annihilate the Jews. Therefore, the temple is very significant during that period.

As we saw earlier, the temple was destroyed when Jerusalem fell in A.D. 70. The Jews rose in revolt against the tyranny of Rome, but Jerusalem was besieged and burned by the Roman general Titus. Many instruments made of gold, which were used for sacrifice in the temple, were burned in this fire and melted into the crevices of the stones. In their search for the hidden gold, the Roman soldiers left no stone unturned, thus fulfilling the prophecy of Jesus in Matthew 24:2.

In the place where the temple previously stood, the Muslims built their own mosque, the Dome of the Rock, between A.D. 687 and 691. Believing it to be the site from which their prophet Mohammed was taken up into heaven, they have made it their second most holy place.

During the Six-Day War of 1967 Israel captured from Jordan the old part of Jerusalem where the mosque stands. Today Israel has finished preparations to rebuild the temple and is ready to start at any time. The money and materials have been collected, and it is the burning desire of the Jews to build a temple on Mount Moriah.

But the Jews, who cannot even go near the present mosque, will surely start a war with the Muslims when they begin to tear it down to make room for their temple. They will only succeed with the help of a unified Europe.

In the second half of the Great Tribulation, God will try those Jewish people with fire who do not believe in Jesus Christ, choosing rather to reject Him. After that, God will measure the sincerity of their faith. He will shelter those who worship Him in the temple and at the altar, according to the measure of their faith; those who are outside the temple He will cast away.

Among the Jews today are pious people who fervently worship the Lord through Judaism. But there are also others who ridicule Judaism, denying the existence of God. In order to separate those two types of people, John measured the temple and the altar and counted the worshipers with a rod-like reed.

THE OUTER COURT (11:2)

HOWEVER, THE LORD told John not to measure the court outside the temple (v. 2). That means God will save only those pious worshipers inside the temple. As for those on the outside, in the temple court, God will abandon them into the hands of the Antichrist for forty-two months, whether they are Jews or Gentiles.

The Antichrist will be making preparation for his rule of the world in the first three and one-half years. Then he will change his shape into a beast and for the following three and one-half years rule the world with full authority. He will break the seven-year treaty he had made with Israel and set up his own idol-image on the altar of the temple, forcing the Jews to worship it. This, as we have already seen, was foretold:

> And he will make a firm covenant with the many for one week, but
> in the middle of the week he will put a stop to sacrifice and grain
> offering; and on the wing of abominations will come one who makes
> desolate, even until a complete destruction, one that is decreed, is
> poured out on the one who makes desolate.
>
> —DANIEL 9:27

And this is also the time of which our Lord warned:

> Therefore when you see the abomination of desolation which was
> spoken of through Daniel the prophet, standing in the holy place (let
> the reader understand), then let those who are in Judea flee to the
> mountains.
>
> —MATTHEW 24:15–16

Since devout Jews will worship only God, not idols, they will, of course, resist. Inevitably, a bloody massacre will ensue. The Bible predicted this in Jeremiah, calling it the tribulation of Jacob: "Alas! for that day is great, there is none like it; and it is the time of Jacob's distress, but he will be saved from it" (Jer. 30:7).

After measuring the temple and altar and counting those who worship there, God will move everyone obedient to His will to the shelter. This scene soon appears.

THE TWO WITNESSES (11:3–13)

TWO WITNESSES, clothed in sackcloth, will appear and prophesy 1,260 days. When a month is counted as thirty days, that's three and one-half years—the second part of the Tribulation. The 144,000 Jews sealed by God on their foreheads to be preachers are seen no more until chapter 14. There we can see they have been taken up into heaven, where they praise God. So now it is time for the two witnesses to come and prophesy.

Of what will they testify? First, they will proclaim that people receive salvation by faith in Jesus Christ through the precious blood of the cross. Second, they will testify that the Antichrist is not the Messiah but a wicked criminal, the son of perdition. Third, they will bear witness of the imminent judgment of God. How the Antichrist will hate these two witnesses! He will grind his teeth with vexation, taking revenge by killing them.

Who do you think the two witnesses are? The Bible says, "These are the two olive trees and the two lampstands" (v. 4). They were seen by the prophet Zechariah about five hundred years before Christ (Zech. 4:1–14). When Zechariah asked the angel the meaning of the two olive trees, he was told, "These are the two anointed ones, who are standing by the Lord of the whole earth" (Zech. 4:14). Thus, the two olive trees have already been worshiping God in heaven for more than twenty-five hundred years. I believe the two witnesses are Moses and Elijah, who comforted Jesus on the Mount of Transfiguration (Luke 9:28–31). Why?

Because when the Israelites became depraved and worshiped idols during the time of King Ahab, Elijah prayed to God that it might not rain, and God shut the door of heaven for three and one-half years. In the second half of the Tribulation the two olive trees will also shut the door of heaven, and it will not rain (v. 6).

When Moses led the Israelites out of Egypt, God first gave him ten plagues to persuade Pharaoh to release the people. One of these plagues was to change the water of the Nile River into blood. During the second half of the Tribulation, the two olive trees will strike the earth with the same plague (v. 6).

The witnesses will return to this world in the flesh and preach about Jesus. The Bible says Elijah did not see death but was caught up into heaven riding a fiery chariot driven by fiery horses (2 Kings 2:1–11). Although it was known that Moses climbed Mount Nebo to die, his body was never found. And the Bible says that Michael the archangel contended with the devil for Moses' body (Jude 9). Because God buried Moses' body, no one was able to find his grave (Deut. 34:5–6). So I believe God hid Moses' body so that He could use him again for His purpose at the end of the world.

Therefore the two olive trees and two candlesticks are unmistakably Moses and Elijah. God sends them again in the flesh to this world to witness of Jesus Christ, showing His love and mercy in order to deliver one more soul from hell.

If anyone tries to hurt the two witnesses while they are prophesying, "fire proceeds out of their mouth and devours their enemies" (v. 5). (Once, when Elijah was on the top of a hill, two bands of soldiers who came to seize him were consumed by fire that fell from heaven [2 Kings 1:9–12]). Thus, while these two witnesses are prophesying, no one can hurt them. And the Antichrist is in constant agony until the second three and one-half years are almost over. Finally, he rises to oppose them.

By this time the two witnesses will have fulfilled their mission. Then the beast that has come up from the bottomless pit, the Antichrist, will kill them (v. 7). The preacher of Christ's gospel will never die before God's appointed time.

The Antichrist will then throw their bodies into the streets of Jerusalem, spiritually called Sodom and Egypt, because it is the adulterous city opposing God by setting up an idol of the Antichrist (v. 8).

All the world's people will congratulate themselves for the death of the two witnesses and refuse to let their bodies be placed in a tomb (v. 9). The people will send gifts one to another and make merry because the two witnesses had harshly rebuked them and brought a judgment of drought because of their wickedness. So it is with great joy that they celebrate their deaths (v. 10).

However, "after the three and a half days the breath of life from God came into them, and they stood on their feet." Then a loud voice from heaven speaks, "Come up here," and they ascend to heaven before everyone's eyes, causing everyone to be very frightened (vv. 11–12).

At the same time, a great earthquake strikes, and a tenth of the city falls, killing seven thousand people. After witnessing such a dreadful scene, the remaining people temporarily give glory to God (v. 13).

THE TRUMPET OF THE SEVENTH ANGEL (11:14–18)

THEN THE SOUND of a trumpet by the seventh angel is heard. This is the last in the series of trumpets by the seven angels who appeared when the scroll's seventh seal was opened by Jesus.

When the trumpet of the seventh angel sounded, John heard the proclamation to take over the world: "And the seventh angel sounded; and there arose loud voices in heaven, saying, 'The kingdom of the world has become the kingdom of our Lord, and of His Christ; and He will reign forever and ever'" (11:15).

As we have seen, the second three and one-half years of the Tribulation were almost finished when the two witnesses died. This is prior to the war of Armageddon. Now that Jesus has regained this world, which had been under the power of Satan, He takes it over. All the procedures to redeem creation have been completed.

As soon as the twenty-four elders sitting on the thrones heard the trumpet, they became overwhelmed with joy, fell on their faces, and worshiped God. They sang this song of praise:

> We give Thee thanks, O Lord God, the Almighty, who art and who wast, because Thou hast taken Thy great power and hast begun to reign. And the nations were enraged, and Thy wrath came, and the time came for the dead to be judged, and the time to give their reward to Thy bond-servants the prophets and to the saints and to those who fear Thy name, the small and the great, and to destroy those who destroy the earth.
>
> —REVELATION 11:17–18

In that song the elders foresee the end of the Tribulation; the millennial kingdom; the general resurrection of all the dead along with the final judgment of Him who sits on the throne; and the coming of a new heaven and a new earth.

Because the gleaning of salvation is come to an end when the two witnesses are taken into heaven, this world will be practically finished.

The Great Tribulation: Part Two

THE ARK OF THE TESTAMENT IN THE TEMPLE (11:19)

WHEN THE ELDERS finished praising God, the temple of God was opened in heaven, and John saw the ark of the testament accompanied by lightning, voices, thunderings, an earthquake, and great hail.

The temple was not opened at regular times. It was opened only once a year when the high priest entered to offer sacrifices.

What does it mean, then, that the temple was opened and the ark of the covenant was seen? Although mankind sinned and fell, God promised that He would forgive our sins, save us, and make a new world for us. By opening the temple, God was confirming that promise.

But after God's assurance of His promise comes a foreboding of the last judgment in the lightning, voices, thunderings, earthquake, and great hail. The world is rushing headlong toward its end during the second half of the Tribulation.

PARENTHETICAL EXPLANATION OF THE FATE OF ISRAEL (12:1–17)

REVELATION 12 EXPLAINS in detail what the fate of Israel will be during the second part of the Tribulation. As I have mentioned several times, this occurs when the Antichrist breaks his seven-year treaty with Israel and sets up his own image in the temple of God, forcing the Jews to worship it. Since they are monotheistic, they strongly resist this demand and suffer for it. If we study chapter 12 with that in mind, we will understand it better.

A GREAT WONDER IN HEAVEN (12:1–2)

WHO WAS THIS woman clothed with the sun? Some say she represents the church. However, the Bible never uses the image of a woman to symbolize the church. The church is the virgin engaged to Christ, not a woman about to deliver a child. But there is a nation that was called "the woman" in the Bible: "'Shout for joy, O barren one, you who have borne no child; break forth into joyful shouting and cry aloud, you who have not travailed; for the sons of the desolate one will be more numerous than the sons of the married woman,' says the LORD" (Isa. 54:1).

Along with this passage, we must also look at the Book of Hosea, which calls Israel the wife who fled from her husband. Israel was sometimes called a married woman when she was obedient to God. At other times, when she disobeyed God, she was called a divorced woman or a widow. Thus, Israel was always compared to a woman rather than a virgin.

Further, in Genesis 37:9–10, Joseph, one of the twelve sons of Israel (Jacob), dreamed a dream. In that dream "the sun and the moon and eleven stars" bowed down to Joseph. That meant that Joseph's father and mother, along with his eleven brothers, would bow down to him. In this dream the sun represented Israel. From these two examples we can deduce that the image of the woman in Revelation 12 represents Israel.

Verse 2 says that birth pangs came upon the woman. That does not mean Israel will deliver something in tribulation. Revelation 12 is a parenthetical, historical explanation of why the devil hates Israel so much and the Antichrist tries to annihilate it.

ANOTHER WONDER IN HEAVEN (12:3–5)

THE SON DELIVERED in verse 5 was Jesus Christ. He was not an ordinary man but One who would rule the nations with an iron rod: "I will surely tell of the decree of the LORD: He said to Me, 'Thou art My Son, today I have begotten Thee. . . . Thou shalt break them with a rod of iron, thou shalt shatter them like earthenware'" (Ps. 2:7, 9).

The red dragon was about to devour the son of the woman. In studying the life of Jesus, we find that the devil followed Jesus constantly, watching for an opportunity to destroy Him. For example, when Jesus was born, King Herod tried to use the Magi to locate the baby so he could kill Him. No doubt inspired by Satan, Herod gave orders to kill all the boys in and around Bethlehem who were two years old and under, but his ploy failed (Matt. 2:1–18). In Bethlehem the tomb still remains where the massacred babies were buried together.

Finally, Satan had Jesus crucified. However, He was resurrected and ascended into heaven, now sitting at the right hand of God. That's why Revelation 12:5 says, "Her child was caught up to God and to His throne."

Who is this "another sign in heaven," the great red dragon? He is a murderer who is called the old serpent, the devil, Satan, or Lucifer. He was one of the cherubim called "the anointed cherub who covers" (Ezek. 28:14). He was also one of the archangels, the highest rank in the hierarchy of angels, but he became proud (Isa. 14:13–14; Ezek. 28:17). This eventually drove him to compete with God (Rev. 12:7). As a result he was driven out of heaven (vv. 8–9) and now rules the power of the air (Eph. 2:2), located between the heavenly throne and the earth.

In the Book of Genesis, when God created heaven and earth and all things in them, He saw that it was all good except for one place: the firmament in the midst of the waters (Gen. 1:6–8). The phrase "it was good" is omitted in the account of that place, and I believe it's because the firmament in the midst of the waters was occupied by the devil and the other evil spirits who opposed God.

Revelation 12 says Lucifer drew a third part of the stars of heaven with his tail and cast them to the earth (v. 4). That signifies he incited a third of the angels to join him when he fell, starting the history of rebellion on the earth. We can be thankful, however, that two-thirds of the angels did *not* fall. Therefore, when one demon attacks us, two angels of God are available to protect us.

Verse 3 describes the red dragon as having seven heads and ten horns. That shows he will oppose God to the end of the world, a point we have already discussed in Daniel and which is further explained in Revelation 13. The seven heads represent the seven nations God raised up that most violently opposed Him: Assyria, Babylon, Media and Persia, Egypt, Greece, Rome, and the Antichrist's country that will be restored. The devil has gone all out to destroy God's people through those seven heads.

The ten horns of this dragon signify the ten countries of unified Europe that will be formed in the early part of the Tribulation. Through that union Satan will make his final struggle to avoid being cast away from the earth.

In Genesis 3:15, however, God declared that Jesus Christ, the seed of woman, would crush the devil's head.

From the time Lucifer heard that word of prophecy, he has exerted all his effort to prevent "the seed of woman" from being born, and thus began humanity's bloody history of constant war and murder. Cain was disobedient to God, but Abel was obedient. So the devil inspired Cain to murder Abel, for he (Satan) was afraid the Messiah might be born from Abel. First John 3:12 clearly says, "Not as Cain, who was of the evil one, and slew his brother. . . ." In other words, Cain killed Abel at the instigation of the devil (Gen. 4:1–8).

Later, when the whole world was judged for its wickedness, Noah found favor in the sight of the Lord (Gen. 6:8–9). Then the devil feared the Messiah would come out of the descendants of Noah, so he caused Noah to become drunk (Gen. 9:20–21) and his offspring to be depraved.

As a result, they fell into a snare. They gathered themselves in the land of Shinar and built the tower of Babel in rebellion against God (Gen. 11:1–4). This was also done at the instigation of the devil.

Afterward, God chose to make a nation out of Abraham's offspring to carry out His will, but the devil again interfered, fearing the Messiah would come out of his seed. So in Egypt he tried to exterminate the people of Israel through Pharaoh.

When the Israelites, led by Joshua, came to the land of Canaan and settled there, Satan repeatedly corrupted them through idolatry, for he was afraid the Messiah might come from them. Therefore, the Israelites were destroyed by Assyria and Persia and carried away as captives.

Through the grace of God, however, many Israelites returned from captivity. Eventually the devil incited them to kill Jesus. But once more God thwarted him by raising Jesus on the third day.

THE WOMAN WHO FLED INTO THE WILDERNESS (12:6)

BECAUSE THE RED dragon has been repeatedly frustrated in attempting to swallow the child throughout the long history of the world, he became furious and hated the woman who gave birth to the child—namely Israel. Therefore, the history of Israel has been a succession of ordeals and sufferings.

Since Christ ascended into heaven, Satan has wreaked his vengeance through many Jew-haters, most notably Hitler and the communists in the former Soviet Union. During the second half of the Tribulation he will launch an unprecedented extermination campaign against the Jews.

Verse 6 says, "The woman fled into the wilderness where she had a place prepared by God, so that there she might be nourished for one thousand two hundred and sixty days." That means God will make a refuge for Israel from the persecution of the Antichrist for one thousand two hundred sixty days, or three and one-half years.

Where is this shelter? The place is revealed in the Book of Isaiah. Several Christian groups from the United States have flown airplane loads of Bibles and canned food there, hiding the material under the earth and between the rocks in preparation for the time when Israel will take shelter there. Isn't that a wonderful thing God did by moving the hearts of the people? He spoke of the time of Israel's need for such protection.

Come, my people, enter into your rooms, and close your door behind

182

> you; hide for a little while, until indignation runs its course. For behold, the Lord is about to come out from His place to punish the inhabitants of the earth for their iniquity; and the earth will reveal her bloodshed, and will no longer cover her slain. In that day the Lord will punish Leviathan the fleeing serpent, with His fierce and great and mighty sword, even Leviathan the twisted serpent; and He will kill the dragon who lives in the sea.
>
> —Isaiah 26:20; 27:1

Mark that scripture, for there God clearly said He will hide the Israelites from the rage of the Antichrist. The passage is preceded by a verse telling about those who believe in Jesus Christ: "Your dead will live; their corpses will rise. You who lie in the dust, awake and shout for joy, for your dew is as the dew of the dawn, and the earth will give birth to the departed spirits" (Isa. 26:19).

The dead of the Lord shall rise again and ascend into heaven first; then the Israelites will hide themselves in the secret chamber. Long ago Isaiah predicted all this accurately. Now look at the place where Israel will hide.

> Then, like fleeing birds or scattered nestlings, the daughters of Moab will be at the fords of Arnon. Give us advice, make a decision; cast your shadow like night at high noon; hide the outcasts, do not betray the fugitive. Let the outcasts of Moab stay with you; be a hiding place to them from the destroyer.
>
> —Isaiah 16:2–4

Here "the destroyer" signifies the Antichrist. When he launches his invasion, the land of Moab will become God's hiding place for Israel.

When the Israelites first crossed the Jordan River and entered the land of Canaan, God ordered them to build cities of refuge on both sides of the river so a person who had accidentally killed someone might flee there to safety (Num. 35:9–15). Those cities symbolize the place where Israel will take shelter during the Tribulation.

Where is Moab located? When I visited Israel some years ago, I went there. About an hour's ride on the highway from Jerusalem will bring you to the highlands of Transjordan. It is there that ancient Moab is located. Once there, you will meet only the blazing sun and swirling gusts of sand.

In the midst of that desert, however, is the strongest fortress in the world.

183

The name of it is Petra. It was discovered in the nineteenth century and is situated between steep mountains. The only entrance is through a narrow, twisting canyon. It is not accessible to tanks, nor can airplanes attack it directly, because the mountains are so precipitous. With the buildings all cut into the rock cliffs, Petra is a formidable fortress. Theologians generally agree it is here that Israel will be hidden during the second half of the Tribulation—in Petra, located in the highlands of Transjordan.

THE WAR IN HEAVEN (12:7–12)

ACCORDING TO VERSE 7, there is war in heaven, a cosmic conflict fought between Michael, the prince of the divine host, and the dragon. The time has come when the antagonistic dragon should be cast out, as all his power was brought to an end when Jesus opened the last seal.

As foretold in Isaiah 24:21, God "will punish the host of heaven on high"—in other words, the red dragon that deceives the whole world. God will punish the kings of the Antichrist. And when He goes to Jerusalem and stands there, the sun will be ashamed and the moon confounded, as the Lord is glorified before the saints who are saved.

In that final, intense conflict in heaven between Michael and the dragon, Satan will be driven out of heaven because he is not equal to the archangel: "And the great dragon was thrown down, the serpent of old who is called the devil and Satan, who deceives the whole world; he was thrown down to the earth, and his angels were thrown down with him" (v. 9).

When the devil is cast out, a great voice in heaven says, "The accuser of our brethren has been thrown down, who accuses them before our God day and night. And they overcame him because of the blood of the Lamb and because of the word of their testimony, and they did not love their life even to death" (vv. 10–11).

Satan still accuses us before God. But we overcome his unceasing accusations by claiming the blood of Christ and the forgiveness it affords.

A church that is under the influence of the devil offers no songs or sermons praising the precious blood of Jesus Christ. However, if a church is full of songs and sermons praising His precious blood, the Holy Spirit will be at work there.

Today modernists, or "new theologians," argue that Jesus Christ died not as Savior, but as a great teacher or a great leader, so His death was self-immolation. This is the voice of the devil. "For this reason, rejoice, O heavens and you who dwell in them. Woe to the earth and the sea; because the devil has come down to you, having great wrath, knowing that he has only a short time" (12:12).

By that time we shall be in heaven. But those remaining on the earth will be hurt by the rage of the devil, who will recklessly attack anyone crossing his path, knowing his time is short.

THE REFUGE OF THE WOMAN AND THE REMNANT (12:13–17)

BEING THUS DRIVEN to the earth, the dragon begins to persecute the woman, the mother of the male child, or Christ, who has brought such a fatal blow to him. His intention is to take his final revenge on Israel. The fate of Israel is indeed miserable. If they had believed in Jesus, such a tragedy would have been avoided. However, they did not accept Him, so they must pass through this ordeal at the end of the world.

Then verse 14 says that "the two wings of the great eagle were given to the woman, in order that she might fly into the wilderness to her place, where she was nourished for a time and times and half a time, from the presence of the serpent." This is why Jesus said:

> Then let those who are in Judea flee to the mountains; let him who is on the housetop not go down to get the things out that are in his house; and let him who is in the field not turn back to get his cloak. But woe to those who are with child and to those who nurse babes in those days! But pray that your flight may not be in the winter, or on a Sabbath; for then there will be a great tribulation, such as has not occurred since the beginning of the world until now, nor ever shall.
> —MATTHEW 24:16–21

Through this scripture Jesus was showing how severe the situation of that time will be. When the Antichrist gives the stern order for all Jews to be put to death, they will flee to Petra without looking back.

The Bible says the woman, or Israel, flew into her place. However, there is no airport in Petra, and it would be impossible for a helicopter to transport such a large company of people to escape the carnage. So how could they go? The Lord will provide a way. In the New Testament we find a miracle that can solve the problem.

Obeying the command of God, Philip went "south to the road that descends from Jerusalem to Gaza. (This is a desert road.)" (Acts 8:26). On his way he met an Ethiopian eunuch. Philip preached Jesus to him and baptized him in water. When they came up out of the water, the Holy Spirit suddenly took Philip away and put him down at Azotus, a city about one hundred miles from Gaza. Thus, when Philip came up out of the water and walked one step, he was transported to a place one hundred miles away.

When the Jews flee from the Antichrist, I believe they cannot go to Petra unless they're helped by a miracle of God. The army of the Antichrist will run after them with tanks and vehicles. The Jews, running on foot, would soon be overtaken and killed unless they miraculously fly with "the wings of a great eagle" as predicted in the Bible.

The Jews take refuge at Petra and are nourished there "for a time and times and half a time" (v. 14)—the second three and one-half years of the Tribulation. The flood of water Satan casts after Israel (v. 15) symbolizes the multitude of people in the Antichrist's army that will charge at Petra.

Then verse 16 says, "The earth helped the woman, and the earth opened its mouth and drank up the river which the dragon poured out of his mouth." The earth's opening her mouth means an earthquake will take place. As the army of the Antichrist approaches Petra, a strong earthquake will cause deep cracks in the earth's surface that swallow the army. Several avenues of attack will be tried, but every time the armies will be engulfed by a chasm in the earth. This day is not far away when all these things will happen.

"The dragon was enraged with the woman, and went off to make war with the rest of her offspring, who keep the commandments of God and hold to the testimony of Jesus" (v. 17). The Jews who believed in Jesus will be transported by God to Petra. So the remaining Jews will be secular, yet they will also keep the commandment of God and do not worship the Antichrist's image. Besides, some Gentiles believe in Jesus belatedly. The dragon now stands ready to make war on those people.

Thus, the Jews and all the Christians are killed during the second half of the Tribulation. No one can escape this annihilation, except those in Petra. Even the two witnesses are killed.

ONE BEAST AND ANOTHER BEAST (13:1–18)

THE BEAST OUT OF THE SEA; COMPARISON TO DANIEL'S VISION (13:1)

JOHN "SAW A beast coming up out of the sea." The sea here signifies the multitude of people. The specific body of water John saw is the Mediterranean

Sea. This verse means that a beast will come out of the coastal region of the Mediterranean Sea—in other words, out of the former territory of the Roman empire. As we previously discovered in Daniel, in the vision of God, beasts represent the kings of the earth. Accordingly, this beast that rises out of the sea in Revelation signifies the Antichrist who rises out of the large crowd of restored Rome.

To understand this beast better, let us review again the image seen by the Babylonian king Nebuchadnezzar in the Book of Daniel.

THE IMAGE NEBUCHADNEZZAR SAW IN HIS DREAM

IN DANIEL 2 we read that King Nebuchadnezzar dreamed a troubling dream in about 606 B.C. In it he saw a great image that had the form of a man. God was prophesying human history through this dream, and Daniel provided the interpretation (Dan. 2:31–45).

The image Nebuchadnezzar saw had a head, breast, arms, belly, thighs, legs, and feet. Then suddenly a "stone was cut out without hands" and hit the image, breaking it to pieces; and the stone that smote the image filled the whole earth (Dan. 2:34–35). That was the vision Nebuchadnezzar saw. Then Daniel gave the following detailed interpretation.

Remember, *the head made of fine gold* represented the neo-Babylonian empire, which conquered the southern Jewish kingdom of Judah and lasted until 583 B.C. As an absolute monarchy, it had absolute political power, like gold, but it was conquered by the Medo-Persian empire.

The breast and the arms. Again, the two silver arms represented a united empire made of two kingdoms. That was the Medo-Persian empire, whose army, under a king named Cyrus, conquered Babylon in 583 B.C.

Media and Persia ruled the empire alternately until 380 B.C. Because its political system was not purely despotic, it was weaker than the neo-Babylonian empire. However, since silver is stronger than gold, it was stronger militarily in spite of its weaker political system.

The belly and the thighs. The belly and thighs of brass signified Greece. Brass is stronger than silver, and Alexander the Great of Greece vanquished the Medo-Persian empire in 380 B.C. By 323 B.C. he had brought all the known territory of Europe under his control.

The two legs. Remember, following the death of Alexander the Great, the Greek empire was divided into four parts that were unified by Rome in 30 B.C. The Roman empire is represented by the legs of iron. Just as iron is stronger than brass, so Rome was far stronger than Greece.

187

By A.D. 364 Rome had conquered all the known world. In 364, however, it was divided in half by religious conflict. The empire in the east was united under the banner of what we know today as the Greek Orthodox Church. The empire in the west flew the banner of the church centered in Rome. Eventually the split empire fell.

The ten toes. Afterward comes the age of ten toes and the description of the image in the form of a man. This signified that the church age would rise in the territory of the Roman empire.

Ten toes mean that ten kingdoms will be united. The feet were made partly of iron and partly of clay. That signified the coalition of nations with totally different political structures. The "strong" structure represented absolute monarchy, and the "weak" structure signified democracy. And, remember we saw that the two will be mixed to form one country—a unified Europe. And this coalition will come together soon.

Finally, in Nebuchadnezzar's dream, *a stone cut out without hands.* "A stone was cut out without hands" (Dan. 2:34), and it struck the image, breaking it to pieces. That stone then became a great mountain and filled the whole earth (Dan. 2:35). Jesus Christ is that stone.

The interpretation is that Jesus will come again and destroy unified Europe, and all the nations in the world will belong to Him.

DANIEL'S DREAM OF FOUR BEASTS

NOW LET US review Daniel's dream involving four beasts. In 555 B.C. Daniel had a dream in which he saw four beasts. Through this dream God showed Daniel future things of the world. Remember, these beasts were predators that bit and tore at each other. The dream is recorded in Daniel 7.

A lion that had eagle's wings. The first beast was like a lion but had the wings of an eagle (Dan. 7:4). Before long, however, the wings were plucked, and it stood erect like a man and spoke. This beast represented King Nebuchadnezzar and showed that he would unify and rule the empire as swiftly as a lion or an eagle.

The vision also referred to Nebuchadnezzar's becoming insane and living in the fields with the wild beasts as punishment for his pride. However, when he repented of his sin, God restored him, and a man's heart was given to him (Dan. 4:24–37).

A bear that had three ribs between its teeth. The second beast Daniel saw was a bear raised up on one side, with three ribs in its mouth between its teeth (Dan. 7:5). This bear signified the Medo-Persian empire.

The statement that the bear was raised on one side means that in the coalition of Media and Persia, Persia was the stronger. This empire was represented by a bear because it had the characteristics of a bear—it was strong but clumsy as it rushed recklessly with its military might. Its army did not win in war through great strategy but by overpowering the enemy with enormous numbers. Xerxes of Persia, remember, mobilized a force of five million in his expedition to Greece. Half the men were in the regular army, and the rest were engaged in the supply area.

Lydia, Babylon, and Egypt fought as allies against the Medo-Persian empire and were defeated. The three ribs the bear had between its teeth signified those three nations.

A leopard that had four heads and four wings. After the clumsy bear passed, Daniel saw a leopard with four heads and four wings (Dan. 7:6). A leopard is a swift animal, and the leopard with wings meant that it would conquer the whole world with lightning swiftness. This was a reference to Greece under Alexander the Great.

The four heads of the leopard signified Alexander's four generals. After his death, the empire was divided among those generals. The four parts were Thrace, Macedonia, Syria, and Egypt.

An exceedingly strong beast. The fourth beast Daniel saw was dreadful and exceedingly strong, with great iron teeth. Remember, it devoured and broke into pieces, and "trampled down the remainder with its feet" (Dan. 7:7). This beast represented the Roman empire. By 30 B.C. Rome subdued Thrace, Macedonia, Syria, and Egypt, bringing all of civilized Europe under its control. It was the most extensive empire in world history.

This beast had ten horns, which correspond to the ten toes of the image in Nebuchadnezzar's dream. As Daniel was looking, a little horn came up out of the ten horns and plucked three of the first horns by the roots. This little horn signified the Antichrist, who will appear and dictate to the whole world, opposing God and causing pain to the saints for three and one-half years before God destroys him.

THE BEAST JOHN SAW (13:1–2)

As WE NOW compare the image and the beasts in the Book of Daniel with the beast out of the sea in Revelation 13, we will better understand their meaning. John's beast also had ten horns and seven heads, and represented the Antichrist, who will appear in the age of the ten toes at the end of history.

THE TEN HORNS THAT WEAR TEN CROWNS

THE TEN HORNS wearing crowns signify the rulers of the ten nations in Europe. In other words, ten nations in Europe will arise in the former territory of the ancient Roman empire. Watch the political development of Europe closely, keeping in mind a unified Europe is presently growing. A recent count showed there were fifteen participating countries, and things are always changing. But when the Antichrist comes out of the sea, he will lead only ten.

THE SEVEN HEADS

THE BEAST HAD seven heads, and on each of them was a blasphemous name. The seven heads with blasphemous names represent seven kingdoms that oppose God and persecute His people.

The fact that seven heads belong to one body shows us that it is made up of parts of six kingdoms and one present kingdom that opposed God. Revelation 17:10 says there are seven kings; "five have fallen, one is, the other has not yet come." It will be explained further in Revelation 17.

THE CHARACTERISTICS OF THE BEAST

JOHN'S PICTURED BEAST that came out of the sea looked like a mixture of three beasts. First, it was said to be like a leopard, which represents the swiftness of ancient Greece. Second, it had the feet of a bear, which means it will possess a large army like the Medo-Persian empire. Third, it had the mouth of a lion, which means it possesses mighty power like that of ancient Babylon, so as to conquer the whole world.

Altogether, this beast symbolizes revived Rome, the union of ten European countries that will become the strongest nation in human history.

THE DRAGON AND THE ANTICHRIST

VERSE 2 SAYS the dragon gave the beast his power, his throne, and great authority. This is the same dragon that was cast out of heaven after he was defeated in his fight with Michael at the end of the first three and one-half years of the Tribulation. When he comes to earth, he will give his power, his throne, and great authority to the Antichrist, hoping he can win in his stead, much as parents anchor their hopes in their children.

THE REVIVAL OF THE HEAD FATALLY WOUNDED (13:3–4)

JOHN ALSO SHOWS that one of the beast's heads is fatally wounded, a prediction that the Antichrist will be killed. Imagine the Antichrist being stabbed to death by a terrorist. As preparations are made for his funeral, suddenly his deadly wound is healed miraculously! He is revived by the power of the devil.

The whole world wonders at such a miracle. The news media around the world had reported the death of the head of the state of united Europe, and the date of his funeral was set. But then all the media suddenly report he has been revived. Wouldn't people be amazed?

Suppose that John F. Kennedy, after he was reported to have died, had been revived. The journalists of the world would have talked about it for weeks, and people all over the world would have admired him, thinking him an extraordinary person.

Besides wondering at the resuscitation of the Antichrist, people everywhere will worship him and the dragon. Pooling their strength, the dragon and the beast will mobilize enormous political, economic, and military power. People will say, "Who is like to the beast, and who is able to wage war with him?" (v. 4).

Since the dragon is Satan, the beast will probably make an insignia of a dragon. Dragons represent evil in the West, but in the East they are revered and worshiped.

Koreans and Chinese call a throne the seat of a dragon; the face of a king, the face of a dragon; and if anyone sees a dragon in his dream, the interpretation is that the person will have a lucky day. (For many years in the Orient, the devil had the stage all to himself because the region had been outside the influence of Christianity.)

People will probably be compelled by the Antichrist to make insignias of the dragon for the purpose of dragon worship. The world will soon be covered with portraits of dragons everywhere: the flag of the dragon, the insignia of the dragon, and the statue of the dragon. Afterward the Antichrist will also be worshiped.

OUTRAGE OF THE BEAST (13:5–10)

THE ANTICHRIST WILL trample the world, wielding great power for the second half of the Tribulation (v. 5). Not knowing his true status, however, he will be proud and utter blasphemy, publicly denouncing heaven and those who are there (v. 6). When he delivers an address over the radio, or when he has a press conference, he will always begin by saying blasphemous words or denouncing the saints in heaven.

Furthermore, he will war against Jewish Christians for forty-two months, ordering them to be killed wherever they are found. But they will be hiding during that time in the fortress of Petra.

Everyone whose name is not written in the Lamb's Book of Life will bow down to the beast, regardless of age, sex, possession, and rank (v. 8). So verse 10 says that the patience and faith of the saints are needed to the end.

John encourages us, however, with the prophecy that "if any one is destined for captivity, to captivity he goes" (v. 10). The Antichrist will go into captivity himself, and with the sword with which many Jews were killed, he also will be killed. Knowing this, we should persevere to the end.

THE OTHER BEAST WHICH CAME OUT OF THE EARTH (13:11–18)

IN VERSE 11 John "saw another beast coming up out of the earth; and he had two horns like a lamb, and he spoke as a dragon."

Notice that this false prophet will mimic Jesus the Lamb. He, however, has only two horns, whereas Jesus has seven. And whereas the Holy Spirit preaches Jesus Christ with all His might, doing honor to Him, the false prophet will try desperately to do honor to the Antichrist.

Further, the false prophet will exercise the power of the Antichrist and publicize his name (v. 12). The Holy Spirit is entrusted with authority given by Jesus Christ and acts in His name. The false prophet makes the earth and its inhabitants worship the Antichrist. The Holy Spirit leads us to worship Jesus Christ. The false prophet will also do great wonders before the Antichrist and all the people:

> And he performs great signs, so that he even makes fire come down
> out of heaven to the earth in the presence of men. And he deceives
> those who dwell on the earth because of the signs which it was given
> him to perform in the presence of the beast, telling those who dwell
> on the earth to make an image to the beast who had the wound of the
> sword and has come to life.
>
> —REVELATION 13:13–14

The false prophet will have the people make an idol of the Antichrist and give life to it so it can speak (v. 15). From a scientific standpoint, this is now easy to do, since electronic devices could be installed to make the image appear to speak. However, the idol not only gained speech, but it seemed to John as though life had been given to it.

The false prophet then makes everyone worship the idol; those who do not are killed. It is a ghastly thought.

As the 144,000 preachers of God were sealed on their foreheads, so the false prophet next causes all the people who are under the reign of the Antichrist to receive a mark on their right hand or forehead. He forbids those without this mark to engage in any kind of commercial activities. In other words, they starve to death because they can't make a living or buy food (vv. 16–17).

In verse 18 the name of the Antichrist is represented by a number, which is 666. This is a satanic number: The number of the dragon is six, the number of the Antichrist is six, and the number of the false prophet is also six. Hence, it represents the evil trinity of wickedness.

The triune God could be represented by the number 777, since seven is the biblical number of completion or perfection.

Thus, those evil ones parody the divine trinity of God. The dragon corresponds to the Father; the Antichrist corresponds to the Son; and the false prophet corresponds to the Holy Spirit. As God the Father gives all His power to Jesus, and the Holy Spirit does honor to Jesus, so the dragon gives all his power to the Antichrist, and the false prophet does honor to him.

PARENTHETICAL PROPHECY (14:1–20)

AS A PARENTHETICAL prophecy, Revelation 14 shows things that will happen during the second half of the Tribulation. A more detailed interpretation will follow in chapter 15.

144,000 AFTER THE FIRST THREE AND ONE-HALF YEARS (14:1–5)

SINCE THE BEGINNING of the second three and one-half years, we have seen no more mention of the 144,000 Jewish preachers who propagated the gospel during the first part of the Tribulation. Now we find them on Mount Zion in heaven, singing a new song no one else could learn (vv. 1, 3).

Why could nobody else learn this song? Because those particular evangelists have endured and overcome the severe trials of the first half of the Tribulation, while those who have not cannot sing the new song.

Verse 4 says they were not defiled with women, which means they did not bow down to the idols. It is spiritual fornication to love the world and worship idols. The verse also says they are chaste, and the Greek word used means "celibate." Hence, the 144,000 are all married faithfully to the Lamb, and they totally obey His guidance. They are the first fruits of the Jews in the Tribulation.

THE ANGEL'S PROCLAMATION OF THE GOSPEL (14:6–7)

JOHN NEXT SAW an angel's proclamation of the gospel. Preaching the gospel is not usually a task assigned to angels. The angel who appeared to Cornelius, for example, did not preach the gospel himself but told Cornelius to call Peter and hear it from him (Acts 10:1–8).

The angel's message was a mixture of hope and warning: "Fear God, and give Him glory, because the hour of His judgment has come; and worship Him who made heaven and the earth and sea and springs of waters" (v. 7).

God was giving those left on earth another chance to respond to the preaching of the gospel from Moses, Elijah, and 144,000 preachers.

THE FALLING DOWN OF BABYLON THE GREAT (14:8)

FOLLOWING THE FIRST angel's preaching of the eternal gospel, the second angel predicted that Babylon the great, which has always rebelled against God, would fall.

Though it is not certain where the Antichrist will make the capital of his kingdom, the city he chooses will become the central city in the world. It is foretold, however, that God will destroy it during the second half of the Tribulation.

Thus, Revelation 14 is a parenthetical prophecy and will begin to be fulfilled in chapter 15.

THE WARNING OF THE THIRD ANGEL (14:9–11)

THE THIRD ANGEL followed and said, "If any one worships the beast and his image, and receives a mark on his forehead or upon his hand . . . he will be tormented with fire and brimstone in the presence of the holy angels and in the presence of the Lamb" (vv. 9–10). The most dreadful judgment is to be cast into the lake burning with fire and brimstone. However, those who do not believe in Jesus now die and go to hell, which is different from the lake of fire and brimstone.

Hell is the place where souls apart from Christ gather together after the death of the body. It is a place of torment. Luke 16 tells us of the rich man who went to hell and saw Lazarus, who was in the bosom of Abraham. The rich man appeals to Abraham to send Lazarus with a bit of water to cool his tongue. If hell is so painful, how great must be the pain when one is later cast into the lake burning with fire and brimstone!

Those who worship the beast and his image and receive his mark in their forehead or hand will be cast into this lake. The word is *Gehenna* in the Greek; it was called the "Valley of the Children of Hinnom" in the Old Testament. This valley was a common dump where all the trash of Jerusalem was burned. At that time human beings will be piled up and burned in the spiritual Gehenna—those who worshiped the beast and his image and had his number on their foreheads or hands.

Jehovah's Witnesses argue that when people die, their souls also die with them. However, verse 11 says that the souls cast into the lake burning with fire and brimstone will be eternally tormented, and the smoke will ascend forever and ever.

People doubt whether there are really such places as heaven and hell. But the Bible clearly states these places exist. All the prophecies of the Bible are being fulfilled. Why, then, would this scripture not be fulfilled? That's why Jesus commented on the soul of the man who betrayed him, "It would have been good for that man if he had not been born" (Matt. 26:24). Jesus knew where that soul would go, and what He said about Judas is just as true for all those who refuse to believe in Him.

THE VOICE IN HEAVEN (14:13)

NEXT JOHN HEARD a voice from heaven saying to him, "Blessed are the dead who die in the Lord from now on!" Then the Holy Spirit confirmed and guaranteed that voice: "Yes, . . . that they may rest from their labors, for their deeds follow with them." Those who belatedly believe in Jesus Christ will all die as martyrs at the hands of the Antichrist. Even the two witnesses die that way. During that time it will be more blessed to take rest

before God and be recognized with the merit of martyrdom than to live—
only to be cast eventually into the lake burning with fire and brimstone.

TWO HARVESTS (14:14–20)

THE FIRST HARVEST

NEXT COME TWO harvests. Verse 14 says a man like the Son of man was
sitting on a white cloud with a golden crown on His head and a sharp
sickle in His hand, and He was reaping. That One is Jesus Christ. During
the second half of the Tribulation Jesus will reap the remaining martyrs.
From then on, no one will be saved. Later we will see those martyrs being
harvested and coming to heaven.

THE SECOND HARVEST

THEN THE SECOND harvest begins. This is the last judgment, which reaps
unbelievers. It is followed by the war of Armageddon, which will be dealt
with in detail in a later chapter. You need to know for now, though, that
the war of Armageddon is a war between the saints of Jesus Christ and
the armies of the earth. When the second three and one-half years begin,
the Antichrist and the people in the world know that the saints will
descend from the air to destroy them. They have already seen the 144,000
preachers and the two witnesses taken away alive into heaven.

The Antichrist, with all the armies of Europe under his command, plus
the eastern kings and their armies, will come to Armageddon to fight
against Jesus and His hosts. At that time Jesus will tread down the winepress. The number of people killed will be so great that blood will reach
up to the bridles of the horses (v. 20). We can easily imagine that John
must have seen a nuclear war. Hail and rain fell down heavily. Many
people were killed—so many, in fact, that their blood, mixed with the
rain, was spread over a distance of sixteen hundred stadia, or about one
hundred eighty miles.

THE PLAGUES AND THE JUDGMENT (15:1–16:21)

THE LAST PLAGUE (15:1)

> And I saw another sign in heaven, great and marvelous, seven angels

> who had seven plagues, which are the last, because in them the
> wrath of God is finished.
>
> —REVELATION 15:1

Things prophesied parenthetically in Revelation 14 are fulfilled exactly in Revelation 15 and 16. These last plagues appear in the form of the judgment of seven bowls and are the final judgment.

THOSE STANDING BESIDE THE SEA OF GLASS (15:2–4)

JUST BEFORE THE final judgment starts, John sees a group of people standing on the sea of glass mingled with fire. These are the people gathered in the final harvest by Jesus. They don't stand *within* the sea but outside of it, for they have come out of that sea. It represents the world that is now calm; the world that had only a short time before sustained severe trials.

These people are the martyrs who were naked and starving who suffered a miserable death because they did not worship the beast and his image. The song those people sing will be "the song of Moses the bondservant of God and the song of the Lamb" (v. 3). It's the same song the Israelites sang when they saw Pharaoh's army being engulfed by the Red Sea. After their song, only dreadful judgment remains.

THE JUDGMENT OF SEVEN BOWLS BY THE SEVEN ANGELS (15:5–16:21)

NEXT, SEVEN ANGELS received seven bowls containing seven plagues; and they came out of the temple to pour them out. From Revelation 16–18, only grim judgments are seen. The people who are judged here will be those left after God reaps every one who can be saved.

THE PLAGUE OF THE FIRST BOWL (16:2)

THE FIRST ANGEL went and poured his bowl on the earth; strong-smelling sores came upon the bodies of those who bore the mark of the beast. Since anyone without that mark could not sell or buy anything, most people had received it. These individuals suffer intolerable pain because of the sores.

A certain skin disease was prevalent just after the liberation of Korea. I had it too, and I applied quicksilver mixed with sulfur all over my body. I still remember the acute pain that made me jump up and down in the room. However, the sores from the plague of the first bowl will be far more painful.

THE SECOND BOWL (16:3)

WHEN THE SECOND angel poured out his bowl on the sea, it became like the blood of a dead man, killing every living thing in the sea. That reminds us of the miracle Moses performed, turning the water of the Nile River into blood according to the command of God (Exod. 7:20–25).

THE THIRD BOWL (16:4–7)

THE THIRD ANGEL poured his bowl upon the rivers and the fountains of waters, and they also became blood. The people will have no drinkable water, so they will suffer from thirst. Then the angel of the waters praised God: "Righteous art Thou, who art and who wast, O Holy One, because Thou didst judge these things; for they poured out the blood of saints and prophets, and Thou hast given them blood to drink. They deserve it" (vv. 5–6).

Then another voice came out of the altar and responded, "Yes, O Lord God, the Almighty, true and righteous are Thy judgments" (v. 7). His judgments really are fair. He is the righteous judge who redresses our grievances.

THE FOURTH BOWL (16:8–9)

WHEN THE FOURTH angel poured his bowl upon the sun, the heat of the sun increased greatly, killing innumerable people. Even now, in a country like India, the sudden assault of brutal heat brings death to many people.

Notice that even though people are scorched to death by this judgment's murderous heat, the survivors still do not repent. Their hearts are hardened to the end. Accordingly, they murmur and blaspheme God.

THE FIFTH BOWL (16:10–11)

THE FIFTH BOWL was poured upon the throne of the beast, the Antichrist, filling his kingdom with darkness. "To be brightened" stands for hope, but "to be darkened" stands for the decline of the kingdom and its power. As a consequence, chaos will arise and the people will be panic-stricken. And although they gnash their teeth and bite their tongues due to extreme pain, they still will not repent of their sins. Instead, they continue to blaspheme God.

THE SIXTH BOWL (16:12–16)

WHEN THE SIXTH angel poured his bowl upon the great Euphrates River, its water dried up in order to make a way for the kings of the East to advance to the west.

As you have read previously, the Orient's army of two hundred million will be watching for an opportunity to invade the West so it can attack the Antichrist. Then the kingdom of the Antichrist will suddenly begin to decline and slip into confusion. The political, economic, and military power the Antichrist will have exerted will be weakened, the balance of power broken, and the army of the East will invade, having the upper hand.

At that time, "I saw coming out of the mouth of the dragon and out of the mouth of the beast and out of the mouth of the false prophet, three unclean spirits like frogs" (v. 13). They go forth to the kings of the West and their kingdoms and seduce them to form an alliance against the Oriental invasion. Then the allied forces will come to a place called Armageddon. The two enormous armies, totaling as many as three hundred million soldiers equipped with ultra-modern weapons, will gather together for a showdown.

Armageddon is the present plain called Megiddo. The last time I visited Israel, I learned that Armageddon is very similar to Kim-hae Plain in Korea—both are surrounded by mountains and located at a strategic transportation center. To the north it leads to Syria and Asia; to the south it leads to Egypt and the rest of Africa.

When a great massacre breaks out on this plain, Jesus Christ will descend, accompanied by His saints. At that point, the armies will cease fighting each other and unite in a struggle against Jesus and His hosts, but they will finally suffer defeat (Rev. 19).

Verse 15 gives a clear warning about Jesus' coming to the battlefield of Armageddon. "I am coming like a thief. Blessed is the one who stays awake and keeps his garments, lest he walk about naked and men see his shame."

THE SEVENTH BOWL (16:17–21)

WHEN THE SEVENTH angel poured his bowl into the air, a great voice sounded from the throne of heaven saying, "It is done." Voices, thunderings, and lightnings filled the air, and the greatest earthquake in history divided Jerusalem into three parts. High mountains were brought low, and deep valleys were filled. Jerusalem was being made fit to be ruled by Jesus Christ, the King of kings and Lord of lords.

Cities all over the earth will be shaken by the earthquake; the configuration of the earth's surface will undergo severe changes, causing calamities everywhere. Among them, the severest judgment will come upon great Babylon, because God will completely destroy that wicked city where the Antichrist rules.

THE RELIGION OF THE GREAT WHORE (17:1–18)

THE NATURAL CALAMITIES end in Revelation 16. But here in chapter 17, the religion of the great whore comes under judgment.

During the Great Tribulation the Antichrist will unite the religions of the world into one. Even today the movement to unite Christianity with other religions is briskly underway. The Antichrist will take advantage of this accommodation to consolidate his foundation for the first three and one-half years. At the beginning of the second part of the Tribulation, however, he will persecute this religious unity and crush it to pieces. Revelation 17 tells how he will set up his own idol and exterminate other religions.

THE JUDGMENT OF THE GREAT WHORE (17:1–2)

IN REVELATION 17 the judgment of the great whore, signifying religion, begins. The Bible calls corrupted religion spiritual adultery (James 4:4). So the great whore represents a depraved and corrupt religion that, like an adulterous bride, follows the idol and the devils, turning away from God. This great whore forms a huge religious body. Taking advantage of its vast organization, she not only worships the Antichrist but also uses him. In turn, the Antichrist politically uses the great whore.

This great whore sits upon many waters. As previously explained, water symbolizes the crowd in every nation, tongue, and people. The great whore already has her roots in the whole of mankind. The religions that do not serve God, including Islam, Buddhism, and Taoism, are the adulteresses.

Verse 2 says this great whore has committed fornication with the kings and inhabitants of the earth. Throughout history, in spite of the modern assertion that politics and religion should be separate, they have actually taken advantage of each other.

In Korean history, for instance, throughout the era of the Three Kingdoms and the Koryo dynasty, Buddhism served as the state religion. During the Yi dynasty, Confucianism was the guiding spirit. And in European history Christianity has been and continues to be the political prop.

History tells us a wholesome religion enlivens a nation as well as an individual. Unwholesome religion, on the other hand, brings misery to the lives of both individuals and the state by stealing away their hearts from God and corrupting them.

A WOMAN SITTING UPON A SCARLET-COLORED BEAST (17:3–18)

THE KINGDOM OF THE WORLD

THE SCARLET BEAST of verse 3, with its seven heads and ten horns, is the Antichrist. The seven heads represent the seven kingdoms and their kings that continuously oppose God. The ten horns represent the ten countries that will ultimately form the union of Europe.

As mentioned earlier, some fifteen European countries are currently making plans to form this union. But when the Antichrist comes into the fullness of his power, there will be only ten.

The great whore sits upon the Antichrist during the Tribulation. This means she will achieve religious unification by using the Antichrist politically.

THE FIGURE OF THE GREAT WHORE

SHE IS SAID to be "clothed in purple and scarlet, and adorned with gold and precious stones" (v. 4). This signifies her great pomp. The golden cup in her hand is a religious cup full of abominations and the filthiness of her fornication. Those who drink from her cup become full of evil spirits. Upon the forehead of the whore was written, "Babylon the Great, the mother of harlots and of the abominations of the earth" (v. 5). She is called "Babylon the Great" because she is the religion started in Babylon,

201

as we saw in Christ's letter to the Pergamum church in Revelation 2.

Every corrupt religion in the world today has been influenced by the Babylonian religion. Even within Christendom, bodies of the old and new church are trying to form an ecumenical council with other religions—not to mention the Christian denominations violating the orthodox faith of the Bible. In this move toward consensus, all the religions of the world are being gradually united. At the beginning of the Tribulation, backed by the power of the Antichrist, union will be achieved quickly. This is the true character of the great whore.

What you must know for certain is that at the end of the world Christendom will be distinctly divided into two groups: One will be the church united politically and institutionally, and the other will be the church united by the Holy Spirit. Churches that genuinely love Jesus will come together, rising above denominations. Christian organizations that follow the trend of modernism and the new theology will be united according to their political concern, advocating social reform.

Denomination has no meaning before God. What matters is whether a church receives the Holy Spirit at its center and surrenders itself to Him.

THE BEHAVIOR OF THE WOMAN

THIS WOMAN IS said to be "drunk with the blood of the saints, and with the blood of the witnesses of Jesus" (v. 6). Her corrupt religion, backed by the power of the Antichrist, will be the first to kill those who have been converted by the evangelization of the 144,000 and the testimony of the two witnesses.

THE MYSTERY OF THE BEAST

AS PREVIOUSLY MENTIONED, the beast of this passage is the Antichrist. It will come out of the bottomless pit. Theologians speculate about him in several ways. But, his identity has not yet been disclosed. One thing is clear: God will one day release him, a spiritual being, out of hell and cause him to be born into this world as a human being, imitating Jesus by putting on flesh.

My belief is that the Antichrist is already in the world. Before long he will emerge and become a conspicuous figure in the political world. Although his appearance on stage is now suppressed by the power of the Holy Spirit, he will be revealed as soon as the church is taken up into heaven.

Verse 9 says the seven heads of the Antichrist are seven mountains. Seven hills always refer to Rome, for Rome was built on seven hills. So, some people speculate that Rome will be the headquarters from which the Antichrist will rule the world. Verse 10 also says that among the seven heads, or kings, "five have fallen, one is, the other has not yet come." The five kingdoms—Assyria, Babylon, Egypt, Medo-Persia, and Greece—have already fallen. One is, which was Rome—the kingdom existing in the time of John—and the seventh kingdom is yet to come. According to the passage, when this kingdom comes, it will continue for only a brief time. Then the kingdom of the Antichrist will come as the eighth (v. 11).

The seventh kingdom will be the union of the ten European countries that will arise in the former territory of ancient Rome. For the first three and one-half years of the Tribulation, united Europe will keep coalition with the Antichrist through compromise. When that period ends, the eighth kingdom, ruled by the Antichrist, will emerge out of the seventh. He will be supported by three of the ten nations, and the remaining seven will be subdued by his autocratic rule.

Verses 12–14 further say that the ten horns are ten kings and that these kings will give their power and strength to the beast. He, in turn, will oppose the Lamb—the King of kings and the Lord of lords—at the battle of Armageddon, but will eventually be destroyed.

The fate of the great whore sitting on the beast is tragic. This religious organization will get along well with the Antichrist, as they take advantage of each other for three and one-half years. But as soon as the second half of the Tribulation begins the whore will be forsaken. The Antichrist will set up his kingdom and deify himself, erecting his own idol and quickly getting rid of her. In this way religious Babylon falls.

BABYLON THE GREAT (18:1–24)

REVELATION 17 SHOWS the downfall of the great whore, religious Babylon. Now Revelation 18 declares the fall of political and economic Babylon. In other words, the Bible shows here the miserable destruction of the Antichrist.

THE FALL OF BABYLON THE GREAT (18:1–2)

POLITICAL AND ECONOMIC Babylon, the city where the Antichrist has wielded power for the second half of the Tribulation, is now destroyed. It crumbles not only by an earthquake and judgment, but also by nuclear weapons launched by the army from the East. These weapons will blow the city to pieces.

Babylon the great is the place that always rejects God. It opposes Him not only spiritually but also politically and economically.

THE SITUATION OF BABYLON THE GREAT (18:2–3)

VERSE 2 ALSO says that Babylon the great has become "a dwelling place of demons and a prison of every unclean spirit, and a prison of every unclean and hateful bird." As the capital of Satan's Antichrist, it attracts every fallen angel and unclean spirit. They will make it an evil and degenerate city, worse than Sodom and Gomorrah. Every nation will have betrayed God and knelt down to Satan; none can survive if it provokes the Antichrist. He will possess unprecedented economic power (v. 3).

THE WARNING OF GOD (18:4–7)

"AND I HEARD another voice from heaven, saying, 'Come out of her, my people, that you may not participate in her sins and that you may not receive of her plagues'" (v. 4). Thus begins a warning of God to His people against being engulfed in the judgment coming to those who partake of the ungodly assembly of politics and business.

THE JUDGMENT AGAINST BABYLON THE GREAT (18:8–24)

THE BIBLE TELLS in detail the judgment that will come upon Babylon the great: "For this reason in one day her plagues will come, pestilence and mourning and famine, and she will be burned up with fire; for the Lord God who judges her is strong" (v. 8).

In a single day the capital of the Antichrist's kingdom will be burned to ashes by a great explosion. Nothing other than nuclear arms can accomplish that. I believe the two hundred million-strong army coming from China will pound this capital with nuclear missiles launched from both the air and the earth. Mushroom clouds ascending from the site will be seen far and wide by sailors upon the sea (vv. 17–19).

Observing the calamity, the other kings who have been on friendly terms with the Antichrist will then mourn for him. The merchants who have traded in this capital will also weep and mourn over him (vv. 9–11).

Holy apostles and prophets in heaven, on the other hand, are told to rejoice over Babylon's destruction, for God has avenged those who were robbed and killed (v. 20).

"And a strong angel took up a stone like a great millstone and threw it into the sea, saying, 'Thus will Babylon, the great city, be thrown down with violence, and will not be found any longer'" (v. 21). The kingdom of the Antichrist will be so completely ruined that it will have no strength left to rise again.

So far we've seen judgments that have fallen upon the world of nature, against the Antichrist, and against corrupt religion and government. In Revelation 19 we will see Jesus Christ holding the marriage supper of the Lamb before coming down to Armageddon, accompanied by His bride.

JESUS' COMING DOWN TO THE EARTH (19:1–21)

PRAISE IN HEAVEN (19:1–5)

REVELATION 19 BEGINS with a great voice of many people in heaven praising God for judging religious and political Babylon, and rejoicing over the political downfall of the Antichrist.

With the second "Hallelujah," smoke rose up forever and ever (v. 3). It is the smoke of judgment. That means God has cast the Antichrist and his followers into the lake burning with fire and brimstone.

Then the twenty-four elders and four living creatures fell down and worshiped God, saying, "Amen. Hallelujah!" The word *hallelujah* is frequently used among people who have received the Holy Spirit. If you say it to those who have not received the Holy Spirit, they will be perplexed. But to those who have received the Holy Spirit, "Hallelujah, amen!" is our greeting both now and after we go to heaven.

Next, a voice came out of the throne saying, "Give praise to our God, all you His bond-servants, you who fear Him, the small and the great" (v. 5). Praise is the fruit God has put on our lips. Many people come to me complaining, "I don't know how to pray. I have nothing to pray for. Even though I kneel down to pray all through the night, I don't know what to pray for."

I always give them the same answer: "Why don't you sing praises then?" The sacrifice of praise becomes the prayer of great glory.

THE ANNOUNCEMENT OF THE MARRIAGE SUPPER OF THE LAMB (19:6–8)

ANOTHER VOICE, LIKE the sound of many waters and the voice of mighty thunder, announces that the world that will be ruled by God is at hand. The beautiful time will soon come when all opposition to God is crushed, Satan is put into custody, and the whole universe rejoices under the sovereign rule of God. Accepting that through faith, all the saints announce and celebrate the reigning of God.

At the end of the Tribulation the marriage supper of the Lamb is held. We have been engaged to Jesus a long time. Even though we haven't actually met our Bridegroom, Jesus has already made us to sit as His bride. And at some day set aside by God, Jesus will come and lead us into the marriage supper.

> For the Lord Himself will descend from heaven with a shout, with the voice of the archangel, and with the trumpet of God; and the dead in Christ shall rise first. Then we who are alive and remain shall be caught up together with them in the clouds to meet the Lord in the air, and thus we shall always be with the Lord.
> —1 THESSALONIANS 4:16–17

After we are taken up into heaven, we will receive our reward. Today we receive salvation freely by the power of the precious blood Jesus shed for us. But in that day we will receive the white linen clothes of Revelation 19:8 as a reward for our behavior here on earth. When crowns are given, some will receive an unwithering crown, others a crown of glory, still others a crown of righteousness, and others a crown of life. Some will receive a crown of joy with gladness and decorate themselves with it. This will take place seven years after the Rapture, when we join our Bridegroom at the marriage supper.

THOSE WHO ARE CALLED TO THE MARRIAGE SUPPER (19:9)

VERSE 9 SAYS that those who are called to the marriage supper are blessed. And if they're blessed, how much more blessed will be those who have become the bride! Who are those called to the marriage supper? The church is the bride of Jesus Christ. After Jesus was resurrected from death, the Holy Spirit descended and established the church; the church, sanctified by the blood of Jesus Christ, was then taken up into heaven before the Tribulation began. Therefore, the church is qualified to be the bride—no one else. All who were not caught up into heaven with the church are those who are invited to rejoice with the bride at the marriage supper.

The first group of these are the friends of the Bridegroom. In the Old Testament God called Abraham His friend. John the Baptist was the last of the prophets who came in the spirit of the Old Testament, and he said, "He who has the bride is the bridegroom; but the friend of the bridegroom, who stands and hears him, rejoices greatly because of the bridegroom's voice. And so this joy of mine has been made full" (John 3:29). Therefore, the Old Testament saints are not the bride, but friends of the Bridegroom. The next group of guests are those who are saved after the church has been taken up into heaven. These have died as martyrs during the Tribulation; after going through the sea of glass mingled with fire, they will attend the marriage supper as the bridesmaids.

THE GREAT EXCITEMENT OF JOHN (19:10)

When John saw this scene, he was so overwhelmed by emotion that he tried to worship the angel who had spoken. Of course, John knew well the commandment that we should worship only God. Nevertheless, he was so excited by the news the angel had brought that he tried to worship him. But the angel restrained him saying, "Do not do that . . . worship God."

DESCENDING OF JESUS TO THE EARTH (19:11–16)

AFTER THE MARRIAGE supper, the church, which has become the bride of Jesus, accompanies Him when He comes down to the earth.

A MAN WHO SITS UPON A WHITE HORSE

JOHN SAW HEAVEN open followed by a man riding upon a white horse. This was Jesus Christ. In Revelation 6 the Antichrist imitated the figure of Jesus, but this is the real Christ. He is called "Faithful and True," since He was faithful to God unto death, and all His words are true (v. 11).

Besides, "in righteousness He judges and wages war." When Jesus comes down to this earth again, He will wipe out all evil. His eyes will see everything, and since He is the King of kings and Lord of lords, He will wear many crowns (v. 12). Further, "He has a name written upon Him which no one knows, except Himself. And He is clothed with a robe dipped in blood" (vv. 12–13). Since the name is secret, we don't know it. The vesture dipped in blood refers to the same precious blood Jesus shed to save mankind.

THE COMING DOWN OF THE HEAVENLY HOST

VERSE 14 TELLS us that "the armies which are in heaven, clothed in fine linen, white and clean, were following Him on white horses." These people following the Bridegroom are the bride. When Jesus shouts while coming down from heaven with words like a sharp sword, His enemies will fall as leaves in the autumn. The Lord will also smite all the nations of the Antichrist with a rod of iron and tread the winepress of the fierceness and wrath of almighty God against those who followed the devil in rebellion (v. 15). This battle of Armageddon becomes the last war of mankind.

THE WAR AT ARMAGEDDON (19:17–21)

VERSES 17 AND 18 tell about the things that will happen at Armageddon. This is how I believe it will take place. The army advancing from the East is two hundred million strong, and the opposing army of the Antichrist will probably not be less than one hundred million. While they advance against Jerusalem, Jesus descends to the earth. The earthly forces quickly stop fighting each other and are allied under the leadership of the Antichrist to resist the heavenly host (v. 19). However, Jesus will annihilate all the earthly forces. Therefore the angel beckoned the birds of the air to come and eat the flesh of the slain (vv. 17–18).

At the same time, the false prophet who had lured people to worship the beast will also be taken, along with the Antichrist, and both will be cast into the lake of fire burning with sulfur (v. 20).

From one end of the earth to the other, when the word of Jesus Christ goes out of His mouth, those who received the mark of the beast on their forehead or hand will all die. As Ananias and Sapphira died immediately by Peter's pronouncement of judgment against them (Acts 5:1–11), so shall all those people with the mark of the beast be killed (v. 21).

Besides the Jews who escape to the desert, only a handful of Gentiles will survive. These are people who live outside the domain of the Antichrist. Since they are self-sufficient, like farmers, they will not have needed to receive the mark of the beast. As the rule of the Antichrist will concentrate on Europe, the poor people living on other continents will probably belong to this group. The God-rejecting rich and business-class people, however, will have received the mark for the sake of their businesses, and they will be killed.

This handful of Gentiles, along with the Jews who survive the Tribulation, will enter the millennial kingdom, but there will also be distinction there.

19

The Millennial Kingdom
and the Great Judgment

THE IMPRISONMENT OF SATAN
(20:1–3)

A T THE BATTLE of Armegeddon, the Antichrist and the false prophet were cast into the lake of fire. The same fate will eventually be given to the old serpent that enticed the world—the dragon called the devil and Satan. First, though, John saw "an angel coming down from heaven, having the key of the abyss and a great chain in his hand. And he laid hold of the dragon" (vv. 1–2). Then he threw this dragon into the bottomless pit. But Satan is not yet cast into the lake burning with fire, for there is still one more thing left for him to do: He must be released. The dragon is bound in the pit for one thousand years, but then he is loosed again for a short time.

During this millennium the earth is once again populated with people. They neither commit any sin nor are afflicted with any illness, as they are not tempted by Satan or under his influence. They flourish and fill the face of the whole earth.

Therefore these people who will have lived in a world free from the influence of Satan will need to decide for themselves whether they truly

211

love God. To test them, Satan is released from the bottomless pit for a little while. This testing will be no worse than what has already been experienced by many of God's saints.

THE THRONES OF JUDGMENT AND THE FIRST RESURRECTION (20:4–6)

THE THRONES OF JUDGMENT

JOHN NEXT SAW thrones that gave judgment to the people before they entered the millennial kingdom. Why should it be "thrones" instead of "a throne?" Because Jesus does not give judgment alone; His bride, the church, will sit with Him and judge. Hallelujah! This is what is meant by the words, "They . . . reigned with Christ for a thousand years" (v. 4).

How will those thrones give judgment? As we have already seen, the people who were sealed by the Antichrist were all killed, but those who were not sealed by him and the remaining Jews will enter the millennial kingdom. Out of those God will separate the sheep from the goats as Jesus said in Matthew 25. The standard by which the two will be separated is how they treated Jesus Christ:

> But when the Son of Man comes in His glory, and all the angels with Him, then He will sit on His glorious throne. And all the nations will be gathered before Him; and He will separate them from one another, as the shepherd separates the sheep from the goats; and He will put the sheep on His right, and the goats on the left. Then the King will say to those on His right, "Come, you who are blessed of My Father, inherit the kingdom prepared for you from the foundation of the world. For I was hungry and you gave Me something to eat; I was thirsty, and you gave Me drink; I was a stranger, and you invited Me in; naked, and you clothed Me; I was sick, and you visited Me; I was in prison, and you came to Me. . . ." Then He will also say to those on His left, "Depart from Me, accursed ones, into the eternal fire which has been prepared for the devil and his angels; for I was hungry, and you gave Me nothing to eat; I was thirsty, and you gave Me nothing to drink; I was a stranger, and you did not invite Me in; naked, and you did not clothe Me; sick, and in prison, and you did not visit Me."
>
> —MATTHEW 25:31–36, 41–43

The sheep on the right side of Jesus will be the people who, though they did not believe in Him, nonetheless treated Christians well by taking care of their needs. The goats, however, will be punished, for they did not accept Christians in the name of Christ.

THE FIRST RESURRECTION

AT THIS FIRST resurrection (v. 5), those who died during the Tribulation rise first. Those who partake in this resurrection are blessed, for they will not enter the second death. The first death is the death of the body, and the second is the death of the soul, which means that one is forsaken by God and dies forever.

Those who participate in the first resurrection, however, are received by God and will reign with Christ for one thousand years. How blessed those people will be!

The rest of the dead do not come to life until the thousand years are ended. All the sinners since the beginning of the world will remain in hell; they will not enter the millennial kingdom. After Jesus' reign of one thousand years has ended, those unbelievers will come to life again and be judged. Then they will be cast forever into the lake of fire.

Therefore the resurrection of sinners becomes a resurrection to judgment and destruction. But the resurrection of those who have participated in the first resurrection is a rising to eternal life.

SATAN IS LOOSED OUT OF HIS PRISON (20:7–10)

AT THE CONCLUSION of the millennium, God will release Satan from the bottomless pit. This gives Satan a free hand to go about the world and entice people as he once did. Realizing this is his last chance, he will gather his people to oppose God. "Gog and Magog" refer to the people who oppose God (v. 8).

Among the people who follow Satan will be those who have enjoyed the reign of Jesus and His saints for one thousand years. Nevertheless, when they are exposed to the temptation of the devil, they will sympathize with him and follow him. They baffle me. Verse 8 says the number of those who follow the devil is like the sand of the sea. Therefore, even out of this group, God will select His people through a test.

As a thief turns on his master with a club, so the people following Satan will come to besiege the holy city of Jerusalem, where Christ and

His saints dwell. At this time, the world will be sharply divided into two groups, those who are inside the city, and those on the outside—wheat and tares—sheep and goats (v. 9).

God will destroy, like tares, those people who are encamped outside the city, and their souls will fall headlong into the lake of unquenchable fire. Moreover, the evil trinity that deceived them—Satan, the Antichrist, and the false prophet—will also fall into the lake of fire, where they will be tormented forever and ever (v. 10).

On the other hand, those who followed Jesus in the millennial kingdom will enter the eternal new heaven and the new earth.

THE JUDGMENT OF THE GREAT WHITE THRONE (20:11–15)

THEN SUDDENLY, THE heaven and the earth disappear (v. 11). Will the earth be gone forever? No. Ecclesiastes 1:4 says, "A generation goes and a generation comes, but the earth remains forever." Therefore it's not that the earth will be gone forever, but that our Lord is going to transform it. The scene of transforming the earth is recorded:

> But the day of the Lord will come like a thief, in which the heavens will pass away with a roar and the elements will be destroyed with intense heat, and the earth and its works will be burned up.
> —2 PETER 3:10

Thus, there will be found no place for the heaven and the earth, and a throne of judgment will be set at a certain place within the universe. This is the white throne, and when the judgment finally begins, all the dead will rise and stand before it. Then the books in which are recorded the deeds of every man and woman will be opened. There will be no hiding at this point.

Verse 12 next says that another book was opened—the Book of Life. Why is the Book of Life needed to judge the dead? Because God is righteous, and after He points out every unrighteous behavior of sinners, He opens the Book of Life and shows them that their names are not recorded. Everyone whose name is not recorded in the Book of Life will fall into the lake of fire without being able to say anything for vindication.

This is the second death—that is, the soul is permanently separated from God and tormented forever. The lake of fire is a place of no hope. Jesus said concerning it, "Where their worm does not die, and the fire is not quenched. For everyone will be salted with fire" (Mark 9:48–49).

Those drunken and wanton people who are given to all kinds of filthiness and wickedness today will die like withering grass on the day when they hear the shout and trumpet call of the archangel. Their souls will wait in hell, and after they are judged before the great white throne, they will fall into the lake of fire, where they will be tormented forever.

In the Old Testament, the harlot Rahab saved the lives of her parents, brothers, sisters, and relatives by gathering them at her house and warning them not to go out when Jericho fell at the hands of the Israelites (Josh. 6:17–25). How much more should we then make our best efforts to save our loved ones! Our efforts must be extended to include our neighbors as well. The reward for what we have done to save souls will be great, and we shall be happy and joyful in heaven.

20

The New Heaven and the New Earth

THE NEW HEAVEN AND THE NEW EARTH
(21:1)

PEOPLE ALWAYS LIKE new things—new food, new clothes, new furni-
ture, and new experiences. Whenever they can afford it, they look
with eagle eyes for new things.

The heaven we shall enter is new forever. It will be new every morning
that we wake up and get newer day by day. The more we see it, the
fresher it will look to us. That is why its name is the new heaven and the
new earth. Nobody gets old, nor does anyone grow weak. There is
nothing filthy there.

In this world everything gets old, stale, and weak. Human beings also
grow old and feeble. Everything we use gets stained, soiled, and shabby.
But the new heaven and the new earth God gives will be new forever.

Isn't that our wish and hope? Don't we strive every day to live a good
and righteous life since we have received salvation through the precious
blood of Jesus Christ? Isn't that what we seek to obtain while fighting the
good fight and finishing our course, keeping ourselves from the pleasures
and comforts of the world? Praise the Lord! God will grant our wish so

richly that there will not be room enough to receive the blessing. God is faithful, and His Word is true. We cannot imagine what the blessed new heaven and new earth will be like. Our hearts will leap with joy, and we will be spellbound by its splendor. We will sing praises of *hallelujah* forever.

In this new heaven and new earth everyone will retain freshness and youth forever in the presence of the Lord. Now the human body inevitably grows old, but not when the new heaven and new earth come into being.

There is no sea in the new heaven and the new earth (21:1). Why? We sometimes call life the sea of trouble. The sea stands for bitterness and sorrow. But there is no pain of any kind in the new heaven and the new earth.

THE NEW JERUSALEM (21:2–4)

JOHN ALSO SAW descending from heaven the new Jerusalem, the capital of the new heaven and the new earth.

Who will live in the new Jerusalem? The church that is the bride of Jesus Christ will enter it with her Bridegroom and live there forever. The Jews and those who are saved during the millennial kingdom will also live in the new heaven and new earth.

The new Jerusalem is so beautiful it is said to be like a bride adorned for her husband (v. 2). Imagine the beauty of a bride as she appears wearing many precious jewels. In the not-too-distant future we shall enter this amazing city ourselves and live there forever, admiring its beauty. We will worship and praise God forever, He will wipe away all tears from our eyes, and there will be no more death (v. 4).

When I was pioneering my ministry at Pulkwang-dong, a couple from Choongchung Province came to live in the community. The husband was a carpenter. They accepted Jesus and began to attend my church. Unfortunately, however, the carpenter fell ill with stomach cancer and eventually died. Upon hearing news of his death, I rushed to his house and found a shocking scene. The small rented room was packed with children who were utterly destitute. In the midst of extreme poverty, the bread earner had died. The wife, holding the body of her dead husband, was wailing, "Why did you go alone, leaving me behind in this world with all these little children? Why?" The children were also weeping.

Suddenly the husband opened his eyes, seized both of his wife's hands as well as my hands, and said, "Dear, why are you crying? Is this our eternal separation? I will go first and wait for you to come, praying there to Jesus that God will keep you and our children. So do your best in taking care of our children and bringing them up well. Then come to the place where I am."

As soon as he finished speaking those words, he died again. His countenance looked so bright, as if he were leaving his wife at the airport for a trip to the United States. It was not long before the wife stopped crying. From that time on her spirit revived, and she was able to exert all her effort to improve her life and take good care of the children. The result was that she lived a better life than she had when her husband was alive.

That couple could part without much sorrow because they had hope that they would meet again in the kingdom of God. But to those who do not harbor such a hope, death means the end of everything. We who will enter the new Jerusalem will no longer experience death or even sorrow. In that place there will be nothing sad and no more pain, for the former things will pass away, and it will become a completely new world.

THE PROCLAMATION OF GOD (21:5–8)

I ONCE HEARD an extraordinary testimony from Maxine Hurston, the wife of a missionary of our church. She wrote of her experience in a Christian magazine called *The Evangel*. I read her testimony and later even met her. Here is her story:

While kneeling in prayer at the altar of the church one Sunday, Mrs. Hurston was slain in the Spirit and given a vision.

Led by an angel, she went upward until she arrived at a place called the new Jerusalem. As she prepared to enter, she saw Jesus standing at a gate made of one great pearl. He stretched forth His hand and welcomed her, saying, "Maxine, welcome."

Entering the gate, she first saw Stephen passing beside her. She called to him, "Deacon Stephen! May I ask you a question? I read in the Bible that you died in a heap of stones. Was it painful?"

With a smile on his face, Stephen answered, "When the stones rained thick and fast around me, heaven opened, and Jesus stretched out His hand. When I took that hand, I was in heaven. I didn't feel any pain at all."

After a while, she met David and Peter. Both of them welcomed her. Then a man who was a total stranger greeted her as if she were a close relative. Wondering, she asked who he was.

He answered, "You may not know me. You are not to stay here. You will soon return to the world below, and when you go back, please talk to my mother who lives there. I am the younger brother of your husband,

219

John Hurston. I died several months after I was born." Because Maxine had never heard about this brother of her husband's, she thought it strange.

Then Jesus showed her many places in heaven, and it was just the same as recorded in the Bible. The glory of God shone so brightly that anyone who saw it was dazzled by the light. The river of the water of life flowed in the midst of the street, and on both sides of the river was the tree of life. Under the tree were benches upon which sat saints who had come there earlier. They were chatting intimately with angels.

Maxine saw the marriage supper of the Lamb prepared in a great hall that was so huge you could not see one end from the other. An angel stood outside the hall looking around. He seemed to be waiting for someone. When she asked him, he said, "I am waiting for the bride, and she will come soon."

As she was led back outside, finishing her tour of heaven, someone called to her, "Maxine! Maxine!"

Turning around, she saw Abraham running to her. Taking her by the hand, he pleaded, "Maxine, please don't fail to tell my words to my descendants when you go down. Please tell them to remember that a beautiful place is already prepared here. Tell them that they should by all means come here, not giving in to the temptations of the world. Now go and work hard."

When she awakened several hours later, she found herself in the arms of her sobbing husband. She immediately questioned him: "Dear, you have something you have kept from me. I just returned from a visit to heaven where I met someone who called me the wife of his elder brother. Do you have a younger brother who died as an infant?"

Her husband answered, "I had a younger brother who died only a few months after he was born. I had forgotten about him, but maybe my mother still has one of his pictures."

When she recovered from her illness, Maxine went to her mother-in-law and asked to see the picture. Later she told me she saw similarities to the face she had seen in heaven. That is the experience I heard from Mrs. Hurston, after begging her several times to tell it to me, for she was not the kind of person who would tell such a story to just anyone.

As Mrs. Hurston's testimony affirms, heaven is finished adorning itself and is ready to accept us. The marriage supper is also ready. We don't know at what time or hour the Lord will come. The scriptural heaven John saw was also seen and testified of by many people after him, and the testimonies are always the same.

Therefore the proclamation of God, "Behold, I am making all things new," is faithful and true (v. 5). God, who is the Alpha and the Omega, said that those who overcome the world and accept Jesus as Savior shall drink freely from the fountain of the water of life (v. 6). "But for the cowardly and unbelieving and abominable and murderers and immoral persons and sorcerers and idolaters and all liars, their part will be in the lake that burns with fire and brimstone, which is the second death" (v. 8).

THE NEW JERUSALEM, THE BRIDE OF THE LAMB (21:9–22:5)

OUR ADORNMENT TODAY, the adornment of the bride of Jesus Christ, is the same as the adornment of the new Jerusalem. Therefore the appearance of the new Jerusalem is the same as our appearance spiritually. That is why the Bible calls the new Jerusalem the bride of Jesus Christ:

> And he carried me away in the Spirit to a great and high mountain, and showed me the holy city, Jerusalem, coming down out of heaven from God, having the glory of God. Her brilliance was like a very costly stone, as a stone of crystal-clear jasper.
>
> —REVELATION 21:10–11

The green color of the precious jasper stone stands for divinity and life, the spiritual green pasture that provides eternal life. Therefore the new Jerusalem will be a place full of infinite divinity, inexhaustible satisfaction, and endless life.

> It had a great and high wall, with twelve gates, and at the gates twelve angels; and names were written on them, which are those of the twelve tribes of the sons of Israel. . . . And the wall of the city had twelve foundation stones, and on them were the twelve names of the twelve apostles of the Lamb.
>
> —REVELATION 21:12, 14

That description refers to the twelve tribes of Israel and the twelve apostles of the New Testament age. Therefore the names here are the names of the twenty-four elders—in other words, the saints who are saved.

> And the one who spoke with me had a gold measuring rod to mea-
> sure the city, and its gates and its wall. And the city is laid out as a
> square, and its length is as great as the width; and he measured the
> city with the rod, fifteen hundred miles; its length and width and
> height are equal.
>
> —REVELATION 21:15–16

The length, the breadth, and the height of the new Jerusalem are all
about fifteen hundred miles. The architecture of heaven is obviously inscrutable, for by human design that kind of structure would be impossible.

> And he measured its wall, seventy-two yards, according to human
> measurements, which are also angelic measurements.
>
> —REVELATION 21:17

The wall of this heavenly city is very thick. Verse 18 says the wall of the
city "was jasper; and the city was pure gold, like clear glass." How
splendid it will be! The twelve foundations of the wall are made of all
kinds of precious stones, and the twelve gates are twelve pearls; each gate
is one big pearl (vv. 19–21).

There is a reason for the gates of the new Jerusalem being made of
pearls. Pearls are produced from oysters in the sea. When sand creeps
into the oyster's shell, it injures the body of the oyster. So the oyster pro-
duces a secretion with its saliva to cover the intruder, and in the process,
over a long period of time, a lustrous pearl is formed.

Likewise, the gates of the new Jerusalem are made of pearls because
the people who enter all possess faith like pearls. While they lived in the
world, they were not discouraged by the numerous trials that came their
way. Rather, they overcame them through prayer. They covered the trials
and tribulations by producing perseverance and faith.

The city's being made of pure gold means that all the people who enter
it will have a divine nature, throwing away their human nature, and will
live forever. Besides divinity, gold stands for a king.

> And I saw no temple in it, for the Lord God, the Almighty, and the
> Lamb, are its temple. And the city has no need of the sun or of the
> moon to shine upon it, for the glory of God has illumined it, and its
> lamp is the Lamb. And the nations shall walk by its light, and the
> kings of the earth shall bring their glory into it. And in the daytime

(for there shall be no night there) its gates shall never be closed; and they shall bring the glory and the honor of the nations into it; and nothing unclean and no one who practices abomination and lying, shall ever come into it, but only those whose names are written in the Lamb's book of Life.

—REVELATION 21:22–27

In the Old Testament God dwelled in the holy of holies of the temple. In the new Jerusalem, however, because God is with us, there is no need for the temple. Moreover, because the glory of God shines in it and Jesus is its light, we will need neither the sun nor the moon. Hence, there will be no more night. In addition, outside the new Jerusalem, the citizens of flesh who enter the new heaven and the new earth after the millennial kingdom become fruitful and multiply. They will rule over nations, having kings at their head. Those kings will continually come to the new Jerusalem, the capital, to make reports and receive orders. But only those whose names are recorded in the Lamb's Book of Life will be able to enter the city.

And he [the angel] showed me a river of the water of life, clear as crystal, coming from the throne of God and of the Lamb.

—REVELATION 22:1

Under the thrones of the Lamb of God and the Father flows a river as clear as crystal. It winds through the midst of the streets, and on each side is a tree of life that bears twelve "manner" of fruit. The tree yields its fruit monthly, and each piece of fruit tastes different (22:2). People will eat this fruit only for the joy of eating, not to fill their stomachs. Because in heaven, we will be able to live without eating. Many people ask me, "Shall we also eat in heaven?" Now you have the answer.

CONCLUSION

A Word of Prophecy

V ERSE 7 OF Revelation 22 says that he who keeps the sayings of the prophecy of this book is blessed. Therefore you who have read this exposition of John's revelation *have been* blessed. And if you put the sayings of this prophecy into your heart and keep them, you will be *more* blessed.

Once again, as in Revelation 19:9, John was so greatly moved in his heart that he fell down at the feet of the angel. The same joy and strong emotion should be in the heart of all who read Revelation. We can shout "Hallelujah!" and be blessed. If you do not have this moving emotion in your heart, pray that you may have a firm faith in the words recorded in Revelation and accept them with an amen. I pray in the name of Jesus that you may have such help from the Holy Spirit.

John's revelation has become an open book to us as the angel desired in verse 10. The sayings of the prophecy have been made known to us, for the time draws near. Our response should be to go and preach, sowing the seed of the gospel.

Now is the age of grace. Therefore, be a witness for Christ. Soon your words will sprout, and in time, they will grow into a big tree. You will reap people of faith. The day of Jesus' coming draws near. Before it is too late, witness with all your might.

The following verses show that the coming of the Lord is much closer than we realize:

> "Behold, I am coming quickly, and My reward is with Me, to render to every man according to what he has done. I am the Alpha and the Omega, the first and the last, the beginning and the end." Blessed are those who wash their robes, that they may have the right to the tree of life, and may enter by the gates into the city.
>
> —REVELATION 22:12–14

Our robes signify life. We must live a life of repentance every day, washed by the precious blood of Jesus Christ. And at whatever time the Lord may come to us, we must be ready to be caught up into the air, saying with the Holy Spirit, "Amen! Hallelujah!" Let us be the blessed people who enter the new Jerusalem, the new heaven and the new earth, where we will serve God forever!

> I, Jesus, have sent My angel to testify to you these things for the churches. I am the root and the offspring of David, the bright morning star.
>
> —REVELATION 22:16

Once again we see in this verse the word *church* that had disappeared since the third chapter of Revelation. However, at the close of Revelation the Lord said to the church:

> And the Spirit and the bride say, "Come." And let the one who hears say, "Come." And let the one who is thirsty come; let the one who wishes take the water of life without cost.
>
> —REVELATION 22:17

The bride is the church that has been taken up into heaven, and the Holy Spirit is the One who initiated it. Thus, this scripture means the Holy Spirit and the church preach the gospel hand in hand. Every church should accept the Holy Spirit and by His power preach the Word of the Lord.

Lastly, the Lord says that plagues will be added to those who add something to this prophecy of the Book of Revelation. Likewise, if anyone takes away from the words of this book, God will take away "his part from the tree of life and from the holy city, which are written in this book" (v. 19). So whatever their motives, people should handle God's Word with great care lest they fall under His curse.

Revelation 22:20 reads: "He who testifies to these things says, 'Yes, I am coming quickly.' Amen. Come, Lord Jesus."

Witnessing things that would happen to the church during the next two thousand years and the things that would happen during the Tribulation following the Rapture of the church John was in fear and disappointment. But after he saw the glorious new heaven and new earth, he was overwhelmed with joy and looked forward to the coming of the Lord. So he concluded his prophetic revelation with a prayer. He prayed, shouting with a loud voice, "Amen. Come, Lord Jesus!"

Let that be our prayer, too. The person who has finished reading this book can shout loudly with me:

"Amen. Come, Lord Jesus!"